APM

Teaching Mission in the Complex Public Arena

Teaching Mission in the Complex Public Arena
The 2017 Proceedings of the Association of Professors of Missions.

Published by First Fruits Press, © 2018
Digital version at http://place.asburyseminary.edu/academicbooks/26/

ISBN: 9781621718130 (print), 9781621718147 (digital), 9781621718154 (kindle)

For all other uses, contact
Association of Professors of Missions
108 W. High St.
Lexington, KY 40507
http://www.asmweb.org/content/apm

Teaching Mission in the Complex Public Arena

The 2017 Proceedings of the Association of Professors of Missions.
    1 online resource (v, 164 pages) : digital
    Wilmore, Ky. : First Fruits Press, ©2018.
    ISBN: 9781621718147 (online.)
    1. Missions – Study and teaching – Congresses. 2. Missions – Theory – Congresses.
    3. Education – Philosophy – Congresses. 4. Teaching – Methodology –
    Congresses. I. Title. II. Danielson, Robert A. (Robert Alden), 1969- III. Hartley,
    Benjamin L. (Benjamin Loren) IV. Association of Professors of Mission annual
    meeting (2017: Wheaton College, IL.) V. Association of Professors of Mission.
    VI. The 2017 proceedings of the Association of Professors of Missions.
  BV2020 .A876 2017eb

Cover design by Jon Ramsay

First Fruits Press
The Academic Open Press of Asbury Theological Seminary
204 N. Lexington Ave., Wilmore, KY 40390
859-858-2236
first.fruits@asburyseminary.edu
asbury.to/firstfruits

APM

Teaching Mission in the Complex Public Arena

The 2017 proceedings of
The Association of Professors of Missions

Edited by
Robert A. Danielson

&

A. Sue Russell

2017 APM Annual Meeting
Wheaton College, Wheaton, IL
June 15 - 16, 2017

About the Association of Professors of Mission

ROBERT DANIELSON, ADVISORY COMMITTEE MEMBER

The Association of Professors of Mission (APM) was formed in 1952 at Louisville, Kentucky and was developed as an organization to focus on the needs of people involved in the classroom teaching of mission studies. However, the organization also challenged members to be professionally involved in scholarly research and share this research through regular meetings. In the 1960's Roman Catholic scholars and scholars from conservative Evangelical schools joined the conciliar Protestants who initially founded the organization.

With the discussion to broaden membership to include other scholars from areas like anthropology, sociology, and linguistics who were actively engaged in mission beyond the teaching profession, the decision was made to found the American Society of Missiology (ASM) in 1972. Since the importance of working with mission educators was still vital, the APM continued as a separate organization, but always met in conjunction with the ASM at their annual meetings.

The APM continues as a professional society of those interested in the teaching of mission from as wide an ecumenical spectrum as possible. As an organization it works to help and support those who teach mission, especially those who often lack a professional network to help mentor and guide them in this task. Through its influence, the APM has also helped establish the prominence and scholarly importance of the academic discipline of missiology throughout theological education.

Table of Contents

Plenary Papers

Conference Papers

Conference Proceedings

Foreword

LARRY W. CALDWELL

Teaching Mission in the Complex Public Arena: Developing Missiologically Informed Models of Engagement

The Association of Professors of Mission was organized in June of 1952 and held its first meeting during that year. This means that 2017 marked our 65th anniversary.

Clearly teaching mission in 1952 was a lot different from teaching mission today. The missiological issues of 1952, during the beginning of the "golden years" of the Eisenhower administration, are not the missiological issues of today. That this is so is reflected in the very membership of the APM. For example, back in 1952 there were no women in the APM (the first woman didn't join until 1962), and very few Roman Catholic professors (most didn't start attending until the late '60s), or professors of color. And, back in 1952, the teaching of mission was quite simple for most: mission professors teaching missionaries and missionary candidates *here* how to do cross-cultural ministry somewhere *over there*. There was very little emphasis on local engagement.

The theme of 2017's meeting was "Teaching Mission in the Complex Public Arena: Developing Missiologically Informed Models of Engagement." In 1952 there wasn't much discussion, or really any discussion, about missiologically informed models of engagement. Sixty-five years later this certainly is no longer the case. For if we professors of mission today do not develop missiologically informed models of engagement, what we teach will likely fall on ears that will not hear.

Why is this so? Because today our North American context constantly immerses us in complex contemporary issues that arise from the public arena: issues of racial justice, immigration, gender and sexuality, ecology and environment, to name but a few. Speaking to such issues responsibly from a missional perspective requires awareness of how religious language is heard, as well as how to have gracious dialog and loving engagement.

Thus, during our two days together, we sought to consider this question: What should mission and the teaching of mission look like in our increasingly complex public arena? We considered how to negotiate contemporary landscapes in North America and worldwide with faithful Christian witness in our mission teaching and scholarship, including models of dialog and engagement.

Embodying a missionally informed perspective in today's world can be challenging. We can be uncertain about what will offend and what will resonate, what is respectful of social difference and what is faithful to what we have seen and heard. This is especially pertinent as we prepare students for mission work globally; equipping them to appropriately interact with their various complex environments. Our students are wondering how to effectively engage in their complex public arenas in both biblically and missiologically informed ways.

The following papers help address some of these issues as we attempt to faithfully teach mission in the public arena.

Conference Theme

**Association of Professors of Mission
Annual Meeting
15-16 June 2017**

Teaching Mission in the Complex Public Arena: Developing Missiologically Informed Models of Engagement

Our North American context immerses us every day in complex contemporary issues that arise from the public arena: issues of racial justice, immigration, gender and sexuality, ecology and environment, to name but a few. Speaking to such issues responsibly from a missional perspective requires awareness of how religious language is heard, as well as how to have gracious dialog and loving engagement. This conference will seek to consider this question: What should mission and the teaching of mission look like in our increasingly complex public arena?

Embodying a missionally informed perspective in today's world can be challenging. We can be uncertain about what will offend and what will resonate, what is respectful of social difference and what is faithful to what we have seen and heard. This is especially pertinent as we prepare students for mission work globally; equipping them to appropriately interact with their various complex environments. Our students are wondering how to effectively engage in their complex public arenas in both biblically and missiologically informed ways.

We seek papers that consider how to negotiate contemporary landscapes in North America and worldwide with faithful Christian witness in our mission teaching and scholarship, including models of dialog and engagement.

Plenary Speakers:

D.A. Carson – Research Professor of New Testament, Trinity Evangelical Divinity School

Michal Meulenberg

Daniel White Hodge – North Park University Chicago

Call for Papers: The Association of Professors of Mission extends an open call for paper presentation proposals for its 2017 annual meeting. Anyone interested in presenting at APM should submit a proposal title with a 150-200 word abstract and a 30-word biography to Larry W. Caldwell, APM President, at lcaldwell@sfseminary.edu by February 15, 2017.

Themes for Proposal: This year's meeting will consider the teaching of mission in the complex public arena, seeking to provide biblical and missiological models for those teaching mission that will help them retain their core missional understandings while at the same time engage the culture at large in ways that are both understandable and in offensive. To this end, we invite papers that consider the relationship between mission teaching and public engagement. Examples of topics in line with the theme might include:

• Models of engagement (biblical, historical, and/or missiological) that help demonstrate how one respects social difference while remaining missionally faithful.

• Descriptions of classroom challenges in the teaching of mission, in regards to some of the complex contemporary issues, and how those challenges were met.

• Case studies of how campus responses to specific contemporary issues have impacted the teaching of mission in the classroom.

Other subjects: Topics of particular interest to APM contributors but not directly related to the conference theme may still be submitted and will be considered by the conference organizers.

Submission and Presentation Requirements:

Paper proposal deadline: February 15, 2017

Notification of accepted papers: March 1, 2017

Submission of completed papers and confirmation of meeting attendance: May 22, 2017.

For the purposes of online publication of presentations, submitted papers may be up to 5,000 words in length including notes and references (about 20 double-spaced pages) and should conform to the style guide of the journal *Missiology: An International Review*, available at: http://asmweb.org/assets/pdf/Style-Guide-2011.pdf. The full text of all papers approved for the conference will be made available to the members of APM online as *The Proceedings of the Association of Professors of Mission, 2017*.

Presentations at the meeting will be limited to 15 to 20 minutes (about 5-7 pages of text, if read), plus additional time for discussion depending on the number of presentations accepted.

Please direct all submissions and questions to **Larry W. Caldwell, APM President,** at lcaldwell@sfseminary.edu.

Registration materials will be available on the website in the Spring 2017.

We look forward to seeing in June!

APM

Plenary Papers

What We Should Look for in Those Who Teach Mission[1]

D. A. CARSON

---

1   This is an edited version of a plenary address given to the Association of Professors
of Mission, held in Wheaton, Illinois, on June 15, 2017.

The topic of this conference, "Teaching Mission in the Complex Public Arena: Developing Missiologically Informed Models of Engagement," almost dares me to adopt the title I have chosen: "What We Should Look for in Those Who Teach Mission." At the same time, it is a bit adventuresome on your part to invite someone like me, someone outside your discipline, to address you on the topic, and it is a bit of a cheek on my part to accept the invitation.

Doubtless all of us could easily check off a list of cultural developments that make the teaching of mission more problematic than it used to be. In no particular order of importance:

(1) Biblical illiteracy in the Western world is spreading quickly. The Bible is the best-selling un-read book in the Western world. As is well known, the researches of Christian Smith and others as to the beliefs of the nation's young people, including the young people in the shrinking Bible belt, show that their God is better characterized by MTD (Moralistic Therapeutic Deism) than by the attributes of the God of the Bible.[2] When I speak at university missions, most of my unconverted hearers do not know the Bible has two Testaments; they have never heard of Abraham, and are likely to confuse Moses with Charleton Heston or with his more recent cartoon analog.

(2) Not only change, but the rate of change, is accelerating. Much of this is the inevitable fruit of the digital revolution. I am not a Luddite: much of the change brought to the world is wonderfully positive: new fields of learning, new ways of dispersing knowledge and accessing sources, new found abilities to communicate with people around the world, technologies scarcely imagined that open up entirely new fields of science and research, and much more. But pundits from all over the political spectrum are warning us that virtual communities that displace personal communities leave us emotionally crippled and relationally immature. Those who for reasons of poverty or inferior education that cannot make the leap into any technology more robust than an individualistic use of smartphones are often condemned to remain in the shadows, victims of the deepening divide between the haves and the have-nots. The same technology that circulates the gospel *gratis* to poor people who live behind totalitarian gates also delivers free porn, with God-only-knows what depredations on our families.

(3) Charles Taylor has powerfully contrasted the "default" cultural assumptions of, say, three hundred years ago with current default assumptions. Three centuries ago, anywhere in the Western world the default assumption was that God made us, that we must one day give an account to him, that fundamental differences between right and wrong are tied up with both God

---

2   Christian Smith and Melinda Lundquist Denton, *Soul Searching: The Religious and Spiritual Lives of American Teenagers* (New York: OUP, 2005).

and human flourishing, and that we are wise to lean upon God's power and providence. This is not to say that there were no atheists, and no philosophical materialists; rather, it is to say that this theistic universe, somewhat Christianized, was the atmosphere in which we lived and moved and had our being. Today, Taylor rightly observes, this is not the case. Even among those in the West who profess Christian faith, such Christian faith is often maintained in highly privatized forms, while at the broader level of public cultural discourse we are practical atheists. It is not difficult to see that such developments make the task of teaching mission more than a little difficult.

(4) Not only is virtually every culture in the world showing signs of rapid urbanization, but the combination of digital exposure to the rest of the world, relatively cheap travel, plus endless regional strife, natural disasters, and famines, means that massive migrations of various sorts have taken place—are still taking place. That means that many (especially Western) countries have become a good deal less monochrome than they once were. Especially is this so in our great urban centers. On the one hand, we can make the claim that New York and London are more like the New Jerusalem today than they were two centuries ago: they have people from every tongue and tribe and race and nation. Some of us thoroughly enjoy the cultural enrichment, the diversity of foods and smells and accents and kinds of humor and dress. On the other hand, some, inevitably, are threatened by these changes, and even the most charitable observer acknowledges that the political and religious stresses that these changes generate are not being accommodated very smoothly. So while it is easier today than it used to be for a professor of mission to take his students down to a nearby mosque and enjoy a chat with the local *imam*, the culture-wide challenges aroused by a resurgent Islam cannot be ignored.

(5) A relatively small but articulate and vociferous minority still continues to think about contextualization in rather old-fashioned and un-self-critical ways. They can talk fluently about how the Bible is itself enmeshed in culture (true enough) and must be interpreted by people who are themselves inevitably enmeshed in culture (true enough) that they become very hesitant to talk about the truthfulness of the gospel (rather worrying) and, so far as content is concerned, commonly get no farther than the affirmation that the Bible has many diverse ways of speaking to power. What they gain in epistemological sophistication they lose in clarity as to what the gospel is, this gospel that was (Jude tells us) once for all delivered to God's people (Jude 3). The result is a generation of would-be missionaries who are either side-tracked away from the gospel in favor of perennial discourse on culture, or who, rather discouraged, give up on the missionary enterprise.

(6) Whatever the causes—and they are highly disputed—the emphasis on tolerance today is not only sharper than it used to be, it has changed its meaning somewhat. When my book *The Intolerance of Tolerance* was published in 2012 (a bare five years ago), I was one of only a handful of people talking about these things. Nowadays most of the observations I made at the time are taken as commonplace; indeed, some of them have been eclipsed by more recent developments.

It is still worth pointing out that tolerance, in the old or traditional sense, operates at some level or other in *every* culture. *Every* culture adopts certain widely espoused beliefs and customs, and some deviations from such beliefs and customs are tolerated. If the deviations become too extreme or obnoxious, social and/or legal pressures may be brought to bear. Obviously, then, all instances of this old or traditional tolerance are essentially parasitic: that is, they feed off the accepted norms, practices, and convictions of the broader culture. By contrast, the new tolerance sets itself up as the supreme good, commonly claiming a high ground above culture.

Moreover, the old, traditional tolerance presupposes that what is tolerated is not liked. You hold that those who deviate from the cultural norm are wrong, but decide to tolerate them rather than oppress them. The new tolerance, however, commonly dictates that it is wrong to say that the other party is wrong, even to think that they are wrong. That is to be intolerant. Suddenly one glimpses what a massive shift in the very meaning of "tolerance" has taken place. It becomes difficult to engage ideas with which one disagrees if the entire discussion is side-tracked with the charge of intolerance.

In reality, of course, Western culture's adoption of the new tolerance is highly selective. Some issues evoke the demand for a display of the new tolerance; some don't. The heaving culture displays a thin crust of venomous hostility against all things Christian, covering a vast sea of dogmatic apathy. Realistically, the new tolerance can be credited with diminishing a significant number of abusive and demeaning labels, even while it displays gargantuan intolerance toward those who do not buy in to the new tolerance. In the name of this new tolerance, many would be prepared to ride roughshod over the First Amendment, which in fact upholds the old tolerance.

The major impact of these developments on the teaching of mission is their bearing on the exclusiveness of the gospel. The God of the Bible brooks no idols and no rivals (e.g., Isaiah 40-45). Jesus insists that no one comes to the Father except through him (John 14:6), and the apostle Peter dogmatically concurs (Acts 4:12). The apostle Paul insists that those who teach some other gospel are *anathema* (Galatians 1:8-9). In the views of most people in our culture, that stance is intrinsically intolerant, so it is easy to dismiss the gospel without even trying to understand it in its own terms. It is beyond the pale. The new tolerance functions as a powerful "defeater belief" (to use the expression amply treated by Tim Keller). Teachers of mission face the challenge of faithfully getting across to their students the non-negotiables of the gospel, including its claims to exclusivity, while gently but persistently and winsomely undermining this particular defeater belief.

(7) Probably the most important book by Charles Taylor is his *A Secular Age*,[3] nicely summarized and reflected on by James K. A. Smith, *How (Not) to be Secular: Reading Charles Taylor*.[4] One of the astute observations that Taylor makes is that we live in the age of authenticity. A genuinely authentic person is widely admired. Authentic people are those who live out their chosen identities. They choose what and who they want to be, and determinedly press toward living out those choices. Even when observers do not like the choices themselves, in an age when authenticity is much admired we are inclined to applaud such people for their authenticity rather than bemoan the foolishness of their self-chosen courses. As a result of this value system, we harbor deep suspicion of all voices of authority, except those that reinforce our right to our own personal values. Our culture broadly holds suspect the authoritative claims of family, tradition, and government. Individualism runs rampant in the Western world, apart from two exceptions: (a) those that form enclaves of like-minded "individuals" who identify themselves in the same way as others belonging to a well-identified group;[5] and (b) counter-cultural groups that are trying to fight the larger trends, whether they understand themselves to be following the Benedict option or not.

As I said earlier, everyone in this room could have created this list, or something like it, and certainly added to it. Those who teach mission are certainly aware of the challenges they face. But there is another dimension to these challenges that we must not overlook. Unless I am reading it wrongly, the three paragraphs describing the goals of this conference focus primarily on the "Complex Public Arena" *in North America*: after all, that is, I imagine, where most of the professors of mission in this room teach. So most of our students, similarly, are North Americans, with all the strengths and weaknesses, all the current cultural biases and reactions against them, attached thereto. Most have become aware that North American Christians who opt to evangelize and engage in church planting in North America, especially along the coasts, in the New England states, in New York City, in the Pacific Northwest, need some

---

3   Cambridge: Belknap, 2007.
4   Grand Rapids: Eerdmans, 2014. Cf. also Collin Hansen, ed., *Our Secular Age: Ten Years of Reading and Applying Charles Taylor* (Deerfield: TGC, 2017).
5   See, for example, the amusing send-up of Cambridge, MA, in Dominic Green, "City of the Chosen," *First Things* 282 (April, 2018): 11-12: "'02138: The World's Most Opinionated Zip Code,' but all our opinions are the same."

help with cross-cultural communication, precisely because Western culture has been changing so quickly. Whether we are teaching our students to preach and teach the gospel to Buddhists or Muslims who happen to live in Thailand or Turkey respectively, or in NYC, makes relatively little difference. What we easily overlook, however, is that we are culturally located; *our students* are culturally located. For example, when I am speaking to university students in North Africa or the Middle East, very few are wrestling with whether or not there is such a thing as public truth, or arguing that it is intolerant to say that any religion is wrong. *Of course* there is public truth; the only questions are, Who has it? and What is it? *Of course* tolerance is a parasitic virtue, not the supreme good. Thus, by preparing students to "read" and respond to Western culture (a needed cross-cultural venture), we may sometimes make them insensitive to the very different cultures one finds elsewhere. And even the word "elsewhere" I utter with my tongue firmly planted in my cheek, for nowadays there are small enclaves of, say, typically Muslim or Buddhist or Hindu cultures within our cities.

So who is sufficient for these things? What should we look for in those who teach mission?

(1) A rich, biblically faithful, grasp of the gospel.

It is a mistake to assume that those who teach mission—or any other faculty member, for that matter—enjoy a rich, biblically faithful, grasp of the gospel. For a start, many of those brought up in a Christian home have no more than a formulaic grasp of the gospel, what I call a shibboleth gospel: e.g., "The gospel is accepting Jesus as your personal Savior." Quite apart from the fact that this formula is not found in Scripture, in substance it stipulates how to respond to the gospel without actually identifying, still less explaining, the gospel.

There are many shibboleth gospels. A very common one is to confuse the great commission and the great commandments. A fine example of this is found in the influential book by Richard Stearns, *The Hole in Our Gospel*.[6] Stearns argues that, on the basis of the commandment to love our neighbors as ourselves and other elements of Jesus' teaching, we should stir up much more concern for the poor, for otherwise we are left with "a hole in our gospel," even while we evangelize and plant churches. Doubtless he is right that we can and should do more than we do, and his own example is stirring. Nevertheless, those who keep track of the monies we spend tell us that Christians contribute about six times more mission dollars toward meeting the physical needs of people than we do toward evangelism and church planting. Judging by such figures,

---

6   Nashville: Thomas Nelson, 2014.

the hole in our gospel, as one wag has put it, is the gospel. More importantly, in such discussions we are in danger of confusing, once again, the gospel with the entailments of the gospel.

More serious yet is the danger of assuming the gospel. Both pastors and missionaries easily fall into this trap, especially if the people to whom we are speaking are primarily professing Christians: they already know the gospel, we tell ourselves, so we should go on to other topics. Pretty soon the gospel is rarely talked about; it is merely assumed. The reasoning is poor in any case: when we examine how the "gospel" functions in the New Testament, we discover that it is to be applied not only to unbelievers but to believers. Moreover, experienced teachers and preachers know that our students and other hearers do not learn all that we teach them; rather, they learn what we are excited about. If we assume the gospel while remaining excited about, say, cultural analysis and the challenges of contextualization, we will produce a generation of mission teachers for whom cultural analysis and contextualization are at the center of the enterprise, while retaining only the fuzziest and most amateur understandings of what the gospel is—even though, at the end of the day, it is the gospel that saves and sanctifies. That's why we must have professors of mission who are excited about the gospel: only in that way will their students maintain the gospel at the center of their priorities.

The gospel is first and foremost news. It is good news, massive news— the news of what God has done in Christ, supremely on the cross and in his resurrection, to rescue us from sin and death, reconcile us to God, providing the gift of the Spirit, the corporate life of the church, the transformation begun in the new birth that enables us to see and enter the kingdom, the promise of resurrection existence in the new heaven and the new earth, the home of righteousness. It follows that we must also include instruction on how to respond to this good news, beginning with repentance and faith, but we ought not displace the news about what *God* has done in Christ with what *we* must do by way of response. Indeed, precisely because the gospel is news, the awesome news of what God has done in Jesus Christ, the most fundamental thing Christians must do with it, apart from believing it, is to proclaim it. That's what you do with news. The old adage, frequently but mistakenly attributed to St. Francis of Assisi, "Preach the gospel; if necessary, use words," makes as much sense as telling a newscaster, "Tonight, give people the news; if necessary, use words."

If you want to flesh out the content of the news that needs to be believed and proclaimed, there are several excellent ways of going about the project. For example, one could begin by focusing on passages that purport to summarize the gospel, e.g. 1 Corinthians 15:1-19. There the apostle tells his readers, "I want to remind you of the gospel I preached to you, which you have received and on which you have taken your stand. By this gospel you are saved, if you hold firmly to the word I preached to you. Otherwise, you have believed in vain" (15:1-2). From this anchor, Paul lays out the matters "of first importance" (15:3)—that "Christ died for our sins according to the Scriptures, that he was buried, that he was raised on the third day, according to the Scriptures,"—and so forth. In brief, Paul makes clear in what ways the gospel is theological, christological, historical, biblical, transformative, and more.[7] Or one could focus on Matthew, Mark, Luke, and John, reminding ourselves that in the first century they were not regarded as four "gospels" but as cumulative witnesses to the *one* gospel, the gospel according to Matthew, the gospel according to Mark, and so forth. Only in the second century were the individual books called "gospels."[8] Or one could focus study on individual books that confront some particularly pernicious error, enabling us to discern what the New Testament writers saw as utterly non-negotiable (e.g., Galatians). Or again, one could follow the course of a pastor I know who, when he takes on a new set of half a dozen interns, promptly sets them to the task of summarizing the gospel in one word, one phrase, one sentence, one paragraph, one page, ten pages. The results are predictable, but instructive. The demand for one word inevitably produces "Jesus" or "grace" or "atonement" or the like—answers that are not wrong, but not particularly insightful, precise, or disciplined. Something like "Jesus and his death and resurrection" is a little better, but there is no mention of the Spirit, the Trinity, justification, new birth, the church, the consummation, and much more. One quickly learns that although a child may identify the gospel in brief order, mature Christians will want to flesh out as much as possible of the good news, never satisfied with the reductionisms and potential inaccuracies of a mere bare bones approach. We want our professors of mission to display a rich, biblically faithful, grasp of the gospel.

Do I need to add that no responsible grasp of the gospel will pit one part of the canon against another part? I'm thinking of claims such as "I prefer the gospel Jesus preached to the gospel Paul preached." One must work toward gospel summaries that try to reflect the whole counsel of God.

---

7   Cf. D. A. Carson, *Prophetic from the Center: The Gospel of Jesus Christ in 1 Corinthians 15:1-19* (Deerfield: TGC, 2016).

8   Matthew, Mark, Luke and John are unique in mutually supporting one another with one storyline of the life of Jesus, beginning with Jesus being baptized by John the Baptist and ending with Jesus' death and resurrection. The many apocryphal gospels from the second, third, and fourth centuries are derivative documents, and not one preserves the same storyline: see Markus Bockmuehl, *Ancient Apocryphal Gospels* (Louisville: Westminster John Knox Press, 2017).

(2) A love for people that hungers to win them to Christ more than it hungers to win arguments

The most sophisticated courses on apologetics, the most mature understanding of the gospel, the best-designed material on cross-cultural communication, are all virtually worthless if we do not love the people we seek to evangelize. That is why Christians with little or no training may be more effective in sharing their faith than well-trained scholars, for no other reason than that their message becomes winsome in proportion to the love they display as a matter of course. Since professors of mission are usually attempting more than the passing on of mission theory to their students, but are trying to recruit new missionaries from among their students, they need to be Christians whose love for the lost shines forth transparently.

That brings up two more reflections to round out the important role of love. *First*, one of the ways you can test the sincerity of a Christian's love for lost people is to inquire into how much they are trying to save them from hell. It is good to dig wells in the Sahel, fight malaria in equatorial jungles, introduce better farming techniques, and teach the skill sets of micro economics so as to start some small businesses. These and many similar things may all be an index of one's love and compassion for needy people. But where such salutary activities are not accompanied by the articulation of the gospel in a winsome and persuasive fashion so as to save people from eternal judgment, one may reasonably ask how deep and insightful is our love for these people. *Second*, another overlooked dimension in the love we must show in our missionary endeavors is the recognition that not everyone raises the same hurdles, or experiences the same roadblocks to saving faith. Some are just plain ignorant, and primarily need the gospel explained; others operate out of an alien frame of reference, so need some worldview transformation; others have bought into a deeply-held alternative religion, such that there are identifiable points that will have to be challenged; others have been offended by Christians, and in consequence have erected large-scale personal barriers; and still others are loaded with a sense of guilt, and are frankly hungry to meet a guilt-bearing Savior. A one-size-fits-all apologetic is likely to get in the way. One crucial element intrinsic to loving people is good listening coupled with humble spiritual diagnosis.

In short, to be effective, professors of mission must have a love for people that hungers to win them for Christ more than it hungers to win arguments.

(3) A recognition that we are in a cosmic struggle, and that it is a privilege to carry the cross and fill up the sufferings of Christ

Not only in the Apocalypse, where the church is portrayed as in an epochal struggle with Satan and his beasts (Revelation 12-14), but elsewhere in the New Testament, Christians understand themselves to be in a cosmic struggle "against the rulers, against the authorities, against the powers of this dark world and against the spiritual forces of evil in the heavenly realms" (Ephesians 6:12). The struggle against "the world, the flesh, and the devil" means that Christians are to expect opposition and persecution. Did not the Lord Jesus teach his followers, "If they persecuted me, they will persecute you also. If they obeyed my teaching, they will obey yours also" (John 15:20)? All of his followers are commissioned to take up their cross and follow him (Matthew 16:24-28), which in context sounds massively threatening. Just as the exalted Lord Jesus identifies with his followers (e.g., Acts 9:4), so his followers identify with him—with him in both his power and his suffering (Philippians 3:10), since after all "it has been granted to [us] on behalf of Christ not only to believe in him, but also to suffer for him" (Philippians 1:29). Christ Jesus not only "bore our sins in his body on the cross, so that we might die to sins and live for righteousness:" (1 Peter 2:24), but in that same death left us "an example that [we] should follow in his steps" (2:21). When the apostles first faced physical battering, they rejoiced "because they had been counted worthy of suffering disgrace for the Name" (Acts 5:41). Small wonder that when Paul suffers for Jesus' sake, he can testify, "I fill up in my flesh what is still lacking in regard to Christ's afflictions, for the sake of his body, which is the church" (Colossians 1:24).

The history of world mission must not be passed on as a narrative of almost unbroken expansion and gospel triumphs. It is important to learn of those triumphs, of course, but it is no less urgent to learn of the martyrs, and of the faithful but lonely servants of Christ who have persevered in dark and discouraging times and places. We must raise up a generation of missionaries—indeed, of Christian witnesses everywhere—who know they are called not only to make disciples everywhere, but also to suffer for Jesus' sake.

(4) A deepening knowledge of the culture where we serve

The initial warrant for such competence is displayed in the ministry of the apostle Paul. There are good reasons why his sermon in a synagogue in Pisidian Antioch (Acts 13) sounds rather different than his sermon in Athens (Acts 17). The audience in Acts 13 shares with Paul many common theological commitments: e.g., monotheism, understanding that sin is first of all offense against God, a linear view of history, the prospect of the consummation as the home of righteousness and a new heaven and a new earth, the authority of the revealed Word of God written down in books, a shared participation in salvation history, the importance of faith, the ties between theology and ethics. Because Paul and his audience in Acts 13 share so many things, Paul does not have to dwell on those points; he can proceed pretty promptly to the identity of the Messiah, and especially to his death and resurrection, events grounded in Scripture. The audience in Acts 17 shares none of these stances with Paul, so it is unsurprising that he feels he must start farther back and establish a biblically-shaped framework in which alone the incarnation, life, death, and resurrection of Jesus the Messiah make sense.

It may be useful to offer five reflections on this point. *First*, teaching cross-cultural communication, or, more broadly, contextualization, is complex and challenging work. It is difficult to know one culture (even one's own) well; it is much more difficult to know two or three, and still more difficult to develop mental frameworks for moving from one to another. Inevitably, such work churns up not only the challenges of cross-cultural communication, but cross-cultural leadership, meaning-systems, sense of humor, personal identity, linguistic and tribal identity, and much more. Throw in graduate-level reading in epistemology and postmodernism, and there is plenty to keep a student (and a professor) busy.

Second, this aspect of the life and teaching of a professor of mission can be usefully divided into two parts. One part is general and theoretical; the other part is specific to particular cultures and peoples—e.g., Muslim Arabs, Thai Buddhists, Hindus in northern India, Japanese secularists, and so forth. Clearly it is helpful for a student who is hoping to serve in, say, Japan, to be able to sit under a specialist in Japanese language and culture.Some specialists know remarkably little theory; some general theorists have remarkably little experience of specific cultures other than their own. Students gain from being exposed to both sorts of professors of mission.

Third, one of the key evidences that one is becoming ready to communicate cross-culturally is the ability to observe and listen to another person's "take" on something and then explain it or defend it with no less empathy and credibility than that demonstrated by that other person. This is simply an expanded version of what might be called the Tim Keller school of apologetics: before refuting an opponent's position, show that you can articulate it better than he or she. Such discipline will eschew argument by stereotyping. The same principle easily extends to assessing cultural differences.

Fourth, however challenging this aspect of the task of the professor of mission, that professor must never see himself or herself as *primarily* a cultural commentator or a professor of intercultural studies. Relying on a rather old-fashioned form of postmodernism, some teachers of contextualization are so caught up in the epistemological challenges of confessing truth that they drift toward the relativizing of all values and truth claims, save only the truth of the supremacy of radical contextualization. They may speak of meaningful interpretations, and talk fluently of diverse ways in which the biblical texts may confront power, but they cannot speak of the truth of the gospel in the same way that the New Testament does. We are all caught up in the hermeneutical circle, they say, so we cannot truly know anything (save that we cannot truly *know* anything) because we are finite and culture-bound by an unavoidably limiting horizon.

The initial responses to such cynicism are well known: (a) To argue that we cannot know anything truly unless we know something exhaustively is to erect an impossible standard. It is to claim that knowledge belongs exclusively to Omniscience. In the most absolute sense, of course, that is true—yet transparently the Bible speaks of finite human beings knowing many things. In other words, it is entirely appropriate to speak of human knowing within the limitations of non-omniscient cognitive powers. Human knowing is possible, even though it is not divine knowing. To dismiss human knowing as knowledge because it is not divine omniscient knowing is not humility, but hubris. (b) Anyone who has begun the study of a new discipline, whether Attic Greek, theoretical physics, or the reproductive system of sea turtles knows (that word again) that growth in knowledge is possible, which demonstrates that knowledge is possible. (c) Nowadays we are not confined to the hermeneutical spiral. Much more convincing models have been set forth: the hermeneutical spiral, or asmyptotic approaches to true knowledge.[9] (d) For the Christian with a high view of Scripture (which is what Jesus espoused), there is considerable reassurance in the fact that Omniscience has condescended to disclose true things to us in words that we humans can study, learn, and reflect on. In itself that cannot guarantee faultless interpretation, but it does suggest a goal worth striving after when this omniscient God has taken the trouble to make truth known to us.

All this is to say that although one of the most important tasks of professors of mission is the teaching of cross-cultural communication, both in theory and in specific practice, that task must be undertaken not as an end in itself, but with the goal of training Christian missionaries to be faithful and empathetic communicators of the glorious gospel once for all delivered to the the Lord's people.

---

9   Cf. Grant R. Osborne, *The Hermeneutical Spiral: A Comprehensive Introduction to Biblical Interpretation*, 2nd edition (Downers Grove: IVP, 2006); D. A. Carson, *The Gagging of God: Christianity Confronts Pluralism* (Grand Rapids: Zondervan, 1996).

And *fifth*, as indicated earlier, this task similarly rests on the shoulders of many pastors who discharge their ministry within North America, not least in our cities where we may come across numerous competing and conflicting cultures. Indeed, the task of cross-cultural communication now falls on the shoulders of most ordinary Christians who desire to bear faithful and fruitful witness to increasingly diverse neighbors. As a result, we need more professors of mission, not fewer.

(5) A growing ability to bridge the gap between the dominant categories in our target cultures, and the dominant biblical-theological categories

Many have observed that the dominant trajectories of the Bible, the strands that hold the Bible's storyline together, have little resonance with much of Western culture. Covenant, temple, kingdom, blood sacrifice, priesthood, creation/new creation, Jerusalem/new Jerusalem, shepherd/sheep, shame, sin, justification, eschatology, consummation—all have this in common: they spark little excitement to the person on the street. Where they do resonate with the culture, they usually mean something different from the emphases in the Bible. But if we focus instead on the dominant interests of our culture, it is easy to transmute the biblical message into false gold. So one of the things we must do is teach pastors and missionaries how to bridge the gap between the dominant categories in our target cultures, and the dominant biblical-theological categories.

For example: Most people in the Western world do not incorporate blood sacrifice into their thinking of what might be appropriate in approaching God (unlike Islam with its animal sacrifice during the *Hajj*). On the other hand, every culture reserves admiration for certain kinds of sacrifice: for instance, the mother who loses her life to save the life of her child from a raging house fire. Indeed, this might even be a wholly admirable substitutionary sacrifice. Or again, when helping students to understand both guilt and shame, it may be useful to draw lines of both continuity and discontinuity with the relevant cultures. In Western predominantly guilt-cultures, it is important to distinguish between subjective feelings of guilt and actual guilt before a holy God. Both must be dealt with, but one remains unprepared for the gospel until one perceives the awfulness of real guilt before God. In a shame culture, virtually all the shame that a person feels is loss of face before peers. By contrast, as early as Genesis 3 the Bible depicts both shame before peers (the covering of fig leaves) and shame before God (trying to hide from him in the garden)—and that must be grasped before we will become clear as to what expressions such as "Jesus bore our guilt *and shame*" really mean.

In short, one of the things we look for in a professor of mission is the ability to bridge the gap between the dominant categories in the target culture and the dominant biblical-theological categories.

(6) People who are actually doing evangelism and church-planting, and not just talking about it

Just because this point is obvious doesn't mean we should fail to articulate it. In exactly the same way that programs that train pastors need professors who love pastoral ministry, so also programs that train missionaries need professors who love cross-cultural evangelism, disciple-making, and church planting. Some things are better caught than taught. Professors of mission who love and engage in such work will inevitably bring anecdotes and personal experiences into the classroom in such a way that not a few students will hunger to emulate them.

That is a huge part of the importance of the short book by J. Mack Stiles, *Marks of the Messenger: Knowing, Loving and Speaking the Gospel*.[10] This is a book that makes Christians *want* to make disciples, without making them feel guilty because they are not very good at it. The professors who keep doing such work are the ones most likely to keep up to date in a practical sense. They are also the ones most likely to inflame the hearts and minds of the next generation.

(7) A passion to identify ourselves as those who bear witness to Jesus

To establish this point, I shall do nothing more than demonstrate the flow of thought in Matthew 11:2-19. The passage can usefully be divided into three parts, and the three parts need to be read together to establish the point that must be made. The crucial verse, as we shall see, is Matthew 11:11, but the run-up must be grasped.

First, a portrait of a discouraged Baptist (11:2-6). I am not, of course, speaking denominationally; rather, I am referring to John the Baptist, who, judging by his actions, is having second thoughts as to whether Jesus is the promised Messiah (11:2). Jesus does not seem to be the kind of Messiah John the Baptist had announced, one who would separate the wheat and the chaff, burning up the latter with unquenchable fire (3:12). Jesus' answer, passed back to John through John's disciples, is bathed in Scripture (esp. Isaiah 35:5-6; 61:1). The essence of Jesus' response is this: my words (chaps. 5-7) and deeds (chaps. 8-10) demonstrate that I am truly bringing in the blessings of the messianic age. And if the judgments are delayed—well, "Blessed is anyone who does not stumble on account of me" (11:6).

---

10 Downers Grove: IVP, 2010.

Second, a portrait of a defended Baptist (11:7-11a). Apparently the exchange between Jesus and the Baptist's emissaries took place in front of the crowd. So now, as John's disciples depart, Jesus talks to the crowd about John (11:7). The context suggests they've been muttering about how John the Baptist is turning out to be something of a disappointment, some kind of wimp—and Jesus comes to John's defense. He poses a series of rhetorical questions. When they went into the desert to take a look at John the Baptist, what were they expecting to see? "A reed swayed by the wind" (11:7)—some creature without backbone? Of course not! The reports to which they were responding pictured

the Baptist as a rugged prophet, not a wimp—so the crowd does not have the right to look askance at him now. So what else might they have been expecting? Eventually Jesus suggests, "A prophet?" (11:9). Yes, indeed, Jesus asserts, "and more than a prophet" (11:9). And how is John the Baptist "more than a prophet?" Jesus provides the answer: the Baptist is himself the subject of a prophecy, the prophecy about one who prepares the way for the Lord (Malachi 3:1; Matthew 11:10). And then comes the stunning conclusion: "Truly I tell you, among those born of women [a pretty comprehensive bracket] there has not risen anyone greater than John the Baptist" (11:11a). In other words, in Jesus' estimate, John the Baptist is greater than Abraham, Moses, David, Isaiah, and everyone else. Why? What makes him so great? The preceding verse gives the answer: the Baptist is greater than all who came before him because it fell to him to introduce Jesus with greater immediacy and clarity than they could. In some ways, of course, Abraham pointed to Jesus, and so did Moses, David, Isaiah, and the rest. But it fell to John to say, in effect, "There! There's the man whose sandals I'm unworthy to loosen." And that's what makes him great.

Third, a portrait of an eclipsed Baptist. John the Baptist is the greatest man born of woman to this point in redemptive history—and now Jesus insists that the Baptist has himself been eclipsed: "yet whoever is least in the kingdom of heaven is greater than he" (11:11b). That's because even the least in the kingdom can point out who Jesus is with greater clarity and immediacy than John the Baptist. In three more chapters, John the Baptist is going to lose his head. He would not live long enough to become a witness of the cross and resurrection, or a member of the post-resurrection community. But the least Christian, however ill-taught and immature, can say, "I don't understand very much yet, but I know that Jesus died on the cross for my sins, and that he lives today, and has forgiven me. I trust him." All the rest of the passage, down to 11:19, contributes to solidifying this point. In other words, the least Christian is greater than John the Baptist, who is greater than Moses and David and Isaiah. If logic means anything, that means that the least Christian is greater than Moses and David and Isaiah. Transparently, that does not mean "greater in every respect." Christians are unlikely to claim to be greater legislators than

Moses, greater military personnel than David, or greater prophets than Isaiah. But on the axis that controls this context—viz, the clarity and immediacy with which they point out who Jesus is—they are indeed greater than Moses and David and Isaiah.

And that's what establishes this eighth point. If bearing witness to Jesus is, according to Jesus, precisely what makes Christians "great," it is shocking beyond words to find Christians who never bear witness to him. And in particular, we want professors of mission as those who identify themselves as people who bear witness to Jesus. That is their heartbeat; that is their life's blood.

(8) A vision for the centrality of the church

After Pentecost, it is impossible to find in the pages of the New Testament a Christian who is not baptized, or a baptized Christian who is not a member of a local church. True, *individuals* come to faith—but when they come to faith, they become part of the body of Christ manifest in that locale. Jesus declared, "I will build my church" (Matthew 16:18), not "I will collect my individuals." The overwhelming preponderance of the New Testament uses of the word "church" refer to the local church. In the New Testament, one repents, believes, is baptized, and becomes a member of the local church, all in one package. That is why an expression such as "all who have been baptized" is more or less the equivalent of "all who have been converted" (cf. Galatians 3:27).

It would take quite a while to provide convincing evidence of these claims. But if they are right, they really ought to shape how we talk about conversion, becoming a Christian, discipleship, church membership, living in a counter-cultural community, even how we think about a number of pastoral challenges (such as combating big city isolation). Should not professors of mission be steeped in such a vision? Is it enough to talk about people movements and not about the church?

(9) A sense of the glory and sheer transcendence of God

Although I'd be happy to defend everything I've said so far in this address, I draw it to a close vaguely dissatisfied. There is a perennial danger of sounding too mechanical, too procedural, too much like a list-maker who creates points to check off but who loses sight of the mission. What we must have, not just among professors of mission, and not just among Christian leaders, but among all Christians, is a growing sense of the utter transcendence and glory of God. It is very rare for that to develop without leaders pointing the way under the authority of holy Scripture. And professors of mission constitute part of this strategic leadership in the church.

Conclusion

So these things, I submit, are among the things we should look for in those who teach mission. There are other things that could have been brought up. For example, some professors of mission devote themselves to the specialization of mission history, which so far I have not mentioned. They become a specialized subset of the band of church historians. Like church historians, ideally they will display exemplary scholarship, great care with research and sources and judgment, while at the same time thinking and writing in such a way as to commend the gospel of our blessed Redeemer.[11]

What is obvious from this list, however, is that most of the entries apply equally to pastors who discharge their ministry in North America within the culture with which they are most familiar. Indeed, most of these points apply to Christians everywhere, who remember their responsibility to evangelize, make disciples, plant churches, and live out their lives in passionate hunger for the glory of God and concomitant death to self and service to others. And the specialty bits that belong peculiarly to professors of mission (e.g., explaining other religions and cultures), as vitally important as they are, must never be discharged at the expense of the biblical sweep of what it means to be a Christian.

---

11 One thinks, for example, of the book by Scott M. Manetsch, *Calvin's Company of Pastors: Pastoral Care and the Emerging Reformed Church, 1536-1609*, Oxford Studies in Historical Theology (New York: Oxford University, 2013).

No Church in the Wild

Missiological Education in a Post-Civil Rights Era

DANIEL WHITE HODGE, PHD
NORTH PARK UNIVERSITY CHICAGO

Good day friends and colleagues. I come to you with a heavy heart. As I sit preparing this talk, the current time, context, climate, and culture in the United States is fraught with racial, gender, and cultural strains the likes of which have not been seen since the Jim Crow Era. It is a time unlike any other. While the period prior to the 1970's was direct and intense racism, the present context utilizes social media, with passive and micro-aggression to create its hegemony and culture of hate. I struggle as a racially Black male living in the U.S. and trying to live out a faith rooted in Christianity—particularly when the history of Christianity has been shown to be objectionable to not only the color of my skin, but my narrative, body, and life.[1] The events that have taken the main stage in the media's public sphere started to erupt, at least personally, during the Troy Davis campaign. Here, a young Black male, who was convicted of shooting and killing a White police officer, sat on death row. When I began to research the issue and the Davis case, I found little physical evidence was actually found, and the "eye witness" later recanted the story of seeing Davis murder the police officer.[2] Amid a strong social media campaign and even phone calls to elected officials, Troy Davis was executed on September 21, 2011. Then came Trayvon Martin and later Michael Brown[3]; both the Ferguson and Baltimore uprisings; and the terrorist acts of Dylann Roof in Charleston, South Carolina. Roof mercilessly murdered nine Black church members of the historic Emmanuel A.M.E Church. Then came Tamir Rice, Dante Parker, John Crawford III, Sandra Bland, and in Chicago, Laquan McDonald. This list could continue with names as it seems the killing of Black bodies has become an epidemic sport in the U.S. All of this time the use of Christian discourse is used to continue the subjugation of Black bodies in the use of phrases and words such as "forgive," "love your enemies," and "bless those that curse you." And while in allegory, at least, those are hoped for and desired, the reality is that when White America feels threatened or is attacked (e.g. 9/11), the opposite of these

---

1   One must consider the use of Christianity as both a racist and violent tool of oppression towards many Africans and African Americans—not to mention other ethnic-minority groups such as Mexicans, Chinese, Japanese, and Native Americans. This will be engaged more later in this text as it relates to missions and colonialization.

2   I do realize this is a controversial case. In fact, most Black and White cases typically are. From my research and investigation, Troy Davis should have had another trial and the new evidence should have been admitted into that trial. I am fully aware that many White evangelicals took issue with the Davis trial and sided with the courts. This is part of the ongoing tensions in the U.S. and especially in Christian evangelical circles.

3   This is in no way minimizing the women and other Black youth who have been murdered and/or killed at the hands of either police officers or "vigilante" White citizens. What I suggest here are the capstone events that have shaped both our nation and where I personally stand as a Black Christian male.

phrases is taken and a type of "holy violence" is often utilized.[4] And while I see White evangelical youth dancing to Lecrae at one of his concerts, the irony comes when those same youth tell me things like "Michael Brown wasn't innocent and probably deserved to die." Or "These 'thugs' were asking for it." Or the classic, "This was part of God's plan."[5] They say such things as they enjoy and embrace Black culture.

Further, the events that culminated on November 8, 2016, shook many of us in the ethnic-minority community when Donald J. Trump was elected as the 45th president of the United States.[6] The election of such a figure in the office of presidency, sent a direct message to ethnic-minority communities that their voice did not matter.[7] Our foretold "hope" of the Obama legacy was

4   The use of violence and the construct of a "just God" is a matter we will be engaged with briefly in this text. For a greater examination see Daniel White Hodge, *Hip Hop's Hostile Gospel: A Post-Soul Theological Exploration* ed. Warren Goldstein, vol. 6, Center for Critical Research on Religion and Harvard University (Boston, MA: Brill Academic, 2017), 122-47.

5   These are all direct quotes taken from two summer youth events in 2014 and 2015. The latter quote came from George Zimmerman's interview with Sean Hannity (2012) in which he stated that the killing of Trayvon was part of "God's plan" and that he "prays for them [Martin's family] daily." This type of discourse is common and is part of the ideological structure that many post-civil rights millennials refuse to engage with and/or adopt. This has ramifications for Evangelicalism as many in the post-civil rights millennial generation view Evangelicals as outdated, racist, sexist, and having a very skewed reality of who "God" is.

6   While the goal here is not to condemn those who favor a conservative perspective, it is, however, important to note that Trump's rhetoric, policies, and many of his appointed cabinet members are aligned with an Alt-Right worldview which is in direct contradiction to any social justice or intercultural work. Therefore, it is difficult to entertain the notion of Trump being "for all Americans" when it is clear, by his actions and cabinet, that he is only for the continuation of Whiteness as a standard for "American." I would challenge anyone who voted for Trump to defend someone like Steven Bannon, for example, and the rhetoric of hate he has spewed over the years towards Jews, Blacks, Palestinians, and even women that his perspective fits as a "Christian worldview." It is imperative that we critically wrestle with these matters because they are of utmost importance for anyone who regards Christianity as their faith.

7   It is also noted in emerging research that the presence and notion of "growing diversity" creates fear in many Whites who concern themselves with the changing electorate. This also illustrates the fear which has existed in many White churches for decades regarding growing ethnic-minority populations, Brenda Major, Alison Blodorn, and Gregory Major Blascovich, "The Threat of Increasing Diversity: Why Many White Americans Support Trump in the 2016 Presidential Election," *Group Processes & Intergroup Relations* 21, no. 6 (931-940). A type of warning, if you will, was issued in the classic text *Divided by Faith : Evangelical Religion and the Problem of Race in America* (Oxford: Oxford University Press, 2001) by Michael Emerson and Christian Smith which, even then, outlined the growing

shown to be mythological in nature and the optimism that was of the coming "demographical changes"[8] in which minorities were to finally triumph and take "power" for justice was just another neo-liberal delusion. It also shook those of us who have dedicated our life to intercultural and racial justice work that 81% of White Evangelicals voted for such a person like Trump and continue to support his policies.[9] That was an awakening for me and it made me question the work I do. Had it mattered? Did any of it sink in? How could all the material published and spoken on just go ignored?

All these questions developed while attempting to prepare this talk. My heart is heavy and my mind full. I ask for your prayers as we enter into this discussion.

I ask, what does faith look like in this context? What does a missiological response feel like when the bodies of Black youth are celebrated and adored on one platform, yet hated and seen as of little worth on the other? What does all of this mean for those doing short term missions in domestic urban contexts—specifically if that ministry favored Trump in the election? How might the dissonance towards multi-ethnic life be salient in popular culture yet manifested in an artist like Lecrae? Do we as mission-minded people take race, gender, and class into account when we "evangelize?" In addition, how does one contend with someone like Darren Wilson who spoke of Michael Brown as a "demon" coming after him? Does the Christian faith, as the mystic and Black Christian theologian, Howard Thurman states, "make room" for concerns such as racism and the disinherited?[10] Some still argue that the only "ministry" or "missions" worth doing is preaching the "gospel" to the "lost" and that is where our mission ends.

I would take issue with ministry and mission defined so narrowly. Woven into that definition is a construct around missions and who those missions are directed at, who does missions, and why those missions are conducted. I would

---

gap within Evangelical churches.

8   Those that are rooted in the notion that somehow the rise of the ethnic-minority population in the U.S. will somehow skew voting to reflect a more "diverse" country and one that has an emphasis on social justice. While no one can accurately predict the future, and I too would argue that possibly in two or three generations we may very well be in such a place within the U.S., as of now, it is not the case and if we have learned anything from the history of South Africa, we know that those in power do not have to have the majority in ethnic numbers.

9   See Gregory A. Smith and Jessica Martínez, "How the Faithful Voted: A Preliminary 2016 Analysis," in *Fact Tank: News in the Numbers* (Washington D.C.: Pew Research Center, 2016); Myriam Renaud, "Myths Debunked: Why Did White Evangelical Christians Vote for Trump?," in *The Martin Marty Center for the Advanced Study of Religion* (Chicago, IL: The Univeristy of Chicago 2017).

10 Howard Thurman, *Jesus and the Disinherited* (Boston, MA: Beacon Press, 1976).

contend with Richard Kyle that, "Reflecting the old Puritan heritage and American individualism, evangelicals focus on abortion and sexual immorality while downplaying the issues of poverty, racism, and social injustice. When they address such problems, they believe that the problems can be solved primarily through individual, church, or local efforts."[11] Further, the agency of race, gender, and class are lost within that narrow definition. Given the current state of American Christianity, race, gender, and class can no longer be avoided. I would argue that one of the reasons Christianity is viewed as irrelevant, useless, sexist, racist, and exclusive is a result of this narrowly defined concept around ministry and missions. The simplicity it depicts is much too utopian in a world that has rejected almost any form of utopianism[12] and rather give creed to complexity, mystery, ambiguity, and a disruptivist worldview. "The Gospel" means nothing to someone who lives in a constant state of terror from institutional racism personified in a police uniform. "Jesus' good news" is just empty discourse to those whose lives are disrupted by short-term missionaries who are only around for selfies, newsletters, and narcissistic emotions taking advantage of a people's misery and despair. Therefore, we find ourselves in a quandary at this point in Christian history, a quandary of values and morals. Whose narrative will win—conservative or liberal?

I would suggest that the issues we face as Christians and missiologists alike are much more multifaceted and broader than those binary constructs such as left vs. right. They are much broader than simply saying ministry and missions ends at the acceptance of Jesus into one's life. I would assert that the issues we face in terms of racism, sexism, fascism, and classism are worsened by a myriad of media outlets claiming to be "fact-checking" or "truth tellers" which drive people deeper into their binary corners and thereby ignore a plethora of complexity in the middle. Thus, a church in the wild is needed. A church that embraces a mission of complexity, mystery, ambiguity, and high concentrations of doubt. The same mindset that makes up large portions of this era and this generation's ethos. A church in the wild bold enough to disrupt the commonplace of American Evangelicalism and create a much more contextual approach to Jesus. A church in the wild creative enough to

---

11 Richard G. Kyle, *Evangelicalism : An Americanized Christianity* (New Brunswick, N.J.: Transaction Publishers, 2006), 314.

12 In fact, most post-soul theorists resist simplicity and utopianism as a form of thinking and life. See Dick Hebdige, "Postmodernism and 'the Other Side'," in *Cultural Theory and Popular Culture: A Reader*, ed. John Storey (London, England: Pearson Prentice Hall, 1998). Also, Garth Alper, "Making Sense out of Postmodern Music?," *Popular Music and Society* 24, no. 4 (2000); Nelson George, *Post-Soul Nation : The Explosive, Contradictory, Triumphant, and Tragic 1980s as Experienced by African Americans (Previously Known as Blacks and before That Negroes)* (New

use Hip Hop and its theological core13 as a missiological premise. A church in the wild confrontational enough to interrupt White supremacy in American Christianity.

A church in the wild, that does not yet exist.

There is No Church In The Wild

Jay Z and Kanye West's song from their 2011 album *Watch The Throne*, "No Church In The Wild" lays out the genesis for this book:

> Human beings in a mob
>
> What's a mob to a king?
>
> What's a king to a god?
>
> What's a god to a non-believer?
>
> Who don't believe in anything?

Note the progression of the chorus. It follows a linear hierarchy of reasoning. Human beings as a group, a community, and/or a specific locality, but what does that even matter to someone like a king or high-established official? In other words, with all the issues and problems someone has on a moment-by-moment basis, why would a king—and I would add queen to this equation—care one bit about those issues? How might something like the Laquan McDonald murder by a police officer affect a high city official like the mayor? How might something as trivial as a parking ticket—whose monetary effect could devastate a family on a very tight budget—distress someone like the president of the United States? But the chorus continues; what is a king to a god? This type of analogy and symbolism repeats itself continually throughout our Bible. Matthew 6:33 urges us to seek first, the kingdom of God, John 18:36 shows Jesus saying how his kingdom is not of this world, Daniel 2:44 tells of God setting up a kingdom that will never be destroyed, and Zechariah reminds us that one day God will be king over all of the earth. Throughout the Bible, there are references which give credence to God not caring much for the kingdoms that humans create God's kingdom is much more important and much more tangible. So, what's an earthly king to a god? Yet, the chorus

---

York, NY: Viking, 2004); Mark Anthony Neal, *Soul Babies: Black Popular Culture and the Post-Soul Aesthetic* (New York: Routledge, 2002); Paul C. Taylor, "Post-Black, Old Black," *African American Review* 41, no. 4 (2007); Joseph Winters, "Unstrange Bedfellows: Hip Hop and Religion," *Religion Compass* 5, no. 6 (2011).

13 A theology of suffering, a theology of community, a theology of the Hip Hop Jesuz, a theology of social action and justice, and a theology of the profane Daniel White Hodge, *The Soul of Hip Hop: Rimbs Timbs & A Cultural Theology* (Downers Grove, IL: Inner Varsity Press, 2010).

line comes back, almost to a singularized point in asking, what is a god to a non-believer—taking the escalating meta-question back to a micro-singular position; what does all that even matter if you do not believe in anything?

This, then, is where Christianity finds itself in the present era: post-civil rights and post-soul.[14] In a place wanting to prove itself relevant; desiring to argue the "truth"; engaging in an "us vs. them" debate. It is in this era that Christianity, in all its complexity, beauty, force, intricacy, and faith is reduced into binary corners: good and bad; moral and immoral; conservative and liberal—or the more recent term of "progressive." Yet, what does this matter to someone who: 1) has lost faith in God altogether, 2) has been oppressed and disenfranchised by Christians, 3) has read, and possibly lived, the destructive history of Christian faith being weaponized for violence and death, 4) has been psychologically affected by the damaging effects of fundamentalism, and 5) simply does not believe there is a God? Given the current age of information and interstellar exploration, God may not even be a literal figure, possibly one created in the minds of humans, right?

I will just say it: it does not matter! It does not matter that the debate continues on regarding abortion. It does not matter if prayer is allowed in school or not. It does not matter that the debate of creation vs. evolution rages on. It does not matter which day is the "right" day to worship God; Sunday or Saturday. It does not matter whether or not your church has an American flag planted in the sanctuary. It does not matter whether or not there is a rapture or a time of suffering. It does not even matter whether or not being LGBT is a sin or not. It does not matter! These side issues are merely noise to a non-believer who does not believe in anything. As Christians and missiologists this should be of greatest concern.

Christian theologians, pastors, priests, be it Protestant, Catholic, Evangelical, or Orthodox, seem to want to convince those non-believers that those things, and other issues, are important. Somehow if the "kingdom" is shown, if somehow the argument and articulation of the Christian faith is done in just the right manner, then they will believe. Jay-Z and Kanye, however, got it right. They ask the pertinent question. They force us to wrestle with those five little lines and within those lines, create an intricacy of dilemmas for anyone wanting to "preach the Gospel" or carry out any form of missions in the United States. Simply put, there is no church in the wild. A church that can sit with more questions and doubt than it can answers and solutions. A church, which disrupts its own thinking on race, gender, and class. A church

14 While these definitions will be defined later in the introduction, I am using these two terms here to name 1) the current generation of young people between the ages of 14 and 29 and 2) the era of the past thirty-five years which questions meta-narrative, meta-ideology, and agency defined from hegemonic positions.

which is able to transcend tradition, dogma, and rigid theological stances and push for relationships, community, and the mystery-enlightenment of who God is in this present age. Is there a church that can do that? Is there a church that pushes past the age-old arguments for the sake of a conversation with a person? Is there a church inside of the Hip Hop generations? Is there a church for the thugs, the pimps, and the drug pushers? Jay-Z and Kanye are wrestling with this! They ask us to grapple with it as well.

The Christian church has been out of the wild for quite some time. The 1960's, (the decade that ushered in the post-soul era[15]) was the last stage for binary Christian thought. It is argued that WWII was the last "just war" and one in which the enemy and the hero were clearly defined—one of the many reasons almost every year there is a new film dealing with some facet of that era. The era prior to the 1960's was a "hay-day" for missionaries; a time when a White heterosexual male was the model for Christian missions and the

---

15 While an exact date and time is not clear, most scholars suggest that the decade of the 1960's gave rise to a deconstruction of which we are still wrestling with, in many regards this was labeled as "post-modernism" and is said to have re-structured the way church and state relate and began what we can now term as the "culture wars." For the purpose of this book, I will use this decade as ground-zero for the post-soul era, see: Zygmunt Bauman, "Postmodern Religion?," in *Religion, Modernity, and Postmodernity*, ed. Paul Heelas (Oxford, UK; Malden, MA: Blackwell, 1998); Daniel Bell, *The Coming of a Post-Industrial Society: A Venture in Social Forecasting* (New York: Basic Books, 1973); David Jacobus Bosch, *Transforming Mission : Paradigm Shifts in Theology of Mission*, American Society of Missiology Series (Maryknoll, N.Y.: Orbis Books, 1991); Don Cupitt, "Post-Christianity," in *Religion, Modernity, and Postmodernity*, ed. Paul Heelas (Oxford, UK; Malden, MA: Blackwell, 1998); Norman K. Denzin, *Images of Postmodern Society: Social Theory and Contemporary Cinema* (Thousand Oaks CA: Sage Publications, 1991); D. Escobar, "Amos & Postmodernity: A Contemporary Critical & Reflective Perspective on the Interdependency of Ethics & Spirituality in the Latino-Hispanic American Reality," *Journal of Business Ethics* 103, no. 1 (2011); George, *Post-Soul Nation: The Explosive, Contradictory, Triumphant, and Tragic 1980s as Experienced by African Americans (Previously Known as Blacks and before That Negroes)*; Hebdige, "Postmodernism and 'the Other Side'"; Paul Martin David Heelas and Paul Morris, *Religion, Modernity, and Postmodernity, Religion and Modernity, Variation: Religion and Modernity*. (Oxford, UK: Malden, Mass., 1998); Jean-Francois Lyotard, *The Postmodern Condition: A Report on Knowledge* (Minneapolis MN: University of Minnesota Press, 1984); Anthony Pinn, *The Black Church in the Post-Civil Rights Era* (Maryknoll, NY: Orbis Books, 2002); Taylor, "Post-Black, Old Black." *African American Review* (Winter 2007) 41(4):625-640.

"sending forth" came from the U.S.[16] to "them, out there." That era was a time when society "made sense."[17] An era when many kept a traditionalist ideology. A time when men were men, children listened, and people—particularly ethnic minorities—knew "their place." It was an era that created America as the powerhouse-sending agent of missionaries.[18] In addition, it was an era which created a sense of the U.S. as the authority for missions and "truth"[19] for those "out there" on foreign soil.

Yet, today, the decline of Christianity as noted by scholars such as Christian Smith, Robert Putman, and David Kinnaman seats the U.S. as a "lost" and "pagan" ground. The church looks more like the godless societies of the 1950's and 60's. It could then be argued that the U.S. is in fact a missiological ground for the sending forth and Missio Dei. This was in fact the shift when Ray Bakke made the case for urban missions and a theology for the city. Domestic missions were not something taken very seriously and not until the last decade

---

16 Soong-Chan Rah, *The Next Evangelicalism : Releasing the Church from Western Cultural Captivity* (Downers Grove, Ill.: IVP Books, 2009), 127-31. Also see William R. Jones, *Is God a White Racist? A Preamble to Black Theology* (Garden City, N.Y.: Anchor Press, 1973); John D. Wilsey, *American Exceptionalism and Civil Religion : Reassessing the History of an Idea* (Downers Grove, IL: IVP Academic, 2015); Richard Twiss, *Rescuing the Gospel from the Cowboys : A Native American Expression of the Jesus Way* (Downers Grove, IL: IVP Books, 2015); Trevor B. McCrisken, "Exceptionalism," in *Encyclopedia of American Foreign Policy*, ed. Richard Dean Burns, Alexander DeConde, and Fredrik Logevall (New York: Charles Scribner's Sons, 2002). It is of interest to note that the majority of missions material between 1950-1961 was written by men, most of whom were White.

17 In particular, for those in the Boomer, Builder, and Civil Rights generations.

18 In Robert Glover's text, *The Progress of World-wide Missions*, he notes the missionary's motives and while those motives are, in some regard, rooted in a Biblical manner, the "sending agents" were primarily from North America; the U.S. to be precise. To further this, a majority of these missionaries were White males coming with a strict evangelical perspective. As I will note later, those perspectives do not come without bias, prejudices, racial constructs, and/or racist presuppositions and thereby, create a settler colonialist missiological space. This practice, continued over decades, is debilitating and does not allow for a full view of the breadth of what Christianity is.

19 This is noted throughout the documentary *God In America: How Religious Liberty Shaped America* (2010) and also by William Ernest Hocking who noted the "error" and "mistaken" approaches of many missionaries abroad *Re-Thinking Missions; a Laymen's Inquiry after One Hundred Years* (New York; London: Harper & Bros., 1932), 29-32.

has it become an area of study for missionaries.[20] But what do we do with the shifting of Christianity in the 20th century and now 21st? How might we then contend with a generation of ethnic minority Millennial Gen Y's? This group calls out the White hegemonic structures of inequality, but seek to also disrupt those hegemonic structures of older ethnic minorities as well? How might one see the U.S. as a mission field when a god does not mean a thing to a non-believer?

This is where this talk enters the scene amid the tension of these questions and at a time when many Christians scurry to keep some remnant of what they define as "Christian." We as missiological educators enter at a time when racial unrest is at, or in some cases beyond, the levels it was in 1969.[21]

Societal Shifts and the Context of Missiological Education in the Post-Civil Rights Context

The White homogeneity of missions in North America is problematic. Not because of White homogeneity solely (e.g. White people), but because many Whites are ignorant to the issues surrounding racism, White Supremacy, and systemic racism, and thereby have continued a legacy of colonialism, micro-aggression, and passive discrimination. Those issues conflate under the premise of "Christian mission" and do not have the cultural relevancy or competencies to enact a contextualized culturally proper missiology. Therefore, my thesis can be broken down into two parts, 1) current missiological approaches are impaired

---

20 When I first attended Fuller Theological Seminary's School of Intercultural Studies (Formerly School of World Missions), I was required to have at least five years of "cross cultural" work in a mission's field. While I thought about using the fact that I had been a racially Black man working in predominantly White Christian settings met that qualifier, I decided to use my domestic missions work as my entry in, which at that time was over a decade. I was denied entry and had to appeal, as "local missions" was not a consideration for "missions" work. This will be taken up later, but often, especially for White missionaries, the only "worthwhile" missions work is that overseas. Overseas work, however, ignores the brutality and severity of White Supremacy and White racism, so, in turn, it is much easier to deal with a genocide your ethnic heritage had nothing to do with, than to engage the issues we face in the U.S. currently.

21 I use 1969 as a set point because it is a time in which many scholars argue that "we almost lost our civility" in society due to the racial, cultural, sexual, and political unrest and violence beset in the U.S. at the given time, for examples of this see George Ritzer, *The Mcdonaldization of Society* (Thousand Oaks, Calif.: Pine Forge Press, 2004); Robin D. G. Kelley, *Race Rebels: Culture, Politics, and the Black Working Class* (New York Free Press, Toronto, 1994); Gordon Lynch, *Understanding Theology and Popular Culture* (Malden, MA: Blackwell Publishing, 2005); Neal, *Soul Babies: Black Popular Culture and the Post-Soul Aesthetic*; "Sold out on Soul: The Corporate Annexation of Black Popular Music," *Popular Music and Society* 21, no. 3 (1997).

and missiological methods need a difficult yet necessary transformation which allows for ethnic-minority leadership, vision, and theology; 2) a Hip Hop theology is a missiological framework which will help in creating community, Church context, and a stronger relationship to the trinity in a wild context.[22]

I explore missiological engagement within post-civil rights[23] contexts in the U.S. and focus on Hip Hop theology as a missiological tool for radical engagement of emerging adult populations in the wild. I would argue we need to emphasize a missiological perspective, within post-civil rights contexts, and suggest new conceptual models for domestic missions within an ever-growing multi-ethnic demographic. My argument speaks to and from three disciplines simultaneously—missiology, Hip Hop studies, and youth ministry—in an attempt to bring the three together around the themes of my thesis and a hybridity of *lived missiology*[24] grounded in the subject of Hip Hop Studies.

At the commencement of this talk, I must note that while many lectures conclude with a course of action or methodological solution—and I confess I have done that in other talks—this lecture will not. The goal here is to sound the alarm, of sort, and present the issues, arguments, and areas of need. We all have a part in this; you are to help in creating solutions and a praxiological approach to what I am raising today. I will assume that if you are here this it is because you are curious as to what the issues might be and possess the capacity to want to see some type of change. Thus, my goal here is to steer away from a 1-2-3 process of "what to do next" and "positivity" for the sake of positivity. We are in a critical state within missiology—a DEFCON 5. When

---

22 The use of wild here is not to imply that people who are non-Christian, or even those who are Christian but do not fit the traditional evangelical Christian image, are less than or even wild for that matter. The use of this word here continues the conversation raised in the song "No Church In The Wild" and is more a symbolic term that I am using here to describe things outside of a tradition or even stereotypical missiological lens rooted in Western Christianity. The current shift occurring in the U.S. is creating a healthy deconstruction of what it means to be Christian and how a Christian even looks, talks, believes, and loves; this would be an example of what I mean by "wild" and not the literal definition of the word.

23 It is important to note that the post-soul/post-civil rights context is made up of a matrix of people, cultures, sub-cultures, groups, ideologies, theologies, and events. I do not desire to take anything away from these important areas. However, an article, as vast as it can be, has limitations. This article will focus primarily on urban/ city culture with a strong emphasis on Hip Hop, Black, Latinx, and U.S. contexts. There are plenty of works that deal with areas outside of the aforementioned, yet, very little that deal specifically with "our" (meaning ethnic-minorities) areas. Thus, this article will take up part of that canon and have a specific focus.

24 That is, the notion that missions, rather than a sending forth to some foreign land, is lived, breathed, and carried out on a day-to-day basis in the sacred, secular, and profane; a lifestyle and engagement with the everyday within a community.

the American Society of Missiology (ASM) are formed of older, White, cis gendered males and struggle to "find diversity" in speakers, we have a problem. When the Association of Professors of Mission (APM) can count the number of ethnic-minorities in their guild, things are not right. To singularize this text and have it act as the guide, rather than a developing guide, is both precocious and arrogant. Moreover, in the current era we are in throughout the U.S., to have an "expert" be the only voice, is egotistical. If we are to move forward, we need to do so in community. Therefore, the suggestions placed here are to begin what a church in the wild might look like; possibly a generation from now. I present research and findings with some brief thoughts on those and allow you, the audience, to begin to formulate what solutions might be within your own context. This is a shift away from having a one-stop-shop within a text and to create dialog and community while working towards a common goal. Therefore, it should be noted, again, that the conclusion and thoughts about moving forward are merely suggestions and not a 1-2-3 step process of "solving" the "dilemma" of those "leaving the church." Rather, it is an invitation to move beyond the traditional missiological response of "going out there" to "reach them" for God and to commune and sit with those who are in the wild. What this is not, is an authoritative guide to the post-soul, and/or post-civil rights era to be used as a type of lexicon or canon. I come to this work as a participant and learner and ask those of you reading to do the same; let us explore what is in order to better see what may be.

Moving forward, we must lay out definitions that will be used throughout. The "wild," while the dictionary definition defines the word in a more adverse premise, I will use this word to symbolize the uncharted, non-domesticated, non-evangelically tamed area of ideological thoughts, theological principles, and generational motifs that makes up those from the Hip Hop and urban multi-ethnic generations. The generation that is now asking how Christianity can be of any help during a time of Black death. The wild is a context in which Black Lives Matter and the Black Youth Project are part of a missiological space and it offers both spiritual and socio-political formation for those movements. The wild is a not a place of methods, standardized curriculum, and over-simplified theologies that do not consider race, gender, and class as a central principle. Therefore, the wild is a space and place that those who venture in are in full knowledge of it being new, not designed for White Supremacy, seeking a Jesus outside of Evangelicalism, and in continual transformation. The wild will not be a place that is easily grappled with—even in an article like this. In other words, the wild is just that, an ongoing development and creation of ideas pushing away from Western White Evangelicalism and moving toward a more holistic space in which all are truly welcomed and embraced.

Sacred places are those areas held as hallowed, consecrated, and/or revered. The areas that we tend to hold near us and keep as special. In essence, the Sacred can be that space in which God finds you even if it is in a tattered state. Possibly the journey of Christian faith, while being held in tension with the secular world, is not just devoid of a deity representing God presence, but even hints about God's manifestation in our life. Often this means living in and taking up residence in a non-church context and environment. The secular has traditionally been used in Christian discourse as a place that is "un-godly" or "non-Christian." I will, however, suggest that the secular world can also nuance understandings of the Sacred while one is seeking a non-deity. In other words, it is in some sense the notion of being "spiritual, but not religious," and while that particular phrasing is captured by those not wanting to associate with religions, I too would agree that those who are secular and want to remain secular, do not necessarily wish to devoid themselves of all socio-spiritual notions and affiliations.[25] This then brings us to the *profane*,[26] the process of deconsecrating that which was once considered consecrated and sacred; the funk and the treacherous. Those areas in a society labeled or given the designation of being outside the given morals, codes, ethics, and values established as "good" and/ or "right" by the society and culture being studied. When combined (sacred, secular, profane), you have a rich and complex intersection of faith that has the three elements held in tension. It can be, particularly on first contact, an uncomfortable space in which to exist, yet, the wild is in constant tension with all three. Sometimes one more than the other. This is no different than any human experience. The experience of anyone on this planet (if they are honest) has all three of these elements present in their life. It is unwise to think that one can only be sacred all the time, or, profane at the core. Thus, this book will keep the trinary elements of the sacred, secular, and profane in tension as we explore the wild.

I also think it is important to define what *Hip Hop Culture and Theology* will mean for this article. Hip Hop culture is an urban sub-culture that seeks to express a *life-style, attitude,* and/or *urban individuality.* Hip Hop at its core— not the commercialization and commodity it has become in certain respects— *rejects* dominant forms of culture and society and seeks to increase a social

---

25 This was a crucial finding in the interviews I have conducted among Hip Hoppers who insisted that they were not affiliated with a church or denomination, yet desired to pursue a relationship with God in a secular space. As one interviewee exclaimed, "I don't need a church to find God, nor do I need a pastor to get wisdom and insight on the word. I like finding God in the void of everyday life."

26 In addition to these three definitions, this article will implore the use of these definitions of the sacred, secular, and the profane: sacred: those things that are divine or could be construed as divine; the secular: that which is devoid of God or lacks in spirituality; and the profane: that which is nefarious, oblique, and at times, contrary to 'good.'

consciousness along with a racial/ethnic pride. Thus, Hip Hop uses *rap music, dance, music production, MCing, and allegory* as vehicles to send and fund its message of social, cultural, and political *resistance* to dominate structures of norms.[27] Therefore, Hip Hop theology is derived from this latter definition and from the bowels of oppression, marginalization, and disenfranchisement in turn. As such it rejects normative and simplistic responses to such issues. Hip Hop theology is a post-civil rights theology and therefore this book will argue for its use as a missiological premise and construct moving into the wild. A Hip Hop theology is comprised of a theology of suffering, a theology of community, a theology of a Hip Hop Jesuz, a theology of social action, civil disruption, and a theology of the profane.

Thinking about Hip Hop and its culture, I think it is wise to define a word that has become quite coded in missiological contexts, the "urban."[28] For some it means those associated with Black and Latinx are all urban—meaning poor, in need of help, and impoverished. For others, it means something negative and a place in ministry they want nothing to do with because it is loud, aggressive, and non-familiar to their own worldview and cultural backgrounds. Yet, for still others, urban means a new space to exact your wealth; a place where the industry caters to you and the once stereotype of the "inner-city" is now gone—those who live in gentrified urban communities. And yet for other people, the urban is a place of ministry, life, missions, and community within a growing geographical area that, in growing cases, has little to do with an actual city. Therefore, urban, is defined as the conflation of low income, poverty, disenfranchisement, dislocation in society (e.g. anomie), and a sense of depravity from mainstream definitions of success. We will use this term not as a geographical location, but as a societal and cultural one. In other words, urban can be in various locations of a city such as Los Angeles and Chicago; it is not just the "inner city" in many regards.[29] I also find it necessary, although

---

27 Adapted from the works of Hodge, *The Soul of Hip Hop: Rimbs Timbs & a Cultural Theology*; *Hip Hop's Hostile Gospel: A Post-Soul Theological Exploration* 6; Efrem Smith and Phil Jackson, *The Hip Hop Church: Connecting with the Movement Shaping Our Culture* (Downers Grove, Ill.: IVP, 2005).

28 This term was popularized by urban theologians such as Ray Bakke, Roger Greenway, Harvie Conn, and the legendary John Perkins. This does not take anything away from the work that these pioneers laid out. It simply means that our times have changed and we have entered a new era with emerging definitions and in need of further developing the canon of urban missiology.

29 Scholars of urban studies are also agreeing that this term is rapidly changing, see Edward W Soja, *Postmetropolis: Critical Studies of Cities and Regions* (New York, NY: Blackwell Publishing 2000); William E Thompson and Joseph V Hickey, *Society in Focus*, 7 ed. (New York, NY: Pearson Books, 2011); William H. Whyte, "The Design of Spaces," in *The City Reader*, ed. Richard T. Le Gates and Frederic Stout (New York, NY: Routledge, 1996).

not a central premise of the article, to define an emerging term, the post-industrial era. This is the era we in the U.S. find ourselves and it is the era of electronics, digital narrative, commodification, and co-opting of other cultures for the use of dominant White structures. In a theological sense, this is the era in which knowledge is no longer sequestered to those with pedigree and status and it is the era of transmediated deity. An information age encasing industry rooted in the digital age and focusing primarily on the glorification of the self through social media spaces.[30] On the other hand, it is also a time when a rapper like Chance The Rapper can create a masterpiece of work without the help of a major record label. It is also the era in which a social media platform like Twitter helped in forming a powerful movement called Black Lives Matter. It is a time when those in Palestine suffering oppression can connect with those in Ferguson, Missouri suffering similarly and lend advice on how to resist. The post-industrial era is developing and although it is not a term used in missiological literature, it needs to be researched more so that it should. We are quickly leaving the era in which categorizations fit nicely in the scientific lab; the post-industrial era reshapes how we view the very basic elements of the "how" in life.

In addition, it will be helpful to examine a few other definitions to be used in tangent with the above list. *Soul context/er* is the era and context that is typically referred to as the Boomer Generation (1948-1969), but encompasses a much broader multi-ethnic variable. It is the era of the Civil Rights Generation and those born between 1945-1970. This era is steeped in the Church and raised on traditional primarily Protestant Christian values. This era saw the likes of Marvin Gaye, Aretha Franklin, and Ray Charles. Culturally speaking, there was a linear process to "life" and society. The soul era is etched with faith and religious overtones that mark its norms, values, and belief system strongly in the Christian church—especially the Black Christian church. The soul era, embraced an American Dream type of social element which many strived to achieve.[31] Leadership was top down and singularized—meaning one voice for the masses. It was a period that helped shape a large part of the African American diaspora in the U.S. It also situated the Black Church as the authority and socio-political space for justice and civil protests. Without this period, there would be no Hip Hop, soul, funk, disco, or Black liberation movement.

---

30 Craig Detweiler, *Igods: How Technology Shapes Our Spiritual and Social Lives* (Grand Rapids, Mich.: Brazos Press, 2014), 199-210.

31 See Daniel White Hodge, *The Hostile Gospel: Exploring Socio-Theological Traits in the Post-Soul Context of Hip Hop*, ed. Warren Goldstein, Center for Critical Research on Religion and Harvard University (Boston, MA: Brill Academic, 2015), Chapter1; *The Soul of Hip Hop: Rimbs Timbs & a Cultural Theology*, Chapter 2.

Still, even with the optimism of Black middle-class life during the 1950's and great hope of the civil-rights movement of the 1960's, the post-soul context/ era came at a time when Black values in the public sphere were declining and leaders of Black life, iconic even in their own time, were either killed or sent off into exile. The following generation was then raised in that void and in a time when media was creating tropes of Black life in shows like *The Jeffersons* (1975-1985) and *Sanford and Son* (1972-1977). This is the era and context following the soul era and similar to what is termed the postmodern period. The post-soul context/era lost its leadership and this emerging generation, those born from 1971 on, was disconnected from earlier ones. The youth born during this time were disconnected and disjointed from society. Moreover, with the rise in the absence of Black fathers during this time,[32] Black youth, especially, found it difficult to adjust in a world that was not socially, religiously, and morally logical to them and without the guidance of caring adults. This era created the first Hip Hop Generation.[33] This article will use this era as the base to build a missiological premise as we engage *with*, not to, this generation of emerging adults.

A term that received some traction after Obama was elected as president in 2008, was *post racial*. This is a false dichotomy created to insist that American society has somehow moved beyond or past the racial divide. In some regard, it was a wishful hope that suggests we—meaning society—no longer sees "color" or race. In this sense, we would be "post" race meaning we overlook the issues of White privilege, White supremacy, and the legacy of racism this country has endured. This book rejects a post racial society and will maintain that the issues of race are even more pronounced in the 21st century.

The *post-civil rights context/era* will be further clarified later, but, for now, it is the generation of youth born during the post-soul era/context, raised on a transmediated diet, disconnected from previous generations both locally and ideologically, and currently have non-binary issues to contend with in a post-9/11 society living within Western society. This generation of youth does not have the binary issues to contend with that the civil rights generation did (e.g. more Blacks in leadership or the right to vote). While those issues are still present, they manifest themselves in a matrix of problems, which involve sexuality, sexual orientation, socioeconomics, transgender, class, and race.

---

32 Angela J Hattery and Earl Smith, *African American Families* (Thousand Oaks, CA: Sage Publishers, 2007), 9-37. There is a host of literature discussing the denigration of Black fathers and the creation of the welfare system during the late 1960's and early 1970's.

33 We will spend some time later in further exploring these concepts, but this gives us a platform on which to begin.

DANIEL WHITE HODGE, PhD | 45

Another socio-geographic term also needs defining is *suburban*. The movement of resources and people out of the cities—suburbanization. The outer cities, albeit smaller, exist outside a metropolitan area and can vary in size and degrees of distance from a Central Business District (CBD).[34] Wealth, traditional approaches to the "American Dream," legacy prosperity, and the concept that "blessings from God" are encapsulated in these areas, accompanied by an ideological framework which situates the suburban locale as a desired place to dwell. This framework is reflected in a certain manner of division—being outside of, or separated from, the urban. Suburban areas are noted as having gates, guards, privatized resources, and allocated locations for the demonstration of power and wealth. Yet, the nuance to all this is that the geographic location of the "suburbs" is quickly receding back into the city with the rise of gentrification a.k.a "urban renewal."

Lastly, I wanted to define several racial terms. *Black* and *White* are both racialized terminology[35] that I realize are both debated and subjective in relation to how they are defined. However, I use these terms to categorize ethnic groups in a pan-ethnic sense. I also want to make clear that while there is still a discord between how those of African heritage living in the U.S. wish to be defined, I am in no way belittling those definitions. In other words, there are some who desire to be called African American, those who like the term Black while still others who desire to only be referred to by their ethnic heritage. African American is typically preferred in academic settings; however, I wish to focus in on a pan-ethnic term such as Black. Thus, Black is the racial term to identify anyone from a Pan African, Afro Latino, and/ or multi-ethnic background that appears "Black" in race. We contend that race is a socially constructed

---

34 William A. Darity, Jr., "Suburban Sprawl," in *International Encyclopedia of the Social Sciences*, ed. William A. Darity, Jr. (Detroit, MI: Macmillan Reference USA, 2008), 208-09.

35 I will discuss this further in section one, but color prejudice is part of a much larger issue of racism and oppression. The White gaze upon blackness, as a color, stems back into pre-colonial periods when Europeans first laid eyes upon central Africans. It was quickly noted that they were "less than" and that "their religion was un-Christian; their manner of living was anything but English." In essence, the "Negro" was one of lesser being, but one of marvel and rich for study. Early missionaries saw them "in need of God" and European stylized education. Winthrop Jordan notes that prior to the 16th century, Black had connotations of being soiled, muddied, evil, dark, twisted, and foul (from the *Oxford English Dictionary*). This worldview, engrained no less, stretched well into the creation of North American slavery and saw the African as less than human, nowhere near the excellence of the European. These same worldviews have continued on and created great divides and tensions all in the name of the "mission of God" *White over Black : American Attitudes toward the Negro, 1550-1812*, Omohundro Institute of Early American, History & Culture (Chapel Hill [N.C.]. University of North Carolina Press, 2012), 4-11.

category and rooted in colors (e.g. White, Brown, Yellow, Black, & Red). Ethnicity is, conversely, a biological and a much older term used to identity people and cultural groups much more accurately. *White* is the racial term to

identify anyone from a European, Russian, Norwegian, Swedish, or ethnically fair-skinned background. White, can therefore be understood as a position in a racialized social structure; that is, it is a label that is meaningless outside of a social system where racial categories influence access to social, political, and economic resources and in the absence of other socially constructed identities such as "Black" or "Asian."[36] I will assert that race, is always on display, while ethnicity can always be hidden, hence the use of these terms.

Racism, then, is a set of ideologies, beliefs, and worldviews regarding the superiority of one race over the other, and it is rooted in a system which reinforces that doctrine.[37] Those systems extend into education, criminal justice, health care, military, food industry, politics, and religion. The latter being of most importance for us as it relates to the way in which White missionaries have gazed upon Black bodies for centuries. The systemic approach to missions, including funding, social agency, networks, and access to seminary education, has privileged Whites and given them the advantage to "present the Gospel" in a one-dimensional manner.[38] Thus, systemically and often unaware, Whites have created a system in which those who are similar may enter and "do the work." This will be examined further in this article, but it is important to note the use of this word and how it will be applied through this text.

As a qualitative researcher, I am compelled to *tell the story*. While numbers and hard data has its place, my research relies heavily on qualitative interviews and narrative methods. First, is research which began in 2005 while I was completing my doctorate at Fuller Seminary, and working as a youth worker on the Northwest sector of Pasadena, CA. At that time, there were at least a dozen or more White evangelical churches bringing their youth groups to the "'hood" to do "mission work" among the "poor kids" of our community.

36 "Whiteness," in *International Encyclopedia of the Social Sciences*, ed. William A. Darity, Jr. (Detroit: Macmillan Reference USA, 2008), 87.

37 Richard Delgado and Jean Stefancic, "Critical Race Theory," in *New Dictionary of the History of Ideas*, ed. Maryanne Cline Horowitz (Detroit: Charles Scribner's Sons, 2005); Jonathan Marks, "Racism: Scientific," in *Encyclopedia of Race and Racism*, ed. Patrick L. Mason (Detroit: Macmillan Reference USA, 2013).

38 Samuel Perry, "Social Capital, Race, and Personal Fundraising in Evangelical Outreach Ministries," *Journal for the Scientific Study of Religion* 52, no. 1 (2013); "Diversity, Donations, and Disadvantage: The Implications of Personal Fundraising for Racial Diversity in Evangelical Outreach Ministries," *Review of Religious Research* 53, no. 4 (2012); "Racial Habitus, Moral Conflict, and White Moral Hegemony within Interracial Evangelical Organizations," *Qualitative Sociology* 35, no. 1 (2012).

And therefore, I began to document the experience and narratives of those being "ministered to," the "'hood kids," as one short-term missionary kid would later come to say. This is based on five urban[39] former students/mentees of mine between the years 2005-2010. Three females and two males of Mexican American, African American, Caribbean, and a mixture of Euro American ethnic makeup comprised this group. The interviews were conducted bi-monthly from 2005-2007 and then five times a year after. The interviews and research began in late summer 2005. Semi-structured interviews were utilized from 2005-2007. From the fall of 2007 to 2010, active interviews were used in group settings as all but one of the students had graduated from high school. All of the students were living in a gentrified urban/suburban environment and attended a predominantly White/Euro American affluent church which had once been located in a primarily White/Euro American community in Southern California. Each of the students started attending the church in early middle school and continued on through their early college years. I chose these students primarily for five reasons: 1) they were the most outspoken on issues of race, class, and gender in the group, 2) they each represented an ethnic minority group, 3) they were each leaders of their respective peers, 4) each had some type of leadership position in their late high school years, and 5) they represented the feelings of many ethnic minorities who did not have the access each of them did to senior leadership.[40] My wife and I also worked/volunteered for this ministry organization and had access to detailed information in regards to the training and background context.[41]

Second, is the research I started with my book *The Soul of Hip Hop* investigating not just Hip Hop culture, but the Hip Hop generation itself. That research, largely qualitative, has grown and continues to develop given

---

39 While the term "urban" is becoming vaguer by the year and a growing debate about how the term is applied and to whom, in what context, I will limit the use of the word to those who live in and/or engage with the issues of poverty, gang violence, single parenthood, low income housing, lack of adequate education, systemic dysfunction, and violent contexts within families, communities, neighboring spaces, educational constructs, and/or community surroundings. While this definition too can present its racial, gender, and class challenges, it will offer the necessary framework for this article and research.

40 The interviews began with the question "Tell me about your experience in X ministry organization" and then led to deeper probing questions as respondents gave their answers.

41 Please note that all of the names have been changed to protect the identity of the participants. Further, any identifying names and/or attributes to the ministry organization have been removed as well. What follows is not an exhaustive breadth of their experience; rather, using grounded theory, themes and patterns will be highlighted to connect their experiences to the broader issue of what Soong-Chan Rah describes as "Western Cultural Captivity," *The Next Evangelicalism: Releasing the Church from Western Cultural Captivity*, 27-44.

the current racial issues occurring in the country with police terrorism, police brutality, and the continual disdain for Black life. Thus, in the fall of 2011 I began doing active interviews with those in the age range of 17-29[42] targeting specifically, urban multi-ethnic young people and emerging adults. Asking open-ended questions such as:

- Tell me your religious affiliation?
- How do you define Christianity? Evangelicalism?
- How has Hip Hop informed your worldview, if at all?
- How might Hip Hop culture provide a space to think, love, play, pray, and converse?
- How does God speak to you, specifically?
- How do you define salvation? Sin? The devil?
- Where is God at and how does God speak in this current era/ generation?

Demographic data was collected, but the heart of the research was to allow the participants to speak and direct the story. From this, arose central themes which will drive this book:

- God is pluralistic in nature.
- Corporate and institutional sin are much greater than individual sin.
- God loves the marginalized.
- Media speaks of God and media creates a transmediated experience for those seeking God.
- Hip Hop is a way for peace and religious expression.
- Space and place, theologically, exists for all, even those considered 'sinful' by other Christians.
- God will judge, not humans.
- Jesus is who you make of him to be.
- Christianity needs a re-boot.

---

42 This age group is targeted because this is the emerging adult group most research is based on. Further, age 29 is the age that most psychologists are now asserting that brain development ends and adulthood begins. Lastly, this is the largest generation of individuals and the group most Christian churches tend to target.

- Ethnic minorities struggle with and tend to not identify with evangelicals and evangelicalism.

These themes might present challenges for some who are evangelical Christian. Yet, missionally speaking, it is exactly where we need to go and be and where this article takes up exploration.[43] These two sets of research will provide the engine for both this article and its direction.

I utilized a theomusicological approach to study Hip Hop and urban popular culture. As the field of missiology develops, it is imperative that new methodological frameworks be engaged and utilized; this is the objective for utilizing theomusicology.

Established by Jon Michael Spencer,[44] theomusicology is defined as, "…a musicological method for theologizing about the sacred, the secular, and the profane, principally incorporating thought and method borrowed from anthropology, sociology, psychology, and philosophy."[45] It is, as Cheryl Kirk-Duggan and Marlon Hall state, "Music as spiritual practice…[to] hear the challenges and evils in the church and the world as the music reveals."[46] What distinguishes theomusicology from other methods and disciplines such as ethnomusicology[47] is:

43 Such themes can add to the core specializations of missiology, which often aims to contextualize a current context. Glenn Rogers, *A Basic Introduction to Missions and Missiology* (Bedford, Tex: Mission and Ministry Resources, 2003), 79-81.

44 Created initially as a discipline, theomusicology is a methodological inquiry as it seeks to understand the theological inferences within the studied culture's music. This method has been used by scholars to examine other areas of music and popular culture such as issues of sexuality and promiscuity Angela McRobbie, "Recent Rhythms of Sex and Race in Popular Music," *Media, Culture & Society* 17, no. 2 (1995); Heidi Epstein, "Re-Vamping the Cross: Diamanda Galas's Musical Mnemonic of Promiscuity," *Theology and Sexuality* 8, no. 15 (2001), understanding poetry in context-Sandra L. Faulkner, "Concern with Craft: Using Ars Poetica as Criteria for Reading Research Poetry," *Qualitative Inquiry* 13, no. 2 (2007), understanding the basic elements of Hip Hop spirituality Jon Michael Spencer, "Book Notes Rapsody in Black: Utopian Aspirations," *Theology Today* 49, no. 2 (1992), to examine the sacred and profane within Black music Melva Wilson Costen, "Protest and Praise: Sacred Music of Black Religion by Jon Michael Spencer Minneapolis, Fortress, 1990," ibid.48, no. 3 (1991), and examined as a methodology in practice Stephen A. Reed, "Exodus by Terence E. Fretheim Louisville, Westminster/John Knox Press, 1991," ibid.

45 Jon Michael Spencer, *Theological Music: An Introduction to Theomusicology, Contributions to the Study of Music and Dance* (New York, NY: Greenwood Press, 1991), 3.

46 Cheryl Kirk-Duggon and Marlon Hall, *Wake Up! Hip Hop Christianity and the Black Church* (Nashville, TN: Abingdon Press, 2011), 77.

47 There is no universal or singular definition of ethnomusicology, as William Darity states, several words comes to mind for ethnomusicology such as sound,

Its analysis stands on the presupposition that the religious symbols, myths, and canon of the culture being studied are the theomusicologist's authoritative/normative sources. For instance, while the Western music therapist would interpret the healing of the biblical patriarch Saul under the assuagement of David's lyre as a psychophysiological phenomena, the theomusicologist would *first* take into account the religious belief of the culture for whom the event had meaning. The theomusicological method is therefore one that allows for scientific analysis, but primarily within the limits of what is normative in the ethics, religion, or mythology of the community of believers being studied.[48]

Therefore, the theomusicologist is concerned with multi-level data within the context of the people they study, and subsequently analyzes the material within the proper time, culture, and context in which it was created. This book will encompass not just the music, but art, print, context, and artists themselves. This will give us a broader picture of the context and allow room for further development and research given that this is such a new area of research in the field of missiology. Thus trinary approaches of theomusicology utilize the sacred, the secular, and the profane as previously discussed.

This trinary approach and methodology best discloses what spirituality and theology look like within the Hip Hop community. Theomusicology rises above simple lyrical analysis and the imagining of what artists might be attempting to say, and goes into the complex arena where the sacred, secular, and profane intersect. This means that songs which express an explicit sexuality might, in fact, be connecting to a spiritual realm. Theomusicology broadens the discussion of missions within a post-soul context and asks, "What is a post-soul community saying in the context in which the music, art, album, and artist were created in?" The following is also used in this study in order to provide a clearer picture of Hip Hop's theological construction:[49]

• Cultural context

• Political climate

---

music, performance, context, and culture. For some it is the study of music in culture, or, more broadly, the study in context."Ethnomusicology," in *International Encyclopedia of the Social Sciences*, ed. William A. Darity, Jr. (Detroit: Macmillan Reference USA, 2008), 20-22.

48 Spencer, Theological Music: *An Introduction to Theomusicology*, 3-4.
49 Spencer asserts that these areas are crucial in the understanding of the theological message at the time the song was created. *Protest & Praise : Sacred Music of Black Religion* (Minneapolis: Fortress Press, 1990); Spencer, *Theological Music: An Introduction to Theomusicology*.

- Artists upbringing and background
- Album cover and art
- Cultural era
- Religious landscape
- Geographic location

I find it necessary to describe, albeit not exhaustively, the social, cultural, political, theological, and varying geographic conditions in which this music was created, because as missiologists there is a dearth of knowledge around almost any form of media within the current era. One must not overlook the various eras and societal shifts that gave rise to Hip Hop and urban popular culture and their connections, implications, and contributions to missiology for the 21st century.

So, let us begin this exploration and give precedent to a more applicable missiological approach to North American missions. I invite you to be challenged and keep an open heart as we explore a newer expanse for missiology scholarship and practice.

White Supremacy in Missions

Christianity is an African religion. Christianity was shaped by people of color and theologically developed by what we would now consider ethnic-minorities. The roots of Christianity lay in the heart of people who are dark skinned, community-oriented, and focused on a relationship with God, the earth, and family.[50] Long before the influence of Western thought, Christianity was familial, communal, had abilities to deal with the reality of day to day life,

---

50 This is recorded well in history when one does their historical homework, Darlene Clark Hine, William C Hine, and Stanley Harrold, *The African American Odyssey*, 4 ed., vol. 1 (New Jersey Prentice Hall, 2010), 2-26; 80-130, document the religious aspects of central, western, and north east African culture. Here, it is revealed just how intricate Christianity was weaved into African culture long before Western White influence. Darlene Clark Hine, William C. Hine, and Stanley Harrold, *African Americans : A Concise History*, Fifth edition. ed. (Upper Saddle River: Pearson, 2014), 2-33, also describes the elements of a Christian heritage within African culture. This is not to suggest that Christianity was the primary religion, but that it was a part of many civilizations. Andrew Walls has also discussed elements of this as well in *The Cross-Cultural Process in Christian History : Studies in the Transmission and Appropriation of Faith* (Maryknoll, N.Y.: Orbis Books, 2002). It should be noted that Christianity throughout Africa was contextual and relevant for each country, clan, and tribe. There was not a singular version or message of what Christianity was, rather, it was a collective faith that was deeply rooted in Jesus' message and the Old Testament prophets.

and was not centered on a "personal relationship" with Jesus. It was much more intuitive and a respecter of other faiths. This all changed once the faith was centered in Western Rome.

With this in mind[51], how is it that many of the mission organizations in North America are still led by White people—and White males at that? Part of what is problematic in all of this is that White evangelicals have difficulty both embracing and envisioning anything that they did not 1) create and 2) have a strong influence in or on. Therefore, the Civil Rights Movement, for example, is not seen as a Christian evangelical movement. The contributions of missiological influence on Christianity originating from ethnic-minority communities is very often overlooked and not acknowledged. This presents a dilemma in the missiological approach and creates a wall between people, not to mention the racist historical aspects of mission that are rarely discussed in mission circles. The issue of historic and present racism seems oblivious and "non-essential," yet it is extremely essential to the people groups these missionaries claim to serve. Acknowledging that my area of specialty is not in history, I am persuaded to discuss, briefly, some key historical moments[52] that have affected how Christian missions have reinforced racism, colonialism, and vicious ideologies rooted in a skewed notion of theology. I will rely on the work of Winthrop D. Jordan as a guide and work to connect it back to historical moments in Christian missions.

The age of discovery, 1500-1600, was flawed with outright violence and extreme racism. While some have heralded this period, I along with other scholars, would assert that it had a horrendous effect on native people groups and Africans. Jordan notes that, "By the early years of the seventeenth century Englishmen had developed a taste for empire and for tales of adventure and

---

51   While one might argue that this is merely anecdotal and does not equal causation or correlation, I would suggest they read Jones, *Is God a White Racist? A Preamble to Black Theology*; Peggy McIntosh, "White Privilege: Unpacking the Invisible Knapsack," *Independent School* 49, no. 2 (1990); bell hooks, *Yearning : Race, Gender, and Cultural Politics* (Boston, MA: South End Press, 1990); Perry, "Social Capital, Race, and Personal Fundraising in Evangelical Outreach Ministries;" "Diversity, Donations, and Disadvantage: The Implications of Personal Fundraising for Racial Diversity in Evangelical Outreach Ministries;" "Racial Habitus, Moral Conflict, and White Moral Hegemony within Interracial Evangelical Organizations." I would then suggest that those then be applied to mission context; in the work of Perry, his work is a direct examination into White-led Christian organizations.

52   This is but a brief sketch on the history of racism within Christianity-there are great works that I would recommend for an even deeper examination into this very important history. I would emphasize the works of J. Kameron Carter, Race: *A Theological Account*, American Council of Learned, Societies (Oxford [U.K.]: Oxford University Press, 2008); Willie James Jennings, *The Christian Imagination: Theology and the Origins of Race* (New Haven [Conn.]: Yale University Press, 2010).

discovery."[53] This taste came with a host of problems rooted in a twisted unexamined knowledge of the Bible. Moreover, the fetish and obsession with the "oddity" of Blackness—as many Europeans noted—was beginning to already head in the wrong direction.[54] "Englishmen found the natives of Africa very different from themselves. Negroes looked different; their religion was un-Christian; their manner of living was anything but English,"[55] the assumption of superiority here was clear. The European establishment of the "standard of living" was held high as Africans, and those from India, were less and unknowledgeable of the "right way." Exploration continued, but with an intent of mastery and healing of the African communities encountered. Jordan adds,

> In England perhaps more than in southern Europe, the concept of blackness was loaded with intense meaning. Long before they found that some men were black, Englishmen found in the idea of blackness a way of expressing some of their most ingrained values. No other color except white conveyed so much emotional impact. As described by the Oxford English Dictionary, the meaning of black before the sixteenth century included, 'Deeply stained with dirt; soiled, dirty, foul... Having dark or deadly purposes, malignant; pertaining to or involving death, deadly; baneful, disastrous, sinister...Foul, iniquitous, atrocious, horrible, wicked. Indicating disgrace, censure, liability to punishment, etc.' Black was an emotionally
>
> partisan color, the handmaid and symbol of baseness and evil, a sign of danger and repulsion. Embedded in the concept of blackness was it direct opposite—whiteness.[56]

This type of superiority would continue long after the dictionary definition was changed in missions. Those categorized as "black" did not always mean ethnically African. Sometimes it meant South American, Indian, or Native American.[57] Because this placed those with darker skin on a hierarchal continuum, this type of ideological construct would result in the subjugation and, eventually, enslavement of Blacks. The "less than" concept because of skin color would continue and place those groups below the European.

---

53 Jordan, *White over Black : American Attitudes toward the Negro, 1550-1812*, 3.
54 Ibid., 4-7.
55 Ibid., 4.
56 Ibid., 7.
57 *The White Man's Burden : Historical Origins of Racism in the United States*, (London United Kingdom: Oxford Univ. Press, 1980). E-Book. Location 143-289.

As missionary movements spread southward and westward from Europe, the entanglement with race and Christianity became even more distinct. It was the concept of Whiteness as the prime factor in being Christian and moral. In other words, to be White was to be human and Christian.[58] It was the duty, then, of Whites (Europeans) to evangelize the world and help the "savages" in their lost nature.[59] Jordan states that,

> In the long run, of course, the Negro's color attained greatest significance not as a scientific problem but as a social fact. Englishmen found blackness in human beings a peculiar and important point of difference. The African's color set him radically apart from Englishmen. But then, distant Africa had been known to Christians for ages as a land of men radically different in religion.[60]

The ideological stage was being set which would affect worldviews for centuries to come. The age of discovery created an ethos which held anyone of Black skin as less than and in need of dire help. The essence of a Christian hegemony was scaffolding into what was to become a sentiment of missions

---

58 In Jones, *Is God a White Racist? A Preamble to Black Theology*, chapters 1-5. This particular concept carries on today. A direct quote from Revered Buchner Payne is a classic one to this point,

> Now as Adam was white, Abraham white and our Savior white, did he enter heaven when he arose from the dead as a white man or as a negro? If as a white man, then the negro is left out; if as a negro then the white man is left out. As Adam was the Son of God and as God is light (white) and in Him is no darkness (black) at all, how could God then be the father of the negro, as like begets like? And if God could not be the father of the blacks because He was white, how could our Savior, 'being the express image of God's person,' as asserted by St. Paul, carry such a damned color into heaven, where all are white, much less to the throne?" Ibid., 258.

This historical ideological construct has multifaceted implications for domestic missions. One element to this is the approach to the Gospel; how is it interpreted? How might domestic missionaries respond to racial profiling, police killings of Black bodies, Muslim bans, and White racism? Often time these go unnoticed and the sole goal of missionary work becomes "winning souls." Thus, social ills are often looked over and avoided as not being part of "ministry" or even part of the mission ethos.

59 White Europeans saw the African religion as "defective" and of no worth; it was heathenism at its highest and therefore in need of the one "true God." Jordan notes that this was cause for proselytizing of the "Negro" for it then became evident that "his religion was in fact defective." Jordan, *White over Black: American Attitudes toward the Negro, 1550-1812*, 20-22.

60 *The White Man's Burden: Historical Origins of Racism in the United States*. Location 189.

in which ethnic-minorities and their culture were to be seen as inferior. With this sense of inferiority, came the heathenistic virtues of Native Americans and their pluralistic sensibilities, which were seen as a task to be attained in "winning" them over for "God."[61] Willie Jennings, discussing property and control, tells us that,

> The grid pattern of sellable squares of land signified the full realization of property ownership. It also displayed the complete remaking of indigenous land. Now, under the grid system, each space of land could be surveyed and designated for purchase by measurement and location. All native peoples, no matter what claims to land, no matter what designations they had for particular places, no matter their history and identity with specific lands, landscape, and indigenous animals, were now mapped on to the grid system.[62]

In many regards, the notion of "America" being God's chosen land for Whites was deeply embedded into the imagination of Whites. It created a sense of rights in the gaze of White men toward anyone non-White. It created a sense of ownership of both land and body. It created a sense of calling which, with the mandate of western expansion through Manifest Destiny, gave decree to Whites as God's chosen to missionize the lost and create God's Kingdom in the image of Whiteness.[63]

By the time one enters the 1700's, the economic force of indentured servitude had turned into African slavery and one reinforced by a twisted interpretation of the Bible.[64] The idea of missionizing was placed into the context of regulation. Any types of passages in the Bible which discussed injustice, love your neighbor/stranger, and of God's love were inconveniently placed into the trash can.[65] The eighteenth century was one of brute violence and a century which saw the juxtaposition of freedom from an "oppressor," England, and the brutality of slavery. Still, the Black was considered not worth missionizing as much as Native Americans. Dysfunctional in approach, missions to Native Americans was seen as a help to Whites during this century. To this, Jordan says,

---

61 Twiss, *Rescuing the Gospel from the Cowboys : A Native American Expression of the Jesus Way*, 61-70.
62 *The Christian Imagination : Theology and the Origins of Race*, 225-26.
63 Hine, Hine, and Harrold, *The African American Odyssey*, 1, 140-60.
64 Jordan, *White over Black : American Attitudes toward the Negro, 1550-1812*, 101-02.
65 To this Jordan discusses the relevant literature and material which was published in order to support the justification of Black enslavement. Titles such as *Anglican Humanitarianism in Colonial*, or *An Appraisal of The Negro* were created and kept those proof texting verses in the Bible in support of slavery, ibid., 180-81.

Indeed they went so far as to conclude that converting the natives in America was sufficiently important to demand English settlement there. As it turned out, the well-publicized English program for converting Indians produced very meager results, but the avowed intentions certainly were genuine. It was in marked contrast, therefore, that Englishmen did not avow similar intentions concerning Africans until the late eighteenth century. Fully as much as with skin color, though less consciously, Englishmen distinguished between the heathenisms of Indians and of Negroes.[66]

This distinction is important as the sediments of its roots carried over into nineteenth century mission ideology in the form of fear. In some regard, the missionizing of Black peoples was regarded as making them "too smart" or "aware."[67] Some were converted and placed as literate ministers, as was the case with Nat Turner, who were to keep the form of Christianity which kept them oppressed.[68]

The Death & Movement away from White Dominance in Missions

The prevalence of Whiteness in missionary settings is problematic in an era of demographic change that favors an intercultural perspective.[69] Further, the image that has been seared into the minds of those outside of Christianity

---

66 *The White Man's Burden : Historical Origins of Racism in the United States.* Location 207.
67 *White over Black : American Attitudes toward the Negro, 1550-1812*, 181-82.
68 It is this same construct in which many ethnic-minority millennials argue that Christianity is the oppressor's religion and not worth any type of inspection as White's control it and have manipulated it enough that it is in critical condition.
69 In his text, Jones notes that White ignorance of social injustices experienced by ethnic-minorites, is large. He says,

> America's still-segregated modern life is marked by three realities. First, geographic segregation has meant that—although places like Ferguson and Baltimore may seem like extreme examples—most white Americans continue to live in locales that insulate them from the obstacles facing many majority-black communities. Second, this legacy, compounded by social self-segregation, has led to a stark result: the overwhelming majority of white Americans don't have a single close relationship with a person who isn't white. Third, there are virtually no American institutions positioned to resolve these persistent problems of systemic and social segregation.

This is highly problematic for those same White Christians desiring to enter predominantly ethnic-minority communities to do "missions" and bring the "gospel" to this community, Robert P Jones, *The End of White Christian America*, Kindle Edition ed. (New York, NY: Simon & Schuster, 2016), Location 2049.

is that of White-blonde Christians, joyfully doing the work of God in other countries or "working among" the "at-risk" youth in inner cities. Couple that with a social media cannonade reflecting these groups amidst ethnic-minorities, assuming dominance, conferring a victory, and the dominance of White values makes mission a "White thing." These images must cease.

I would also contend that predominately White church plants into ethnic-minority communities are problematical as well. Many times this comes with a type of gentrification into a community that, even though unknowingly at times, destroys any indigenous or local voice. Churches that spring up in the new urban landscape[70] of many U.S. cities create an off balance socioeconomics conjoined with an ignorance of that particular community. A typical scenario is when White suburban mega-churches want to enter an urban context and "teach" those in that context to do "missions" using their methods, practices, and ultimately their theology.[71] A partner of our center at North Park from the South Side of Chicago runs one of the largest Black youth ministries in the city. They have been a cornerstone of that community for decades. A White suburban church approached them desiring to train them on how to do "missions" and "outreach" in their community—for a fee of course.[72] The church was looking to "expand" and work in the "city." My friend told me that they sat down, talked, but in the end, lovingly, yet firmly rejected the idea and proposal. If anything, my friends' church could have taught them how to develop intercultural and multi-ethnic relationships; how to create a Christian

---

70 As discussed previously, urban environments are quickly changing in the U.S. High rents and stratospheric real-estate, have created a type of new urban center. The once-feared inner city is developing into a White, affluent, and green movement toward city living that erases any relic of local history—it is as if the Apple Store and Starbucks have always existed and the ugliness of displacement and inequality never happened. Scholars of urban studies are also agreeing that this term is rapidly changing, see Soja, *Postmetropolis: Critical Studies of Cities and Regions*; Thompson and Hickey, *Society in Focus*; Whyte, "The Design of Spaces."

71 I would assert that this comes from a position of dominance rather than out of a genuine "call" from God. It is done in a manner of superiority to "teach" those without asking, learning, and collaborating with the people in that community who, often, are doing great work.

72 The monetizing of Christian ministry is troublesome on many levels. And while I still support honorariums, pastoral salaries, and the professional component of ministry, yet, the how-to market is treacherous to navigate and those labeled as "experts" in a particular space of Christian ministry can be questionable. Monica Miller contends that this is part of the Christian "marketplace" in which morals and deviant behaviors are monitored and managed; I would agree. Moreover, the focus then becomes about money and profit, rather than on people—a recipe for disaster and exploitation, Monica R Miller, *Religion and Hip Hop* (New York, NY: Routledge, 2013), 6-7.

Community Development (CCD)[73] model; how to live with and among people, even if they never change in a manner that the church prescribes. This is an example of this type of imperialism that has continued to plague missions and missional approaches to community engagement.

The White gaze upon multi-ethnic contexts needs redirection and reconstruction. Death and movement away from White dominance will mean we come at Christian theology the way Willie Jennings describes as a, "Christian intellectual identity that is compelling and attractive, embodying not simply the cunning of reason but the power of love that constantly gestures toward joining, toward the desire to hear, to know, and to embrace."[74] One would not plot a course across the country without consulting a map and acquiring the necessary knowledge prior to departure. The same is true for engagement with any context in which you are not familiar. Do not assume God has not been doing God's work in a context long before you arrive. To assume you are a savior, or any form of rescuer, is to assume dominance and create an imperial status for and in that context. This is why I am in strong favor of the death and movement away from White dominance in any missional setting.

The death of White dominance means that fundraising strategies and models will need to be overhauled. A large part of the dominance for Whites is that donor bases tend to be White and affluent which, in turn, fund other Whites. And because Whites continue to be in privileged positions financially, mission organizations reflect that dominance. Christian mission organizations simply lack diversity and engagement with diverse perspectives. Conversely, volunteer organizations and Evangelical Outreach Ministries (EOMs) are racially homogenous[75]; to place this in another manner, most EOMs are led by White Evangelicals. In his study of social capital and fundraising within EOMs, Samuel Perry found that Whites dominated the ministry landscape; 84.8% compared to just 4.8% Black, 8.3% Asian, and 2.2% Latino.[76] We see some of these similar numbers among young ministry organizations. Numbers such as these present several problematic variables. It has been widely researched

---

73 That is based on John Perkins' now famed model of the three R's: Restoration, Relocation, and Reconciliation. This model is focused on developing the community holistically and not placing the sole emphasis of ministry around salvation and church attendance. It is about community and working with the people already in a space and place, see John Perkins, *With Justice for All* (Ventura, CA: Regal Books, 1982).

74 *The Christian Imagination : Theology and the Origins of Race*, 291.

75 Michael D Lindsay and Robert Wuthnow, "Financing Faith: Religion and Strategic Philanthropy," *Journal for the Scientific Study of Religion* 49, no. 1 (2010): 87.

76 "Social Capital, Race, and Personal Fundraising in Evangelical Outreach Ministries," ibid.52(2013): 164.

and argued that Whites tend to be unconscious and unware of much of the history of race in the U.S.[77] This presents issues on two fronts, because Whites will more than likely be leading an EOM, and be in a supervisorial role. If they are unaware or unconscious of the racial history in the U.S., it will be likely that they will dismiss or minimize racial identity and racism within the EOM, or on national issues such as Trayvon Martin, appear unsympathetic toward the death of a young man. On the second front, it is difficult for a subordinate to discuss issues of racism and racial inequality with their supervisor—even more so if the issue is with their supervisor. Thus, fundraising becomes problematic when issues of social capital are factored into the context. As Marla Fredrick McGlathery and Traci Griffin remind us:

> Further complicating this problem is that upon becoming a part of contemporary interracial evangelical mission organizations, many workers do not know the history of African American evangelical missions or the struggle of the black church in America. Without this knowledge, the appeal of white-conversion Christianity can appear unproblematic. Those who want to share the gospel with the world and be held accountable for living lives of more integrity would 'naturally' become part of such an organization. ...[This] immediately places them in a position that requires them to work against the stigma within African American communities regarding the racist history of white missionary organizations in places like the United States, Africa, and South America.[78]

Lack of diversity presents difficulties for ethnic minorities among donor bases. When I was a young area director with Young Life on the Central Coast of California, my metro director (supervisor), who was Black, lost 75% of his

---

77 Michael O. Emerson, People of the Dream : Multiracial Congregations in the United States, (Princeton: Princeton University Press, 2010), http://carli. eblib.com/patron/FullRecord.aspx?p=664562; Antony W. Alumkal, "American Evangelicalism in the Post-Civil Rights Era: A Racial Formation Theory Analysis," *Sociology of Religion* 65, no. 3 (2004); Wilbert R. Shenk, *Changing Frontiers of Mission* (Maryknoll, NY: Orbis Books, 1999); Tim J. Wise and Twomey Center for Peace Through Justice., *Little White Lies : The Truth About Affirmative Action and "Reverse Discrimination"*, Blueprint for Social Justice (New Orleans: Twomey Center for Peace Through Justice, Loyola University, 1995); Tim J. Wise, *Colorblind : The Rise of Post-Racial Politics and the Retreat from Racial Equity*, Open Media Series (San Francisco: City Lights Books, 2010); *Between Barack and a Hard Place : Racism and White Denial in the Age of Obama*, Open Media Series (San Francisco: City Lights Books, 2009).

78 ""Becoming Conservative, Becoming White?": Black Evangelicals and the Para-Church Movement," in *This Side of Heaven: Race, Ethnicity, and Christian Faith*, ed. Robert J Priest and Alvaro L Nieves (New York, NY: Oxford University Press, 2007), 151.

funding when he assumed the leadership role within the first two months. Further, parents did not want to send their children to our weekly club meetings for fear of the new "urban youth ministry" component, and within the next three months—after losing 75% of their funding—lost over half of his parental support and committee members. While he and I could lament these issues, his supervisors above him were opaque toward the situation and even suggested that he change his approach to "be more like them." Conforming to the hegemony is often a struggle for ethnic minority youth workers in EOMs, as just the mere fact of being an ethnic minority in an EOM can place them in an adversarial stance. But more than likely, the ethnic minority who works for the EOM will have to conform.

> Recent research on race relations within evangelical institutions suggests that white evangelicals, like white Americans in general, tend to embody a complex of covert racial ideologies, attitudes, and practices collectively labeled "white racial identity" or "whiteness" that serve to legitimize and reproduce white structural and cultural dominance within evangelical institutions.[79]

Thus, it becomes difficult when *one* ethnic minority is hired. They are faced with a myriad of issues in regards to race and ethnicity. This "Whiteness" which Bell refers to, complicates the fundraising process, and, as I will argue briefly, facilitates fundraising models that are not suitable for ethnic minority contexts.

Having engagement and being knowledgeable of the historical occurrences of racism, inequality, and oppression toward ethnic minorities in the U.S. could alleviate some of these problems. When one is aware and conscious of their own ethnic heritage and know the continuing significance of race in the U.S., they are able to listen to others' narrative and life experience much better.[80] Further, a diverse staff means diverse views and approaches to Christian Theology and the Gospel within respective contexts. However, what typically happens is that ethnic minorities suffer in silos within EOMs, and if there is a group of ethnic minorities who can organize, they do so in small numbers or once a year at national events such as the CCDA (Christian Community Development Association) or the UYWI (Urban Youth Workers Institute).

White Supremacy does not like to be uncomfortable. Moreover, White Supremacy will not allow itself to be in distress over issues of race. Whites have continually commented on how "uncomfortable" they are the first time

---

79 "Diversity, Donations, and Disadvantage: The Implications of Personal Fundraising for Racial Diversity in Evangelical Outreach Ministries," 398.

80 Alvaro L Nieves, "An Applied Research Strategy for Christian Organizations," in *This Side of Heaven: Race, Ethnicity, and Christian Faith*, ed. Robert J Priest and Alvaro L Nieves (New York, NY: Oxford University Press, 2007), 310-11.

they realize they are the minority. To that, Whites tend to feel stressed, uneasy, nervous, anxious, and even angry after experiencing what many ethnic-minorities have to contend with most of their lives—being the other. Exclude a White person from something and they will let you know immediately. Have an injustice occur to Whites and there will be a claim of "reverse racism." Yet, through all of this, there are many Whites who will sit by in their comfort while ethnic-minorities live out a life of discomfort, stress, anxiety, and even fear of death. So, just because there is ethnic inclusion does not mean there will be ethnic "unity." If we learned anything from the 2016 election, it is that the dream and hope of a multi-ethnic future is still yet to be realized; that hope of having the minority vote away a person like Trump was simply a myth. This is also seen in EOM's when an ethnic-minority is hired—the hope is that somehow the evil of racism will suddenly end and now, because of that one hire, the organization is "reconciled." No. In fact, most White organizations do not even realize their racism and bigotry until an ethnic-minority is present. Therefore, the presence of one, while good, often causes more problems. If that person, say, wants to change the mission statement that reflects a more interculturally sensitive perceptive, how will the organization react? If that person wants to hire more women and ethnic-minorities in positions of power, will funders hold back their money? If that person interprets the cross as having its connection to the lynching tree, will that organization have the strength to engage or wither into a mythical land of "unity" and White fragility? Often the latter is the course of action and White voices remain in control. This means that power and control must be yielded. That is often easier said than done, especially when those in control fear that loss, such as many Whites who voted for Trump in the 2016 election.[81] I am not convinced that by hiring someone of ethnic descent, that somehow the organization then becomes inclusive. If anything, the organization has just begun that process and might not be able to survive the change, if that ethnic hire is freed to actually be culturally ethnic.

---

81 Fear is what often drives many Whites. The 2016 election of Donald Trump was no different. Fear of immigrants. Fear of losing control. Fear of Blacks. Fear that somehow, the U.S. is becoming more "multi-cultural" and that is a problem. This type of fear finds itself embedded deep within the American Christian imagination and the threat of anything other than Whiteness presents a clear and present danger to a supremacy that many Whites simply do not see, nor care to see. Thus, it is with ease that many White people then dismiss a candidate for an EOM position by openly saying race had nothing to do with it, yet power and control remains with Whites. It is also easy for Whites to dismiss anyone who thereby suggests racism is at work. That fear of loss, accounts for a lot, see Major, Blodorn, and Blascovich, "The Threat of Increasing Diversity: Why Many White Americans Support Trump in the 2016 Presidential Election."

I long for a different route and a different face on newsletters, EOM social media pages, and for the voice of ethnic-minorities to be heard. I also desire to see a much broader and different voice within Christian theology—especially in missiology. My goal here is to converse on and present new ideas that resist White dominance in missions. However, I am not inclined to believe that just because my ideas and actions are adhered to, that White supremacy will end and racism will stop. This is a much more complex problem and one that is not simply written off as "the fall of humanity" (e.g. sin). I am not hopeful that Whites will levy power to ethnic-minorities. I am not ambitious enough to believe that somehow God will sprinkle magic dust on U.S. Christianity and things will "work out." There are deep divides and hurts that exist—especially within the ethnic-minority community. Those hurts have gone unaddressed for far too long. When a known rapist and racist is in the highest position of the land, it is not a hopeful time nor a time to celebrate. It is a time of lament, a time for sorrow, and, a time for action. I am not so convinced that White people can partake in that action. And while I believe some, very few, Whites can "get it" and be an ally, the vast majority—especially those in positions of power in EOMs—cannot undo their supremist nature. I am in doubt. The next and final imperative starter will be to nurture and nourish doubt and ambiguity in missiology as we dismantle and move away from White dominion in missions.

Concluding Thoughts

I believe that none of what I am grappling with in this book will be easy, nor is it simple to engage with or develop innovative pathways. Yet, that should not stop any of us. Nothing good is ever within easy grasp nor without tedious labor. And so I would like to propose some dream-making moving forward. Dreams of what might be and could be. Some, are already dreams in action turning into reality, while others are still at a distance. Nonetheless, I would like to bring about some closing thoughts around where I feel we are at and need to go.

Hip Hop provides the space to dream. Hip Hop allows space for dissent, questions, and doubt. So much of our Christian faith is built upon a foundation of assurance and knowledge, moreover, Western Christianity wants to defend God when God needs no defense. The notion of apologetics is not what Jesus had in mind when he laid out the Great Commission. Questions are often for those who need a "stronger walk with God," or for those who are "questioning God" altogether. I would contend that when spaces are created for dissent and disruption, faith grows. At my church, here in Chicago, LaSalle Street Church, those spaces exist. Dissent is allowed and encouraged. Moreover, it is part of the ministry mechanism that is in the ethos of the church. As a result, conservative, centrist, progressive, and liberal are all under one roof. The spectrum of the community is great—it is not a church of all-of-one by any regard. Hip Hop, therefore, allows the room to have that dissent and openly question aspects of the faith that simply do not make sense, or have errors in them. Part of this dissent and disruption will also mean dismantling the dominion of absolutized "truth" concepts and policies.

Embracing Hip Hop means you then begin to work as a community in the process of truth-seeking and knowledge. Knowledge and truth, then, is owned by the community and not an individual. For faith development to develop, one must own their faith for themselves. Far too often, knowledge and truth comes from up front with the pastoral team, without any real connection to what it may actually mean for their one's own life. I am not suggesting a revival of individualism and faith, but that knowledge and truth be looked at as an evolving concept, keeping Jesus at the center of it all. Hip Hop theology does just that. In fact, in some cases, conflict, tension, and communication are all in one package. Tension is sure to come, but, as I have mentioned, it is part of the deal. There is no "kumba-ya" fuzzy feeling about doing the difficult work of faith development in the wild. Yes, we should strive for equality. Yes, we should not always focus on the serious and have a comedic approach. But, in relationships, the messier it gets, the more opportunity that 1) the gospel will be seen, and 2) the relationship will grow.

Hip Hop theology is also a place to experience rather than know. For too long the Christian faith has been about knowing and having that assurance that you are "right." Hip Hop theology continues to shake those foundations while still allowing Jesus to remain central in the conversation. Further, it creates the opportunity for intimacy in the experience, rather than just a knowing of what is "right." That intimacy is part of the experience. Experiential components to faith development are also a central aspect of urban post-soul millennial pedagogy. The days of passive learning in churches where a pastor delivers knowledge from up front, and then assumes it has been disseminated are non-existent for this group. Further, even with previous generations, there is no engagement, interaction, thought development, and embracing of those values. And while I am not suggesting that all sermons be eliminated—they do have a useful purpose in some contexts—they can at the very least be utilized as a starting point in the development of faith. The great thing about a Hip Hop theology is that it truly lives out the sacred, the secular, and the profane; all areas I have argued are important for a missiology and church in the wild.

I return to the opening lyrics of Kanye and Jay-Z's track, "No Church In The Wild," in which the question is posed, "what's a god to a non-believer, who don't believe in, anything?" As argued, nothing. But, if that god is shown to be the God of the Bible (loving, forgiving, challenging, mysterious, ambiguous at times), then, you might begin to have something. The possibility to have a relationship with a God that has not been seen much in the wild. A God that exists in a space of questions and dissent. A God like that is different than a God that is an all-clad perfectionist. And while I am not asserting we dumb God down, or put onto God that which is not God, I am suggesting we show the God of the Bible. A God who can be bargained with, a God who chooses a liar to be the beginning of a nation, a God who allows a book like Jonah to end on a miserable note, a God who would allow sorcerers (the Magi who came to Jesus' birth) into the birth of Jesus, the God who has women at work in all areas of biblical narrative, the God who's origin is unknown, the God who sent Jesus who disrupted all of the religious structures and ideology of his day, and the God who continues to abound even though hate fills the world. That God is a God I would like to get to know. And I know it is the God who could begin the conversation with the person who is not a believer, in the wild. The goal here is not to "convert" that non-believer, but to have a relationship of meaning, significance, and one rooted in God. Allow God to do the work, not you, not the "church," not knowledge, and not "absolute truth." God. God through Jesus using Hip Hop as a vehicle is part of that process.

The neo-secular sacred within Hip Hop gives much more room for individuals to expand their knowledge about God and does not constrain them within narrow religious and doctrinal boundaries. In this manner, the neo-secular sacred could possibly be a better approach to spirituality using Hip Hop as merely one of its vehicles, and allowing for the yin and yang of life to flow more naturally without guilt, shame, and rules which no one can live up to.

My dream is that we can continue this conversation, explore new pathways, dismantle White supremacy, and use Hip Hop as a vehicle to create a missiology with the wild for a new modus of operation for Christianity in the 21st century. The time is now. The time is ready. And I truly believe, God is at work in areas that we simply cannot see with the naked eye until we get up close, intimate, and personal. It's time for a church and missiology in the wild!

References Cited

Alper, Garth.
2000.   "Making Sense out of Postmodern Music?". *Popular Music and Society* 24, no. 4 (Winter 2000): 1.

Alumkal, Antony W.
2004.   "American Evangelicalism in the Post-Civil Rights Era: A Racial Formation Theory Analysis." *Sociology of Religion* 65, no. 3 (2004): 195-213.

Anonymous.
2008.   "Whiteness." In *International Encyclopedia of the Social Sciences*, edited by William A. Darity Jr., 87-89. Detroit, MI: Macmillan Reference USA.

Bauman, Zygmunt.
1998.   "Postmodern Religion?". Chap. 4 In *Religion, Modernity, and Postmodernity*, edited by Paul Heelas, 55-78. Oxford, UK; Malden, MA: Blackwell.

Bell, Daniel.
1973.   *The Coming of a Post-Industrial Society: A Venture in Social Forecasting*. New York, NY: Basic Books.

Bosch, David Jacobus.
1991.   *Transforming Mission : Paradigm Shifts in Theology of Mission*. American Society of Missiology Series. Maryknoll, N.Y.: Orbis Books.

Carter, J. Kameron.
2008.   *Race: A Theological Account* [in English]. American Council of Learned, Societies. Oxford, U.K.: Oxford University Press.

Costen, Melva Wilson.
1991.   "Protest and Praise: Sacred Music of Black Religion by Jon Michael Spencer Minneapolis, Fortress, 1990." *Theology Today* 48, no. 3 (October 1, 1991): 360-62.

Cupitt, Don.
1998.   "Post-Christianity." Chap. 11 In *Religion, Modernity, and Postmodernity*, edited by Paul Heelas, 218-32. Oxford, UK; Malden, MA: Blackwell.

Darity, William A., Jr.
    2008a. "Ethnomusicology." In *International Encyclopedia of the Social Sciences*, edited by William A. Darity, Jr., 19-20. Detroit: Macmillan Reference USA.

    2008b. "Suburban Sprawl." In *International Encyclopedia of the Social Sciences*, edited by William A. Darity, Jr., 208-10. Detroit, MI: Macmillan Reference USA.

Delgado, Richard, and Jean Stefancic.
    2005. "Critical Race Theory." In *New Dictionary of the History of Ideas*, edited by Maryanne Cline Horowitz, 501-07. Detroit: Charles Scribner's Sons.

Denzin, Norman K.
    1991. *Images of Postmodern Society: Social Theory and Contemporary Cinema.* Thousand Oaks CA: Sage Publications.

Detweiler, Craig.
    2014. *Igods: How Technology Shapes Our Spiritual and Social Lives.* Grand Rapids, MI.: Brazos Press.

Emerson, Michael O.
    2010. *People of the Dream : Multiracial Congregations in the United States.* Princeton: Princeton University Press. http://carli. eblib.com/patron/FullRecord.aspx?p=664562.

Emerson, Michael O., and Christian Smith.
    2001. *Divided by Faith : Evangelical Religion and the Problem of Race in America.* Oxford, U.K.: Oxford University Press.

Emerson, Michael O. Smith Christian.
    2000. *Divided by Faith : Evangelical Religion and the Problem of Race in America.* Oxford, U.K.: New York, NY.

Epstein, Heidi.
    2001. "Re-Vamping the Cross: Diamanda Galas's Musical Mnemonic of Promiscuity." *Theology and Sexuality* 8, no. 15 (September 1, 2001): 45-65.

Escobar, D.
    2011. "Amos & Postmodernity: A Contemporary Critical & Reflective Perspective on the Interdependency of Ethics & Spirituality in the Latino-Hispanic American Reality." *Journal of Business Ethics* 103, no. 1 (2011): 59.

Faulkner, Sandra L.
   2007. "Concern with Craft: Using Ars Poetica as Criteria for Reading Research Poetry." *Qualitative Inquiry* 13, no. 2 (March 1, 2007): 218-34.

George, Nelson.
   2004. *Post-Soul Nation : The Explosive, Contradictory, Triumphant, and Tragic 1980s as Experienced by African Americans (Previously Known as Blacks and before That Negroes)* [in English]. New York, NY: Viking.

Hattery, Angela J, and Earl Smith.
   2007. *African American Families.* Thousand Oaks, CA: Sage Publishers.

Hebdige, Dick.
   1998. "Postmodernism and 'the Other Side'." In *Cultural Theory and Popular Culture: A Reader*, edited by John Storey, 371-86. London, England: Pearson Prentice Hall.

Heelas, Paul Martin David, and Paul Morris.
   1998. *Religion, Modernity, and Postmodernity.* Religion and Modernity; Variation: Religion and Modernity. Oxford, UK: Malden, MA.

Hine, Darlene Clark, William C Hine, and Stanley Harrold.
   2010. *The African American Odyssey.* 4 ed. Vol. 1, New Jersey Prentice Hall.

Hine, Darlene Clark, William C. Hine, and Stanley Harrold.
   2014. *African Americans : A Concise History* [in English]. Fifth edition. ed. Upper Saddle River: Pearson.

Hodge, Daniel White.
   2010. *The Soul of Hip Hop: Rimbs Timbs & a Cultural Theology.* Downers Grove, IL: Inner Varsity Press.

   2015. *The Hostile Gospel: Exploring Socio-Theological Traits in the Post-Soul Context of Hip Hop. Center for Critical Research on Religion and Harvard University.* edited by Warren Goldstein Boston, MA: Brill Academic.

2017. *Hip Hop's Hostile Gospel: A Post-Soul Theological Exploration Center for Critical Research on Religion and Harvard University.* edited by Warren Goldstein. Vol. 6, Boston, MA: Brill Academic.

hooks, bell.
1990. *Yearning : Race, Gender, and Cultural Politics.* Boston, MA: South End Press, 1990.

Jennings, Willie James.
2010. *The Christian Imagination : Theology and the Origins of Race.* New Haven, CT: Yale University Press.

Jones, Robert P.
2016. *The End of White Christian America.* Kindle Edition ed. New York, NY: Simon & Schuster.

Jones, William R.
1973. *Is God a White Racist? A Preamble to Black Theology.* Garden City, N.Y.: Anchor Press, 1973.

Jordan, Winthrop D.
1980. *The White Man's Burden: Historical Origins of Racism in the United States.* London, U.K.: Oxford Univ. Press. E-Book.

2012. *White over Black : American Attitudes toward the Negro, 1550-1812.* Omohundro Institute of Early American, History & Culture. Chapel Hill, NC: University of North Carolina Press.

Kelley, Robin D. G.
1994. *Race Rebels : Culture, Politics, and the Black Working Class.* New York Free Press, Toronto.

Kirk-Duggan, Cheryl, and Marlon Hall.
2011. *Wake Up! Hip Hop Christianity and the Black Church.* Nashville, TN: Abingdon Press.

Kyle, Richard G.
2006. *Evangelicalism : An Americanized Christianity.* New Brunswick, NJ: Transaction Publishers.

Laymen's Foreign Missions, Inquiry, Appraisal Commission of, and William Ernest Hocking.
1932. *Re-Thinking Missions; a Laymen's Inquiry after One Hundred Years.* New York; London: Harper & Bros.

Lindsay, Michael D, and Robert Wuthnow.
    2010.   "Financing Faith: Religion and Strategic Philanthropy."
            Journal for the Scientific Study of Religion 49, no. 1 (2010): 87-
            111.

Lynch, Gordon.
    2005.   *Understanding Theology and Popular Culture.* Malden, MA:
            Blackwell Publishing.

Lyotard, Jean-Francois.
    1984.   *The Postmodern Condition: A Report on Knowledge.* Minneapolis
            MN: University of Minnesota Press.

Major, Brenda, Alison Blodorn, and Gregory Major Blascovich.
    n.d.   "The Threat of Increasing Diversity: Why Many White
            Americans Support Trump in the 2016 Presidential Election."
            Group Processes & Intergroup Relations 21, no. 6 (931-940).

Marks, Jonathan.
    2013.   "Racism: Scientific." In *Encyclopedia of Race and Racism,*
            edited by Patrick L. Mason, 445-60. Detroit: Macmillan
            Reference USA.

McCrisken, Trevor B.
    2002.   "Exceptionalism." In *Encyclopedia of American Foreign Policy,*
            edited by Richard Dean Burns, Alexander DeConde and
            Fredrik Logevall, 63-80. New York: Charles Scribner's Sons.

McGlathery, Marla Frederick, and Traci Griffin.
    2007.   ""Becoming Conservative, Becoming White?": Black
            Evangelicals and the Para-Church Movement." Chap. 9 In
            This Side of Heaven: Race, Ethnicity, and Christian Faith, edited
            by Robert J Priest and Alvaro L Nieves, 127-44. New York,
            NY: Oxford University Press.

McIntosh, Peggy.
    1990.   "White Privilege: Unpacking the Invisible Knapsack."
            Independent School 49, no. 2 (1990): 31-36.

McRobbie, Angela.
    1995.   "Recent Rhythms of Sex and Race in Popular Music." *Media,
            Culture & Society* 17, no. 2 (April 1, 1995): 323-31.

Miller, Monica R.
    2013.   *Religion and Hip Hop.* New York, NY: Routledge.

Neal, Mark Anthony.
1997.   "Sold out on Soul: The Corporate Annexation of Black Popular Music." *Popular Music and Society* 21, no. 3 (Fall 1997): 117.

2002.   *Soul Babies : Black Popular Culture and the Post-Soul Aesthetic.* New York: Routledge.

Nieves, Alvaro L.
2007.   "An Applied Research Strategy for Christian Organizations." Chap. 19 In *This Side of Heaven: Race, Ethnicity, and Christian Faith*, edited by Robert J. Priest and Alvaro L. Nieves, 309-34. New York, NY: Oxford University Press.

Perkins, John.
1982.   *With Justice for All.* Ventura, CA: Regal Books.

Perry, Samuel.
2012a. "Diversity, Donations, and Disadvantage: The Implications of Personal Fundraising for Racial Diversity in Evangelical Outreach Ministries." *Review of Religious Research* 53, no. 4 (2012): 397-418.

2012b. "Racial Habitus, Moral Conflict, and White Moral Hegemony within Interracial Evangelical Organizations." *Qualitative Sociology* 35, no. 1 (2012): 89-108.

2013.   "Social Capital, Race, and Personal Fundraising in Evangelical Outreach Ministries." *Journal for the Scientific Study of Religion* 52, no. 1 (2013): 159-78.

Pinn, Anthony.
2002.   *The Black Church in the Post-Civil Rights Era.* Maryknoll, NY: Orbis Books.

Rah, Soong-Chan.
2009.   *The Next Evangelicalism : Releasing the Church from Western Cultural Captivity.* Downers Grove, IL: IVP Books.

Reed, Stephen A.
1991.   "Exodus by Terence E. Fretheim Louisville, Westminster/ John Knox Press, 1991." *Theology Today* 48, no. 3 (October 1, 1991): 362-66.

Renaud, Myriam.
    2017.   "Myths Debunked: Why Did White Evangelical Christians Vote for Trump?" In *The Marting Marty Center for the Advanced Study of Religion*. Chicago, IL: The Univeristy of Chicago.

Ritzer, George.
    2004.   *The Mcdonaldization of Society*. Thousand Oaks, CA: Pine Forge Press.

Rogers, Glenn.
    2003.   *A Basic Introduction to Missions and Missiology*. Bedford, TX: Mission and Ministry Resources.

Shenk, Wilbert R.
    1999.   *Changing Frontiers of Mission*. Maryknoll, NY: Orbis Books.

Singleton, Harry H.
    2012.   *White Religion and Black Humanity*. Lanham, MD: University Press of America.

Smith, Efrem, and Phil Jackson.
    2005.   *The Hip Hop Church: Connecting with the Movment Shaping Our Culture*. Downers Grove, IL: IVP.

Smith, Gregory A., and Jessica Martínez.
    2016.   "How the Faithful Voted: A Preliminary 2016 Analysis." In *Fact Tank: News in the Numbers*. Washington D.C.: Pew Research Center.

Soja, Edward W.
    2000.   *Postmetropolis: Critical Studies of Cities and Regions*. New York, NY: Blackwell Publishing.

Spencer, Jon Michael.
    1990.   *Protest & Praise: Sacred Music of Black Religion*. Minneapolis, MN: Fortress Press.

    1991.   *Theological Music: An Introduction to Theomusicology*. Contributions to the Study of Music and Dance. New York, NY: Greenwood Press.

    1992.   "Book Notes Rapsody in Black: Utopian Aspirations." *Theology Today* 49, no. 2 (July 1, 1992-January 1, 1992): 283-89.

1995. *Sing a New Song: Liberating Black Hymnody.* Minneapolis, MN: Fortress Press.

1997. *The New Negroes and Their Music : The Success of the Harlem Renaissance.* 1st ed. Knoxville: University of Tennessee Press. Biography (bio); Government publication (gpb); State or province government publication (sgp).

Spencer, Jon Michael, ed.
1992. *Sacred Music of the Secular City: From Blues to Rap. Vol. 6.* Durham, NC: Duke University Press.

Taylor, Paul C.
2007. "Post-Black, Old Black." *African American Review* 41, no. 4 (Winter 2007): 625-40.

Thompson, William E., and Joseph V. Hickey.
2011. *Society in Focus.* 7 ed. New York, NY: Pearson Books.

Thurman, Howard.
1976. *Jesus and the Disinherited.* Boston, MA: Beacon Press.

Twiss, Richard.
2015. *Rescuing the Gospel from the Cowboys: A Native American Expression of the Jesus Way.* Downers Grove, IL: IVP Books.

Walls, Andrew F.
2002. *The Cross-Cultural Process in Christian History: Studies in the Transmission and Appropriation of Faith.* Maryknoll, NY: Orbis Books.

Whyte, William H.
1996. "The Design of Spaces." In *The City Reader,* edited by Richard T. Le Gates and Frederic Stout, 483-90. New York, NY: Routledge.

Wilsey, John D.
2015. *American Exceptionalism and Civil Religion : Reassessing the History of an Idea.* Downers Grove, IL: IVP Academic.

Winters, Joseph.
2011. "Unstrange Bedfellows: Hip Hop and Religion." *Religion Compass* 5, no. 6 (2011): 260-70.

Wise, Tim J.

    2009.   *Between Barack and a Hard Place : Racism and White Denial in the Age of Obama.* Open Media Series. San Francisco, CA: City Lights Books.

    2010.   *Colorblind : The Rise of Post-Racial Politics and the Retreat from Racial Equity.* Open Media Series. San Francisco, CA: City Lights Books.

Wise, Tim J., and Twomey Center for Peace Through Justice.

    1995.   *Little White Lies : The Truth About Affirmative Action and "Reverse Discrimination".* Blueprint for Social Justice. New Orleans, LA: Twomey Center for Peace Through Justice, Loyola University.

APM

Conference Papers

Identity and Otherness

Missiological Explorations of Engaging the Other
and Embracing the Otherness in a Pluralistic World

DAVID THANG MOE

Introduction

In Galatians 3:28, Paul told the Galatian Christian community[1] that there are no longer ethnic and religious differences (no longer Jews or Gentiles), no socio-political divisions of status between the oppressed and the oppressors (no longer slave or free), no gendered differences between us (no longer male and female). But in reality, *otherness,* as Miroslav Volf defines in his award-winning book, *Exclusion and Embrace,* as "the simple fact of different in some way"[2] remains and it "has become a disturbing and challenging factor for us today. My assumption is that the contemporary world we live in today is perhaps more pluralistic than Paul's ancient time. The world of today is religiously pluralistic, ethno-culturally diverse and globally interconnected. My aim is not to raise the question: why is the world pluralistic? Rather the question I will be pursuing is: how should we perceive the identities of the other and ourselves? I consider the latter question more important because it raises not only the methodological approaches to otherness, but also the hermeneutical perception of the identities of the self and the other.

In response to that question, my aim is threefold and the paper is divided into three parts. In part one, I will examine the hermeneutics of identity and otherness. I will explore two kinds of identity and three kinds of otherness. In part two, I will explore some methodological ways of how Christians should think of their identity and the other and how they should engage the other and embrace their otherness. In part three, I will examine the teleological issues of mutual transformation through critical engagement and mutual acceptance of Christians and others in the name of Christ. The ultimate goal of this paper is to promote an engaging and embracing missiology in a pluralistic world.

Two Kinds of Identity and Three Kinds of Otherness

When it comes to the issue of identity, what we commonly hold in our mind is a national identity. If you asked someone, what his or her identity is, the common response would be a national identity. In Myanmar, if you put your national identity as the Chin, Kachin, Karen or any other kind of ethnic minority nationality on your identity card, you would unavoidably face discriminatory treatment.[3] My task in this paper is not to regard national

---

1   Brad Ronnell Brazton, *No Longer Slaves: Galatians and African American Experiences* (Collegeville: The Liturgical Press, 2002), 93. Brazton argue that Paul addressed the implications of Gal. 3:28 within the large Christian community in Galatia

2   Miroslav Volf, *Exclusion and Embrace: A Theological Exploration of Identity, Otherness and Reconciliation* (Nashville, TN: Abingdon Press, 1996), see the back cover of the book.

3   Lian H. Sakhong, *In Search of Chin Identity: A Study in Religion, Politics and Ethnic Identity in Burma* (Copenhagen: NIAS Press, 2003). See also my forthcoming

identity as our primary identity, not because such national identity is less important than other kinds of identities, but because we often abuse national identity as a tool to judge or discriminate against the other who is different from us. Rather my task is to see human identity as our primary identity so that we would see inherent human equality despite a variety of socio-religious and national-ethnic differences and otherness.

I argue that our primary identity is rooted in God's creation and in Christ's redemption as new humanity (2 Cor. 5:17). In making my case, I like to address two kinds of identity: human identity and religious identity. Paul Hiebert helpfully proposes two ways of approaching the issue of identity, namely *the oneness of humanity and the oneness of Christianity*.[4] By the oneness of humanity, Hiebert means the universal citizens of one human family. This oneness of humanity is declared in God's creation account as His image bearers (Gen. 1:26; 12; Ps. 72:17). The oneness of Christianity, on the other hand, refers to one body of Christ with many members and different gifts.[5] The former rests upon God's image-centered approach, which emphasizes the commonality of humanity within the inter or "extra-religious cultural context," while the latter rests upon Christ's body approach, which demonstrates the oneness of Christians with many gifts within the "intra-religious context" (2 Cor. 12).[6] To illustrate the former, Hiebert writes;

> Christians must learn that our primary identity is as human beings. When we meet the religious other, we must see them first as fellow humans, only secondarily as males or females, Americans or Arabs, rich or poor. In reaching out to the lost other, Christians must meet them at the deepest level of their common humanity.[7]

According to Hiebert, our first identity is as a member of the human family, secondarily as a member of our national family, such as Americans, Burmese, Chinese and so on, and thirdly as a member of the Christianity family.[8] Or the last two identities could occur simultaneously in some contexts.

---

article, David Thang Moe, "Burman Domination and Ethnic Discrimination: Toward a Postcolonial Theology of Resistance and Reconciliation in Myanmar" in Exchange: Journal of Contemporary Christianities in Context, Vol. 47. No. 2. (April 2018).

4   Paul G. Hiebert, "Western Images of Others and Otherness," in *This Side of Heaven: Race, Ethnicity and Christian Faith*, edited by Robert J. Priest and Alvaro L. Nieves (Oxford: Oxford University Press, 2007), 97-110.

5   Ibid., 106-117.

6   See Mark Kline Taylor and Gary J. Bekker, "Engaging the Other in a Global Village," in *Theological Education* 26 (Spring 1990): 52-85.

7   Hiebert, "Western Images of Other and Otherness," 108.

8   Ibid., 108.

In some contexts, national identity and religious identity are inseparable. For example in Myanmar, if you are from the Chin or Kachin ethnic, you must be a Christian and if you are a Burman, you must be Buddhist. The question we must ask is: who defines our human identity and our religious identity? I argue that the first identity is given by God and the second by human beings. I mean our common human identity is not given by humans, but only by God who creates us to be human. But our national-religious identities are given by both ourselves and others (human beings). In other words, we do not choose to be humans, it is a choice made for us. Yet, we can choose to be Christian, Buddhist, Confucian, Hindu and so on. Hiebert writes how Christians should perceive their religious identity. He puts it this way:

> Christians must learn to see our religious identity as Christians. When we meet other Christians from different countries, races, denominations, we must see them as brothers and sisters in the same family. This familial belonging to a new community is our eternal identity. Our oneness with other Christians is deeper than the identities that divided us on earth, such as ethnicity (Jews and Gentiles), class (slave and free) and gender (male and female), which are not eternal.[9]

This statement echoes the goal of Gal. 3:28, which describes God's salvation or reconciliation in Christ as a relational and an egalitarian aspect of Christians' self-perception of themselves and their view of the other in a new way.[10] In this text, Paul does not mean to describe God's reconciliation of humanity as a means of eliminating the sexual distinction of woman-ness, male-ness and the religio-ethnic distinction of Jewishness and Gentiles-ness, though he tries to eliminate the unequal relationship between slave and free. In Gal. 3:28, Paul's aim is to re-define our new identity as a new humanity (creation out of the old: 2 Cor. 5:17) and new oneness in Christ regardless of social-ethnic otherness and to ask how to relate ourselves to the other who are different from us.[11]

Since otherness remains, the challenge for us is how to perceive the other. Herbert Anderson defines the "other" in three ways, which I call "three kinds of otherness." He defines the "other as not us, the other as not like us, and the proximate other, who is like us, but different from us."[12] It is true that the other is not "us" in terms of nationality, immediate, and religious family. It is not like "us" in term of cultural practices and physical looks. Yet the other is not simply

9   Ibid., 108.
10 Elisabeth Schussler Fiorenza, *In Memory of Her: A Feminist Theological Reconstruction of Christian Origins* (New York: Crossroad, 1983), 213.
11 Ibid., 213. See also Volf, *Exclusion and Embrace*, 21
12 Herbert Anderson, "Seeing the Other Whole: A Habitus for Globalization," in *Mission Studies* 14, (27 and 28): 40-63 (here p. 41).

the absolute other of us. Especially in our globalized world, the other, though they are not like us, is somehow part of our human community. Globalization draws us connected to each other more than ever before. Therefore in this paper, I would like to choose the third metaphor of the proximate other without abandoning some of appropriate implications associated with the first two metaphors.

Lalsangkima Pachuau is right when he said, "Of the three metaphors, the proximate otherness is most troublesome, but is significant that it brings out the complexity of the problem of difference."[13] When or if the other is just a distant other or what I call "the transcendent other" across the countries that other is not bothering us. But it is the "proximate other who is different from us, but is close to us who is both problematic and significant for us," according to Anderson.[14] As I have mentioned above, because of globalization and its interconnected impact of homogenization in many cases, a number of distant strangers or unfamiliar people have become near neighbors to us and the boundaries between "us and them" have been inseparable.[15] Let us take the US as an example where the distant other becomes the proximate other. As Alvin Padilla puts;

> The whole world has come to our doorstep. Learning to live well in the diverse culture of North America is no longer an option, but a necessity. The US census estimates that in 2050 that proportion of the whites in the population will be only 53%. Our children will live and serve in a society in which their classmates, neighbors, fellow disciples of Christ will be equally divided whites and people of color. As new people move into our cities and neighborhoods; the communities undoubtedly will change. The change could be haphazard and filled with misunderstandings, hurt feelings, and even violence, or the change could permit all to reinvent and reinvigorate themselves for the better.[16]

In the past, Americans have had to go to far continents, such as Asia if they wanted to study Buddhism, Confucianism, Hinduism, and other religions. Now the context has changed so that Buddhists, Confucians, and Hindus are becoming the proximate others to Americans. In the US, these proximate others are not merely the religious others, but they are also the proximate marginal

---

13 Lalsangkima Pachuau, "Engaging the 'Other' in a Pluralistic World, Towards a Subaltern Hermeneutics of Christian Mission," in *Studies in World Christianity*, vol. 8. No. 1 (2002): 63-80 (here p. 68).

14 Anderson, "Seeing the Other Whole," 43.

15 Pachuau, "Engaging the 'Other' in a Pluralistic World," 68.

16 Arvin Padilla, "A New Kind of Theological School: Contextualized Theological Education Models," in *African Journal*. 2.2. (November 2012), 5-6.

others. Their marginal and religious otherness poses a missiological concern about how to promote a healthy and harmonious way of engaging with the other and of embracing their otherness. Moreover, the proximate otherness poses a sociological question of whether their otherness has a role in shaping our identity.

Kevin Vanhoozer observes that the "other is a hermeneutical problem in our times."[17] He suggests that the right hermeneutics of the identity of the Trinity serves as the Christian's proper perception of the self and the other.[18] To Vanhoozer, a good focus on both the One and Three (one God with three persons) provides the paradigms for successfully addressing the oneness of humanity with different cultural otherness.[19] Jung Young Lee also argues that humans are created to be different, yet equal, in order to copy the different characteristics of the Trinity within one Godhead with mutual abiding and equality.[20] The different characteristics of the Trinity with the same substance of one divinity provides the framework for rightly perceiving human diversity within the same substance of the *imago Dei* (Gen. 1:26-27) and calls for the oneness of humanity.[21]

Likewise, Christian identity is grounded in the identity of the Trinity or by what Miroslav Volf beautifully refers to when he says "the church is the image of the Trinity."[22] The three-ness of the trinitarian personhood and the oneness (tri-unity) is the model for the oneness of Christianity with one faith by embracing different gifts.[23] Just as "three persons in one divinity exist so intimately with, for and in one another by the power of eternal love," so also is the church as a community with different gifts to be communal by the power of reciprocal love.[24] Volf argues that the "church does not exist only through the narrow portals of ordained ministers, but through the life of the

---

17 Kevin J. Vanhoozer, "Does the Trinity Belong in a Theology of Religions? One Angling in the Rubicon and the Identity of God," ed, Kevin J. Vanhoozer, *The Trinity in a Pluralistic Age: Theological Essays on Culture and Religion* (Grand Rapids, MI: Eerdmans, 1997): 41-71 (p. 43).

18 Ibid., 47.

19 Ibid., see the back cover of the book

20 Jung Young Lee, *Marginality: A Key To Multicultural Theology* (Minneapolis, MN: Fortress, 1995), 42.

21 S. Mark Heim, *The Depths of the Riches: A Trinitarian Theology of Religious Ends* (Grand Rapids, MI: Eerdmans, 2001), 123-127.

22 Miroslav Volf, *After Our Likeness: The Church as the Image of the Trinity* (Grand Rapids, MI: Eerdmans, 1998).

23 Ibid., 208-210.

24 Ibid., 210.

whole congregation. This is because the Spirit does not constitute the church exclusively only through ordained pastors, but through all members serving equally with different gifts" (1Pet. 4:10-11).[25]

Thus, we must look at the one identity of the church and the different gifts and cultures of the church's members for a common ministry. Likewise, we must look at the one identity of humanity and their different religious cultures through the lens of the Trinity, so that we would perceive ourselves and the other rightly. In the past, Western Christians perceived the non-Western other negatively. "The other until the sixteenth century was pagan, during the enlightenment age was the unenlightened, during the nineteenth century was primitive, and during the twentieth century was different."[26] The first three images of the other are negative, while the fourth is positive. Against the first three images, I argue that we must perceive the religious other as neighbor in the twenty-first century.[27] The root of perceiving the religious other as neighbor echoes the twenty-first century's image of neighbor. There are eight references to Lev. 19:18 ("love your neighbors as yourself") within the NT (Matt. 5:43; 19:19; 22:39; Lk. 10:27; Rom. 13:9; Gal. 5:14; Jas. 2:8). In the NT, Jesus, Paul and James refer directly to the Leviticus command of loving neighbor.[28]

Naim Ateek argues that neighbor comes from the Hebrew word *ra*, which can be defined as "friend and fellow companion."[29] Neighbor is not necessarily to be seen as a blood relative person, but as a fellow human.[30] Likewise, Kosuke Koyama states that neighbor is to be defined as a "person who lives close by and is not a member of one's immediate family, but a member of the human family."[31] Neighbor reflects our common human nature, and our world becomes one neighborhood. But one human family does not mean that we are all the same. This echoes Anderson's third metaphor—*the other is like us (sameness), but different (otherness)*. As Dale Irvin argues, Jesus broke the dividing wall

---

25 Ibid., 152.
26 Vanhoozer, "Does the Trinity Belong in a Theology of Religions?" 43. The originate statement is quoted from, Bernard McGrane, *Beyond Anthropology: Society and the Other* (New York: Columbia University Press, 1989).
27 Kosuke Koyama, *Water Buffalo Theology*, 25th anniversary (Maryknoll, NY: Orbis, 1999), 180. In the 1974 edition published by Orbis Books Koyama spelled "Waterbuffalo" as one word in the title, while 1999 edition spelled it as two words, 64-67.
28 Emerso Powery, "Under the Gaze of Empire: Who is my Neighbor?" in *Interpretation: A Journal of the Bible and Theology*, (April 2008): 134-145 (here p. 136).
29 Naim Ateek, "Who is my Neighbor?" in *Interpretation: A Journal of the Bible and Theology*, (April 2008): 156-170 (pp. 157-158).
30 Ibid., 158.
31 Kosuke Koyama, "Neighbor: The Heartbeat of Christ-Talk," in *The Living Pulpit*, (July- September, 2002): 24-25.

of hostility not by eliminating human differences, but by creating a new communion with God and with fellow humans as neighbors (Eph. 2:13-22).[32] In short, the Trinity provides the model not only for affirming the diversity and oneness of humanity, but also for the right relationship among humankind with different cultures within and outside the church. Recent scholarship has focused on the "relational aspect of the Trinity."[33]

In the following section, I will examine how the relational identity of the Trinity calls for rightly engaging the other and embracing the otherness in our pluralistic world.

Engaging the Other and Embracing Otherness

Robert Schreiter provides five ways that Christians' perceive of the other.

> First homogenizing the other (perceiving the other through the lens of sameness and otherness is ignored); second colonizing the other (either dominating the marginal other or assimilating their marginal identity); third, demonizing the other (the other is considered to be a threat to be expunged); fourth, romanticizing the other (seeing the other to be superior in its otherness); and fifth, pluralizing the other (seeing the otherness differently through the multi-cultural lens).[34]

We may observe that the first three not only perceive the other negatively, but also attempt to discriminate against their otherness, while "the remaining two recognize the existence of otherness to some extent, but fail to take it seriously."[35] For the purpose of this paper, I would develop Schrieter's last point, that is pluralizing the religious other as the other. I understand Schrieter's use of *pluralizing the other* as a way of seeing the other as the other by recognizing their otherness. My concern in this section is a balanced emphasis on why we should embrace otherness and how to engage the other.

First, I would argue that we must recognize otherness or difference as God's gift to the world. In his book *The Will of God*,[36] Leslie Weatherhead helpfully provides three different kinds of God's will—God's intentional will (God's

---

32 Dale T. Irvin, "The Mission of Hospitality: To Open the Universe a Little More," in *The Agitated Mind of God: The Theology of Kosuke Koyama*, eds, Dale T. Irvin and Akintunde E. Akinade.173:187. (Maryknoll, NY: Orbis, 1996): 173-187 (p. 182).

33 For example, see Ted Peters, *God as the Trinity: Relationality and Temporality in Divine Life* (Louisville, KY: Westminster John Knox Press, 1993), especially 179-182.

34 Robert J. Schreiter, "Teaching Theology from an Intercultural Perspective," in *Theological Education 26*. (Autumn 1989): 13-34.

35 Pachuau, "Engaging the 'Other' in a Pluralistic World," 71.

36 Leslie D. Weatherhead, *The Will of God* (Nashville, TN: Abingdon Press, 1999),

original plan for the well-being of creation before the fall of humanity); God's circumstantial will (God's current plan for unity or oneness amid diversity: Jn. 17:22); and God's ultimate will (God's final restoration of life: Eph. 1:1-11).[37] According to Weatherhead, diversity is God's circumstantial will. If this is God's will, then seeing the other as the other and recognizing their otherness is imperative. The failure to recognize diversity means opposing God who affirms cultural diversity. Letty Russell rightly argues that "The difference or otherness is not a problem, rather the failure to recognize and embrace that difference or otherness is a problem."[38] The result of the failure to recognize and embrace otherness is exclusion. Volf reminds us that exclusion itself is a contemporary sin.[39]

Many Christians sinfully misunderstand God's election or calling of Christians as a way of excluding the other rather than seeing it as an inclusive privilege for reaching out to the other where they are with their different cultures and for recognizing their differences as ways of glorifying God with different voices.[40] In this regard, it is important to combine God's creation narrative with a Pentecostal narrative. If the creation narrative recognizes God as the creator of diverse cultures, then a Pentecost narrative (Acts 2:1-21) helps us understand how God affirms diversity as His greatest gift to the world, as I have mentioned above. The many tongues of Pentecost invite us to a consideration of the church as one body of Christ with many gifts (1Cor. 12). As Amos Yong observes, "there is a little debate among theologians over the relationship between the many tongues and cultures."[41] But one thing for sure is that a Pentecostal narrative affirms diversity as the opportunity for witnessing to Christ within and across the church in a pluralistic world.

Second, Christians must learn to see otherness not as a dividing line of discrimination between "us and them," but rather as an identity marker of differentiation. In light of the latter, Christians must learn to see "otherness as the privileged meeting place where different people come to form a new and most inclusive humanity in Christ."[42] This echoes the implication of Gal. 3:28 where we should not see the otherness of Jews and Gentiles, men and

21-42.
37 Ibid., 9-60.
38 Letty M. Russell, *Just Hospitality: God's Welcome in a World of Difference* (Louisville, KY: Westminster John Knox Press, 2009), 62.
39 Volf, *Exclusion and Embrace* , 66-67.
40 Russell, *Just Hospitality*, 62.
41 Amos Yong, "Toward A Trinitarian Theology of Religions: A Pentecostal-Evangelical And Missiological Elaboration," in International Bulletin of Mission Research, 40 (4). (October 2016): 294-306 (pp. 299-300).
42 Timothy Matovina, ed, Beyond Borders: Writings of Virgilio Elizondo and Friends (Maryknoll, NY: Orbis, 2000), 183.

women, and slave and free as the dividing line of either assimilating one to the other or dominating one over the other, rather as the identity marker of a new humanity. Too often, Christians choose the former because of their pride. This leads me to offer some suggestions as to how Christians should engage the other.

Third, I would suggest that Christians should engage the other with the mind of humility. Koyama once argued that Christian mission has passed through two kinds of mind. One is with the *crusading mind* and the other with the *crucified mind*. He referred to the crusading mind as "all kinds of crusading against the other who are different from us."[43] The crusading mind approaches mission with an ethnocentric and monological style. The crusading mind of mission tries not only to colonize the other, but also to assimilate their otherness into the dominant culture. This echoes Schreiter's first and second ways of approaching the other (assimilating and colonizing the other).

Against the crusading mind of Christian missionaries, Koyama introduced an engaging mission model of the crucified mind. The crucified mind is not condemning,[44] because it is rooted in Christ's self-giving love. Unlike the crusading mind, the crucified mind approaches mission with a humble and dialogical style. Koyama reminds Christians to reject the crusading mind, which stands in contrast to the mind of Christ. He invites Christians to adopt the crucified mind, which is the mind of Christ. Echoing Paul's exhortation, "Let the same [crucified] mind be in you that was in Christ" (Phil. 2:5), Koyama proposes to use the crucified mind as the mission model of Christians' humble attitudes toward one another in the intra-Christian community and Christians' engagement with the religious other in the extra-Christian community.[45] The crucified mind does not condemn, but loves the other in light of the claim that all humans are created equal. This means that engaging mission with the crucified mind not only loves the other as neighbors created in the image of God, but also recognizes their otherness.

---

43 Kosuke Koyama, *No Handle on the Cross* (London: SCM Press, 1976), see the preface. See also Kosuke Koyama, *Three Mile an Hour God* (Maryknoll, NY: Orbis, 1980), 54. *Italics* are his.

44 Koyama, *Three Mile an Hour God*, 54. See also Kosuke Koyama, "What Makes a Missionary? Toward a Crucified Mind, Not a Crusading Mind," in G.H. Anderson and T.F. Stransky, eds. *Mission Trends No. 1: Crucial Issues in Mission Today* (Grand Rapids, MI: Eerdmans, 1974): 117-132.

45 For a full discussion of Koyama's concept of the crucified mind, see my forthcoming article David Thang Moe, "The Crucified Mind: Kosuke Koyama's Missiology of Theology of The Cross," in *Journal of World Christianity*, Vol. 7. No. 2. (October 2017).

Fourth, Christians must engage the religious other and embrace their otherness with the open arms of hospitality. Hospitality carries several meanings. Theologically speaking, hospitality is both a metaphor of God's reconciliation and His virtue.[46] God reconciles the whole world to Himself through an act of Christ's humiliation and calls the church to witness to this reconciliation to the whole world (2 Cor. 5:19) so that the world or the religious other would experience this reconciliation.[47] In light of God's universal reconciliation, the mission of hospitality requires the church's threefold act of border-crossing of reaching out to the other where they are, mutual relationship with the other, and welcoming the other. Sociologically speaking, hospitality encompasses *attentiveness* (being attentive to the other in love and in respect), *invitation* (inviting the other into our community with generosity) and *spaciousness* (making a wider space within ourselves for the other to come in by de-centralizing the self).[48] These three factors need to be elaborated.

Fifth, "hospitality means paying attention."[49] God is a hospitable God who is attentive to the world as His creation through the incarnation of Christ. Just as God is attentive to the world as His creation and all humans as His image in love (Jn. 3:16), so we are to be attentive to the religious other as our neighbor in love.[50] Especially Jesus' attentive engagement with the marginal other, the Samaritan woman (Jn. 4) in love and respect is crucial for our attentive engagement with the marginal religious other in love. The crucial nature of Jesus' attentive engagement with the Samaritan woman is His willingness to break the social-ethnic boundary of Jew-Samaritan. Likewise, the Samaritan in Luke 10:25-37 breaks social-ethnic boundary and heals the unknown victim as neighbor. The starting point for Jesus and the Samaritan's reaching to the other is different. While the first one is a move from the center to the margin, the latter is a move from the margin to the margin. In both cases, love is the motivating power for their border-crossing.[51]

---

46 Amos Yong, *Hospitality and the Other: Pentecost, Christian Practices and the Neighbor* (Maryknoll, NY: Orbis, 2008). See also Hans Boersma, *Violence, Hospitality and the Cross: Reappropriating Atonement Tradition* (Grand Rapids, MI: Baker Academic, 2004), see esp. 99-204.

47 Ibid., 139.

48 Cathy Ross, "Often, Often, Often Goes the Christ the Stranger's Guise: Hospitality as a Hallmark of Christian Ministry," in *International Bulletin of Missionary Research*, vol. 39, No. 4. (October 2015): 176-179. The *Italics* are the author's and the phrases in the parenthesis are mine. The idea of de-centralizing the self for the other, see also Volf, *Exclusion and Embrace*, 20-21.

49 Ibid., 176.

50 Ibid., 176.

51 See, David Thang Moe, "The Word to the World: Johannine Trinitarian Missiology (John 20:21-22)," in *Journal of Pentecostal Theology*, Vol. 26. Issue 1. (April 2017): 68-85.

Peter Phan and Lalsangkima Pachuau are right when they sum up "mission as all about a border-crossing act."[52] For them, Jesus is the border-crosser and His whole life of Trinitarian mission was border crossing. The incarnation is the border crossing by which the triune God steps out of Himself and crosses into the world "without crushing our human identity."[53] This reminds us that we have a Christian mission of border crossing of reaching out to the marginal other in particular and the religious other in general *without crushing* their identity. I emphasize that this is a missiological imperative of Christians imitating Jesus Christ who crosses the border between heaven and the world in love.[54]

Let us now see engaging mission as invitation. Mission is not only about reaching out to the other to witness to God's hospitality in love, mission is also about inviting the other with generosity. When we reach out to the other, we are the guests and they are the hosts in a sense,[55] but when we invite them we are the hosts. Yong rightly states that "Christian mission of hospitality involves us as both guests and hosts."[56] This is because, for Yong, "Christ is not only the missionary who came into the world as a stranger (Matt. 25:43-44), but also the host of all creation who invites the world to particulate in His banquet of salvation."[57] I agree with Yong, but my focus is on how we should see the church as what Hans Boersma calls "the community of hospitality with fifthfold characteristic."[58] Fifthfold characteristic, according to Boersma, includes;

> Evangelical hospitality (proclaiming the gospel of reconciliation and forgiveness as hospitality); baptismal hospitality (welcoming all the reconciled humans into the body of Christ); Eucharistic hospitality (proclaiming the death of Christ and inviting all reconciled humans into the fellowship of the Lord's Supper); penitential hospitality (confessing our

---

52 Peter C. Phan, "Crossing the Borders: A Spiritual for Mission in Our Time from an Asian Perspective," in *SEDOS Bulletin, 35.* (2003): 8-19 (16-17). See also Lalsangkima Pachuau, "Missiology in a Pluralistic World: The Place of Mission Studies in Theological Education," in An International Review of Mission, 89/355 (October 2000): 539-555.

53 Pachuau, "Engaging the 'Other' in a Pluralistic World," 77.

54 Moe, "The Word to the World," 80.

55 As the ethnic Christian in Myanmar, I deeply understand the alienation of the ethnic as the guests or aliens rather than the hosts. See my article, David Thang Moe, "Being Church in the Midst of Pagodas: A Theology of Embrace in Myanmar," in *Journal of the International Association for Mission Studies*, vol. 31. No. 1. (2014): 22-43 (see especially p. 38).

56 Yong, *Hospitality and the Other*, 132.

57 Ibid., 131.

58 Boersma, *Violence, Hospitality and the Cross*, 205-234.

sins and struggling for restorative relationships) and cruciform hospitality (following the ways of Christ by suffering with fellow humans and anticipating the fullness of the hospitable kingdom).[59]

Although Boersma's fifthfold aspect of hospitality plays a crucial role in defining mission as the practice of hospitality, I have confined myself to employing the *Eucharistic hospitality* as the central idea of the identity of the church as the host for the other. Like Boersma, Christine Pohl rightly argues that "hospitality is basic to who we are (our Christian identity as the community of hospitality) as following Christ,"[60] in a hostile world. Pohl's thesis of Christian hospitality is grounded in three main themes: "remembering our heritage, reconsidering the tradition, recovering the practice."[61] The first two describes the apostolic tradition of hospitality, while the third point prescribes the contemporary Christians' practice of hospitality for the other. In light of this, I like to read the Lukan traditional parable of the great banquet (Lk. 14:15-24) as a good metaphor in which the host broke boundaries and invited the excluded and marginalized groups.

Many New Testament scholars interpret this banquet as an ecclesiastical image of the messianic meal.[62] In the ecclesiastical image, God's *oikos* can be classified as a classless society with both the rich and the poor, the host and the guest, and it must be crowded with different races and ethnicities without excluding one from another.

As I re-read Luke's parable through the lens of a pluralistic context, I view the host in the parable as the metaphor of the church, while the banquet is the metaphor of Holy Communion and the guests coming to the banquet represent the religious outsiders. I am deeply inspired by how the host willingly breaks the boundaries and invites the excluded groups into the house for the banquet, which represents the church's Eucharistic meal.[63] Reconciliation enclosed in the Eucharist becomes the church's responsibility to extend compassion and generosity to the marginal religious other in particular, as the host in the parable does. In order for God's kingdom to be full as the host's house is full of guests (14:23), the task of the church is to invite the guests to come in.[64] But

---

59 Ibid., 208-235.

60 Christian D. Pohl, *Making Room: Recovering Hospitality as a Christian Tradition* (Grand Rapids, MI: Eerdmans, 1999), 150.

61 Ibid., 3-187.

62 David B. Gowler, *Host, Guest, Enemy and Friend: Portraits of the Pharisees in Luke and Acts* (New York: Peter Lang, 1991), 246.

63 Moe, "Being the Church in the Midst of Pagodas," 38.

64 Philip S. Elser, *Community and Gospel in Luke-Acts: The Social and Political Motivation in Lukan Theology* (Cambridge: Cambridge University Press, 1987), 179.

the question is, if our invitation is rejected. What should we do? Certainly, we should not invite them by force. I would suggest that we should pray and wait. This leads us to the next step.

Finally, I would argue that making a space for the other plays a crucial role in an engaging mission of hospitality. In his book *Reaching Out*,[65] Henri Nouwen writes;

> Hospitality means the creation of a friendly space where a stranger can enter and become a friend instead of an enemy. Give the guest a chance to talk. Hospitality is not simply to change people, but to offer them where change can come.[66]

Volf also states the reason why we should make a space for the other. Volf writes;

> At the heart of the cross is Christ's stance of not letting the other remain an enemy and of creating a space in Himself for the other to come in. The arms of Christ are open—a sign of space in God's self and an invitation for the other to come in.[67]

In Volf's view, the two dimensions of God's hospitable act through the crucified Christ are important for the moments of Christians' creation of a space for the other to come in. One is God's *self-giving love*, which overcomes hostility and extends hospitality to the other, and the second is *other-receiving love*, which invites and welcomes the other to come into a friendly space.[68] We must admit that the creation of a space for the unknown is not as easy as the creation of a space for friends we know. Yet following Christ who reaches out to everyone, including the enemy at the risk of His life, we ought to decentralize ourselves and make a space for the other to come in (Matt. 16:24).

Thomas Ogletree reminds us that our costly commitment to following Christ in a risky world must be balanced by "our readiness to enter the world of the other and our willingness to make a hospitable world for the other to come in."[69] Our readiness to reach out to the other and embrace their otherness

---

65 Henri J.M Nouwen, *Reaching Out* (London: Fount, 1975). Nouwen calls the creation of a space for the other is the "second movement of spiritual life," while the first movement is called "reaching out to ourselves from loneliness to solitude" and the third movement is "reaching out to God from illusion to prayer," 3-42; 13-126.

66 Ibid., 68-69.

67 Volf, *Exclusion and Embrace*, 126.

68 Ibid., 127.

69 Thomas W. Ogletree, *Hospitality to the Strangers: Dimensions of Moral Understanding* (Philadelphia, PA: Fortress, 1985), 4.

and our willingness to make the space for the other to come in our community are basic to who we are as following and embodying Christ who first extends hospitality to the other and embraces otherness (Rom. 15:7).

Engaging and Embracing Missiology as Mutual Transformation: The World without the Other

We come to the concluding section right back where we began. We are living in the same one world with different identities of religio-cultural backgrounds. God creates us not to live in self-enclosing isolation from and discrimination against the other, but to have a mutual relationship with one another in respect. This is the imperative of copying the relational nature of the Trinity. Mark Heim helpfully combines the relational nature of the Trinity (God's identity) with the relational aspect of salvation (God's economic work) which defines our new human identity in Christ. For Heim, salvation is a relational communion with God, fellow humans and other creatures.[70] As Christians, we must copy the relational identity and nature of the Trinity through a right relationship with one another as fellow Christians within the church and as fellow humans outside the church.

Right relation with the religious other as our fellow humans is my focus here. By the world without the religious other, I do not mean that our Christian identity depends on the identity of the other. Rather our identity should be shaped by the identity of the other, and also the other should be shaped by our identity. Thus, when we engage the other and embrace otherness, our primary goal is not to include them into our community by force. This I call "an assimilative missiology." In this sense, inclusivism is different from embracivism.[71] What I like to discuss is an engaging and embracing missiology, which reaches out to the other by crossing the borders as the identity markers for enrichment. The goal of engaging and embracing missiology is mutual "transformation."[72]

Some Christians try to transform the other without being transformed by the other because they misunderstand being transformed by the other as a synonym of being conformed to this world (Rom. 12:2). It is true that God does not want us to be conformed to the immoral form of the secular world, but this does not mean that we are not to learn some moral teaching of other religions for cultivating our Christian faith. I would argue that the "religious

---

70 S. Mark Heim, *The Depth of the Riches: A Trinitarian Theology of Religious Ends* (Grand Rapids, MI: Eerdmans, 2001), 49-78.

71 For example, see Volf, *Exclusion and Embrace*, 60-64.

72 A good deal of mission as transformation, see *Mission as Transformation: A Theology of the Whole Gospel*, edited Viney Samuel and Chris Sugden (Eugene, OR: Wipf & Stock, 2009).

other is not the mere object for conversion or transformation, but a neighbor to and from whom hospitality must be both given and received."[73] Hospitality is a key for mutual giving and receiving. Angelyn Dries writes, "Hospitality is about relationships in respect and love. The stories convey some type of reciprocity, of transformation/change and mutual learning."[74]

Angelyn Dries reminds us to see hospitality not only as a relational, but also as a transformative dimension of Christian life. "The New Testament metaphor of salvation as reconciliation,"[75] is not just about the right relationship with God and fellow humans, but also about the transformative acceptance of the self by God and the other by us. From a sociological perspective, hospitality is a mutual benefit of giving and receiving through a relational and transformative act of hosts and guests. When hosts and guests are to meet, they have to share their different stories and exchange their insights. However, I will not argue that Christians are always hosts and the religious other are not always guests. Rather I like to treat them as "neighbors" to whom hospitality must be both given and received for mutual information and transformation. Mutual information through an act of sharing different stories and exchanging their insights creates the mutual transformation of each group.

In making my case, I like to re-read Acts 10 as a contextual text for why an engaging and embracing missiology is urgent for mutual transformation. This text shows the story of respectful engagement and mutual embrace between Peter (Jewish follower of Christ) and Cornelius (Gentile religious outsider). Reading this text through the contemporary lens, Peter represents a Christian, while Cornelius represents a religious outsider. What is significant in this story is the idea of salvation as a universal reconciliation.[76] According to Luke Timothy Johnson, God's embracing story of the Gentile Cornelius expresses "the most critical phase of the expansion of God's people."[77] This demands for the reconciling relationship between Peter (Jew) and Cornelius (Gentile) through engagement of the religio-ethnic border-crossing and mutual acceptance of perceiving one another as God's image and new humanity in Christ.

---

73 Yong, *Hospitality and the Other*, see the back cover.

74 Angelyn Dries, "Hospitality as a Stance in Mission: Elements from Catholic Mission Experience in the Twentieth Century," in *International Bulletin of Missionary Research*, Vol. 39. No. 4. (October 2015): 194-197 (here p. 196).

75 Volf, *Exclusion and Embrace*, see the back cover of the book.

76 Beverly B. Gaventa, *The Acts of the Apostles* (Nashville, TN: Abingdon Press, 2003), 55.

77 Luke Timothy Johnson, *The Acts of the Apostles* (Collegeville, MN: Liturgical Press, 1992), 186.

In order to interact with each other in respect, Peter and Cornelius made a hospitable space where there is no room for hostility. They realized the presence and power of the Spirit in their midst (Acts 10:33). It is through their interaction by the power of the Spirit that Peter and Cornelius were transformed or converted—Cornelius was transformed as a new believer and Peter was transformed into a new way of experiencing God as the "One who shows no partiality" (Acts 10:30). One's transformation is radical, which gives a new space/heart for Jesus to come in, and the other's transformation is by renewal, which "gives a new space for the other to experience oneness in Christ."[78] This story serves a crucial model for the church's continued transformation and her continued "transmission of Christian faith into other faiths."[79] Too often, Christians think that conversion or transformation is just a radical event, but by looking at the transformative life of Peter, we come to realize that conversion or transformation is also a process. From this follows two suggestions for how mutual transformation is possible.

First, it is important to see conversion not just as an event, but also as a process. The event of conversion is a moment when one is convinced psychologically and responds to Christ as his/her Savior. This is a movement of self-realization that we are sinners and Jesus is our Savior. In this regard, conversion is closely related to salvation. Salvation and conversion are not synonymous. Making a distinction between conversion and salvation is important because "salvation is the work of Christ, whereas conversion is the human's work of response to divine salvation."[80] However, the two are closely related to each other in the context of which we see conversion as both an event and a process. Salvation is offered as a gift for all (Eph. 2:8). But human response is needed. Human response is enabled by the work of the Holy Spirit (Phil. 2:13), just as it happened in the conversion of Cornelius.[81] Likewise, the gradual conversion or transformation of Peter is possible through a combination of his own commitment to change and the power of the Holy Spirit. In his book *The Continuing Conversion of the Church*, noted missiologist Darrell Guder argues that conversion is not just an event, but a continuing process. He writes;

---

78   Lalsangkima Pachuau, "Vulnerability and Empowerment in Crossing Frontier: A Christian Theology of Mission," in *Asbury Journal*, Vol. 68. No. 2 (Fall 2013): 78-94 (here p. 85).

79   For example, see Andrew F. Walls, *The Missionary Movement in Christian History: Studies in the Transmission of Faith* (Maryknoll, NY: Orbis, 1995), 16-25.

80   Gordon T. Smith, "Conversion and Redemption," in *The Oxford Handbook of Evangelical Theology*, edited by Gerald McDermott (New York: Oxford University Press, 2010): 209-221.

81   Gerald R. McDermott and Harold Netland, *A Trinitarian Theology of Religions: An Evangelical Proposal* (Oxford: Oxford University Press, 2014), 161.

> The Holy Spirit began the conversion of the church at Pentecost and has continued that conversion through the pilgrimage of God's people from the first century up to now. The conversion of the church will be the continuing work of God's spirit until God completes the good work began in Jesus Christ.[82]

This statement affirms the need of the continuing conversion of a believer. Second, Richard Peace rightly states that "Christian conversion involves repentance from sin, turning to Christ and it results in life gradual transformation."[83] The human response to God's salvation is the beginning of a process in which converted believers are transformed into the image of Christ (Rom. 8:29). In the context of being transformed into the image of Christ, salvation involves sanctification, holiness, and glorification. This sequence of salvation does not just occur after conversion. This began at the moment of God's once-for-all-justification and its gradual aspect of transformation continues to occur in the life of a new believer. We may argue that the event of conversion has more to do with one's psychological or personal transformation, while the process of conversion has more to do with the ethical or moral transformation, but the choice is not either personal or moral transformation. The choice is "both-and," and the ultimate goal is moral transformation in the process of becoming more like Christ.

In their book *A Trinitarian Theology of Religions*, Gerald McDermott and Harold Netland rightly remind us that all religions have "theological differences, yet moral similarities."[84] I agree that there are theological differences, yet moral similarities among religions. In relation to theological differences, Karl Barth writes, "the doctrine of the Trinity is what basically distinguishes the Christian doctrine of God in contrast to all other possible doctrines of gods."[85] Indeed no religious founder, such as Mohammed, Confucius, or Buddha can be claimed to be eternal gods in the flesh. "The Christian central doctrine of the crucified and risen Christ is nonnegotiable in world religions."[86]

---

82 Darrell L. Guder, *The Continuing Conversion of the Church* (Grand Rapids, MI: Eerdmans, 2000, 206.

83 Richard V. Peace, "Conversion," in *Global Dictionary of Theology*, edited by William A. Dyrness and Veli-Matti Kärkkäinen (Downers Grove, IL: IVP, 2008): 196-197.

84 Gerald R. McDermott and Harold Netland, *A Trinitarian Theology of Religions: An Evangelical Proposal* (Oxford: Oxford University Press, 2014), 193-196.

85 Karl Barth, *Church Dogmatics: The Doctrine of the Word of God*, vol. 1.1. (Edinburgh: T&T Clark, 1936), 301.

86 McDermott and Netland, *A Trinitarian Theology of Religions*, 193.

However, all religions have moral teachings. No other religion has ever taught that cheating, stealing, committing adultery, and murdering are all morally permissible. "All the religions agree at least on the second table of the Ten Commandments (Exodus 20:12-17), which teach about the right relationship with fellow human beings and God (or whatever they call ultimate reality)."[87] Although they may interpret and apply them differently, the religions never agree on the basic principles behind the commandments.[88] Thus, in our reaching out to the religious other, it is important for Christians to recognize the ethical bridge between Christians and other religions not only as point of contact for proclaiming the gospel of salvation, but also as a source for cultivating our moral faith.

Learning from the ethics of the religious other is imperative for mutual transformation. McDermott and Netland offer two suggestions. First, Christians must remember that the "full meaning of the Christian faith is greater than our perception of it, and the lives of religious outsiders can sometimes help us see better what actually is inside."[89] The Buddhist eightfold path of morality, meditation, and wisdom could enrich Christian moral life. Christian life is not a lawless life. Moral law plays a crucial role in cultivating our ethical faith for sanctification. In Philippians 2:12, Paul exhorts Christians "to cultivate our salvation." Similarly in Ephesians 2:9, Paul reminds us that Christ does not simply save *from* something (the power of sin and death) but also *for* something good (transformative life into the likeness of Christ). Salvation does not end when we are converted and baptized into Christ. Our conversion and being justified is just the beginning. We need to further allow the Spirit to dwell in our hearts so that we can be transformed into the likeness of Christ by cultivating our minds (Rom. 12:2).

Second, Jesus as a Jew by his human identity deliberately uses the Samaritan from a different religious and ethnic background as a moral exemplar to teach his disciples and "Christians for thousands of years what it means to be a moral neighbor in an immoral world (Lk. 10:25-37)."[90] This shows that God may use the moral religious other as His image to help the moral life of Christianity. McDermott and Netland argue that the Dalai Lama's genuine forgiveness of his enemy, the Chinese murderers of the innocent lives of his fellow Tibetans "helps many Christians to understand what Jesus means by forgiveness,"[91] in a violent world caused by enemies. In addition, Confucian moral virtue plays

---

87 Ibid., 194. See also Ronald M. Green, "Morality and Religion," in the *Encyclopedia of Religion*, edited by Mircea Eliade (New York: McMillan, 1989): 10-99.

88 Ibid., 194-195.

89 McDermott and Netland, *A Trinitarian Theology of Religions*, 199.

90 Ibid., 199.

91 Ibid., 199.

a crucial role in applying Christ's Golden Rule (Matt 7:12) as the reciprocal relationship among human beings. Confucius can enrich Christians by helping them know what we mean by Christ's Golden Rule in our moral relation in our family, church, and society.[92]

If the moral teachings of other religions can shape us to be moral disciples of Christ in partnership with the moral teaching of the Bible, it is no longer possible for us to merely convert the religious other without being transformed by their ethical insights. In the process of interaction with each other and embracing otherness, mutual transformation must occur by the power of the Spirit. This is what happened to Peter and Cornelius and this means that engaging the other and embracing otherness is not only for the sake of the other from the perspective of transmitting the Christian faith, but also for the sake of ourselves from the perspective of ethical transformation.

Thus, we must see mission as a two-way communication between a Christian and the religious other in love and respect. Moreover, it is important for Christians to understand that in our reaching out to the other, we do not simply bring God to the other, rather we bring the gospel. We do not bring God to them because God has already been there prior to our reaching out to them. But since they do not know God (Acts 17:23), we make God comprehensible to them through the gospel and through their moral insights. [93]

Andrew Walls is right when he said, "God accepts all humans as they are and where they are with their cultural identities and God transforms them into the image of Christ."[94] The former is what he calls the "indigenizing principle," which tends to localize the gospel through local religious cultures, and the latter "the pilgrim principle," which tends to universalize the gospel.[95] As God's pilgrims, we are called to continually go beyond our comfort zones to transmit Christian faith into other faiths or proclaim the gospel of salvation as reconciliation and redemption by learning their cultures and by appreciating what is moral in them as sources for transforming our ethical faith and building their new faith. I affirm that the religious other is not the mere object for conversion, but the neighbor to and from whom ethical insights must be both given and received for cultivating a Christian faith of holiness. Christian faith is

---

92 Ibid., 200. For Confucian teaching, see Confucius, *The Analects*, translated and edited by D.C. Lau (Hammondsworth: Penguin, 1979, 7.23; 3.13; 7.35.

93 See my article David Thang Moe, "Adoniram Judson as a Dialectical Missionary who brought the Gospel (not God), and Gave the Bible," in *Missiology: An International Review*, Vol. 45. No. 3. (July 2017). This article appears online first, see the link http://journals.sagepub.com/doi/full/10.1177/0091829617701085 (accessed May 29, 2017).

94 Ibid., 54.

95 Ibid., 53-54.

not only about believing in Christ as Savior and Lord, but also about reflecting the holy nature of the Trinity (Lev. 11:44). Thus, it is right to conclude that the relational and transformative aspect of salvation is imperative for reflecting the holy and relational nature of the Trinity.

Conclusion

In this paper, I have explored three major themes. The first is the hermeneutics of identity and otherness. I have argued that we must learn to see our primary identity as a member of the same human family. This primary identity is grounded in the image of God and is reformed in Christ as new humanity. I have also argued that although our primary identity is grounded in the same creator, we are different from one another. My focus is on religious difference or otherness. In light of this, I have suggested that we must see the religious other as both the image of God and neighbor. In the same way a Christian must be seen as part of the body of Christ without ceasing to see the Christian-self as the image of God. In other words, God's creation and His plan of new creation or reconciliation are the starting points for a right construction of the identity and perception of the self and the other.

The second theme is the methodological question of how a Christian should engage the other who is different from us. Arguing against the assimilative and hostile ideas of homogenizing and colonizing the other, I have employed hospitality as a relational tool for engaging the other and embracing otherness. This theme emphasizes the relational nature of the triune God and the external expression of salvation froom a relational aspect. We must copy the relational aspect of the Trinity as the model for our respectful engagement with our fellow humans—both Christians and non-Christians. What I have demonstrated in this section is the importance of seeing the other as the other and to see otherness not as a diving wall, but rather as an identity marker.

The third theme stresses the teleological concern of mutual transformation through a critical engagement and mutual embrace of one another. This theme emphasizes salvation not only from a relational aspect, but also as a transformative aspect of mutual acceptance and recognition in the name of Christ. The goal of mission is not only to convert other faiths to Christ by the power of the Spirit, but also to allow Christians themselves to be converted morally in a new way of experiencing Christ. Recognizing diversity as God's gift to the world, we must interpret the gospel not only through our eyes, but also through the eyes of the other without compromising the integrity of the truth of the gospel, so that we will see the full meaning of the gospel for the whole world.

Works Cited

Anderson, Herbert.
>1997. "Seeing the Other Whole: A Habitus for Globalization." In *Mission Studies* 14, (27 and 28): 40-63.

Ateek, Naim.
>2008. "Who is my Neighbor?" In *Interpretation: A Journal of the Bible and Theology*, (April 2008): 156-170.

Barth, Karl.
>1936. *Church Dogmatics: The Doctrine of the Word of God*, vol. 1.1. Edinburgh, Scotland: T&T Clark.

Boersma, Hans.
>2004. *Violence, Hospitality and the Cross: Reappropriating Atonement Tradition.* Grand Rapids, MI: Baker Academic.

Brazton, Brad Ronnell.
>2002. *No Longer Slavs: Galatians and African American Experiences* Collegeville, MN: The Liturgical Press.

Confucius.
>1979. *The Analects*, translated and edited by D.C. Lau. Hammondsworth: Penguin, 7.23; 3.13; 7.35.

Dries, Angelyn.
>2015. "Hospitality as a Stance in Mission: Elements from Catholic Mission Experience in the Twentieth Century." In *International Bulletin of Missionary Research*, Vol. 39. No. 4. (October 2015): 194-197.

Elser, Philip S.
>1987. *Community and Gospel in Luke-Acts: The Social and Political Motivation in Lukan Theology*. Cambridge, England: Cambridge University Press.

Fiorenza, Elisabeth Schussler.
>1983. *In Memory of Her: A Feminist Theological Reconstruction of Christian Origins*. New York, NY: Crossroad.

Gaventa, Beverly B.
>2003. *The Acts of the Apostles*. Nashville, TN: Abingdon Press.

Gowler, David B.
  1991. *Host, Guest, Enemy and Friend: Portraits of the Pharisees in Luke and Acts.* New York, NY: Peter Lang.

Green, Ronald M.
  1989. "Morality and Religion." In the *Encyclopedia of Religion*, edited by Mircea Eliade. 10-99. New York, NY: McMillan.

Guder, Darrell L.
  2000. *The Continuing Conversion of the Church.* Grand Rapids, MI: Eerdmans.

Heim, S. Mark.
  2001. *The Depths of the Riches: A Trinitarian Theology of Religious Ends.* Grand Rapids, MI: Eerdmans.

Hiebert, Paul G.
  1987. "Critical Contextualization." In *International Bulletin of Missionary Research*, Vol. 11. No. 3. (July 1987): 104-112.

  2007. "Western Images of Others and Otherness." In *This Side of Heaven: Race, Ethnicity and Christian Faith*, edited by Robert J. Priest and Alvaro L. Nieves. 97-110. Oxford, England: Oxford University Press.

Irvin, Dale T.
  1996. "The Mission of Hospitality: To Open the Universe a Little More." In *The Agitated Mind of God: The Theology of Kosuke Koyama*, ed. Dale T. Irvin and Akintunde E. Akinade. 173:187. Maryknoll, NY: Orbis.

Johnson, Luke Timothy.
  1992. *The Acts of the Apostles.* Collegeville, MN: Liturgical Press.

Khong, Lian H.
  2003. *In Search of Chin Identity: A Study in Religion, Politics and Ethnic Identity in Burma.* Copenhagen, Denmark: NIAS Press.

Lee, Jung Young.
  1995. *Marginality: A Key To Multicultural Theology.* Minneapolis, MN: Fortress.

Koyama, Kosuke.

    1974.   "What Makes a Missionary? Toward a Crucified Mind, Not a Crusading Mind," in G.H. Anderson and T.F. Stransky, eds. *Mission Trends No. 1: Crucial Issues in Mission Today.* 117-132. Grand Rapids, MI: Eerdmans.

    1976.   *No Handle on the Cross.* London, England: SCM Press.

    1980.   *Three Mile an Hour God.* Maryknoll, NY: Orbis.

    1999.   *Water Buffalo Theology*, 25th anniversary. Maryknoll, NY: Orbis.

    2002.   "Neighbor: The Heartbeat of Christ-Talk." In *The Living Pulpit*, (July-September, 2002): 24-25.

McDermott, Gerald R. and Harold Netland.

    2014.   *A Trinitarian Theology of Religions: An Evangelical Proposal.* Oxford, England: Oxford University Press.

McGrane, Bernard.

    1989.   *Beyond Anthropology: Society and the Other.* New York, NY: Columbia University Press.

Matovina, Timothy ed.

    2000.   *Beyond Borders: Writings of Virgilio Elizondo and Friends.* Maryknoll, NY: Orbis.

Moe, David Thang.

    2014.   "Being Church in the Midst of Pagodas: A Theology of Embrace in Myanmar." In *Journal of the International Association for Mission Studies*, Vol. 31. No. 1. (2014): 22-43.

    2017.   "The Word to the World: Johannine Trinitarian Missiology (John 20:21-22)." In *Journal of Pentecostal Theology*, Vol. 26. Issue 1. (April 2017): 68-85.

    2017.   "Adoniram Judson as a Dialectical Missionary who Brought the Gospel (not God), and Gave the Bible." In *Missiology: An International Review*, Vol. 45. No. 3. (July 2017). See http://journals.sagepub.com/doi/full/10.1177/0091829617701085 (accessed May 29, 2017).

2017. "The Crucified Mind: Kosuke Koyama's Missiology of Theology of The Cross." In *Journal of World Christianity*, Vol. 7. No. 2. (October 2017).

2018. "Burman Domination and Ethnic Discrimination: Toward a Postcolonial Theology of Resistance and Reconciliation in Myanmar." In *Exchange: Journal of Contemporary Christianities in Context*, Vol. 47. No. 2. (April 2018).

Nouwen, Henri J.M.
1975. *Reaching Out.* London, England: Fount.

Ogletree, Thomas W.
1985. *Hospitality to the Strangers: Dimensions of Moral Understanding.* Philadelphia, PA: Fortress.

Pachuau, Lalsangkima.
2000. "Missiology in a Pluralistic World: The Place of Mission Studies in Theological Education." In *An International Review of Mission*, 89/355. (October 2000): 539- 555.

2002. "Engaging the Other in a Pluralistic World, Towards a Subaltern Hermeneutics of Christian Mission." In *Studies in World Christianity*, Vol. 8. No. 1 (2002): 63-80.

2013. "Vulnerability and Empowerment in Crossing Frontier: A Christian Theology of Mission." In *Asbury Journal*, Vol. 68. No. 2. (Fall 2013): 78-94.

Padilla, Arvin.
2012. "A New Kind of Theological School: Contextualized Theological Education Models." In *African Journal.* 2.2. (November 2012), 5-6.

Peace, Richard V.
2008. "Conversion," in *Global Dictionary of Theology*, edited by William A. Dyrness and Veli-Karkkainen. 196-197. Downers Grove, IL: IVP.

Peters, Ted.
1993. *God as the Trinity: Relationality and Temporality in Divine Life.* Louisville, KY: Westminster John Knox Press.

Peter C. Phan.
  2003. "Crossing the Borders: A Spiritual for Mission in Our Time from an Asian Perspective." In *SEDOS Bulletin*, 35. (2003): 8-19.

Pohl, Christine D.
  1999. *Making Room: Recovering Hospitality as a Christian Tradition.* Grand Rapids, MI: Eerdmans, 1999.

Powery, Emerso.
  2008. "Under the Gaze of Empire: Who is my Neighbor?" In *Interpretation: A Journal of the Bible and Theology*, (April 2008): 134-145.

Ross, Cathy.
  2015. "Often, Often, Often Goes the Christ the Stranger's Guise: Hospitality as a Hallmark of Christian Ministry." In *International Bulletin of Missionary Research*, vol. 39, No. 4. (October 2015): 176-179.

Russell, Letty M.
  2009. *Just Hospitality: God's Welcome in a World of Difference.* Louisville, KY: Westminster John Knox Press.

Samuel, Viney and Chris Sugden, eds.
  2009. *Mission as Transformation: A Theology of the Whole Gospel,* Eugene, OR: Wipf & Stock.

Schreiter, Robert.
  1989. "Teaching Theology from an Intercultural Perspective." In *Theological Education* 26. (Autumn 1989): 13-34.

Smith, Gordon T.
  2010. "Conversion and Redemption." In *The Oxford Handbook of Evangelical Theology*, edited by Gerald McDermott. 209-221. New York, NY: Oxford University Press.

Taylor, Mark Kline and Gary J. Bekker.
  1990. "Engaging the Other in a Global Village." In *Theological Education* 26 (Spring 1990): 52-85.

Vanhoozer, Kevin J.
   1997.   "Does the Trinity Belong in a Theology of Religions? One Angling in the Rubicon and the Identity of God." In Kevin J. Vanhoozer, ed, *The Trinity in a Pluralistic Age: Theological Essays on Culture and Religion*. 41-71. Grand Rapids, MI: Eerdmans. 41-71.

Volf, Miroslav.
   1998.   *After Our Likeness: The Church as the Image of the Trinity*. Grand Rapids, MI: Eerdmans.

   1996.   *Exclusion and Embrace: A Theological Exploration of Identity, Otherness and Reconciliation*. Nashville, TN: Abingdon Press.

Walls, Andrew F.
   1995.   *The Missionary Movement in Christian History: Studies in the Transmission of Faith*. Maryknoll, NY: Orbis.

Weatherhead, Leslie D.
   1999.   *The Will of God*. Nashville, TN: Abingdon Press.

Yong, Amos.
   2008.   *Hospitality and the Other: Pentecost, Christian Practices and the Neighbor*. Maryknoll, NY: Orbis.

   2016.   "Toward A Trinitarian Theology of Religions: A Pentecostal-Evangelical And Missiological Elaboration." In *International Bulletin of Mission Research*, Vol. 40. No. 4. (October 2016): 294-306.

Teaching Civility in an Age of Conflict

A. Sue Russell

Introduction

I stood in front of my class and the tension was palpable. People were on the defensive. I knew I needed to say something to diffuse the tension. The election season had brought out the worst in people and I knew that last night's results made at least half of my class unhappy. Being a native Californian and teaching in Kentucky, my Facebook feed had been inundated with strong attacks and support of the candidates and policies on both sides. Students on our campus had been hurt by some of the rhetoric of other students and others were unwilling to listen to how their rhetoric was hurting another. Here we were, brothers and sisters in Christ training for the ministry, yet there seemed to be a greater desire to promote a particular political voice than hearing how it hurt their brothers and sisters in Christ. I knew my class well enough that I knew I had students who were on both sides of the political divide and somehow, I needed to reunite my class. As I prayed about what I could say that would diffuse the tension and help us find a middle ground; something that both sides could agree on. Finally, I quietly said, "No matter how you voted last night, I think one of the things this election showed us is how many people on both sides of the political divide feel disenfranchised and marginalized. Our role as the church is to reach out and minister to those people."

As professors of mission preparing students for vocational ministry, we challenge our students to look at the world differently. We challenge our students to listen and learn from the cultural 'other'. We teach our students to make connections with those who are very different than themselves, those who have a different belief system, different lifestyles, and different language and culture. We teach our students to be culturally sensitive and to dialogue with others who are unlike themselves. Yet, in our own environment we often forget to apply those same principles when reaching out to those who are different than ourselves. It has never been more important for us to be able to teach civility in this age of conflict if we are to reach people for Jesus Christ.

In this paper, I first discuss some theological foundations I use for teaching civility to students. I then use cross-cultural training principles to help us teach students to learn to engage their cultural "other" in their own context.

Theological Principles

There are two theological foundations that are important for helping our students learn to love others and respond in ways that are glorifying to God and his church. The first principle is to understand who we are as people created in the image of God, as image bearers in the world. Civility must be an extension of what we think of ourselves and of others. If we think of ourselves primarily as belonging to a group; white, conservative, liberal, feminist; and those who do not belong to our group as the repugnant 'other' there cannot be civil discourse. We will seek to include or exclude based on whatever is the particular identity marker of our group. The starting point for civil discourse is our shared humanity as created in the image of God and bearers of His image. There are several facets to consider.

First, we are image bearers, created in God's image to reflect his nature. God has created us as individuals with unique gifts and talents to participate in redemption in our unique way. Newbigin states, *"I believe that the reign of God is present in the midst of this sinful, weak, and divided community, not through prayer or goodness of its own, but because God has called and chosen this company of people to be the bearers of his gift on behalf of all people"*[1] We are bearers' of God's goodness to all people. As a missional community, we are image bearers who are representing God to the world. As individuals, we are unique image bearers who are able to reflect that image in our own unique way, in our unique network of relationships. What we do matters because as image bearers we are to represent God in the world.

When I talk about being image bearers to my classes, I often stop and ask my class if any of them have ever been servers in a restaurant. I then ask them what their fellow servers think about serving on Sunday. After 16 years and asking the question to over 6000 students the answer is always the same. People hate serving on Sundays because the 'church crowd' is stingy. Christians do not tip well and sometimes not at all, but may leave a religious tract instead of a tip. We have witnessed by our actions, but probably not the way that was intended.

How we live is important. The church, speaking in terms of you and me, is to represent the presence of God. Newbigin also argues that the church is in the midst of history as a sign, an instrument to further God's reign in the world. It is not just about conversion, but the church is to represent the presence and reign of God, to represent and bring God's love to both the righteous and unrighteous.[2] The church is to carry out God's mission of redeeming the world to Himself. We are not just to do this inside of the walls of the church, but everywhere. I think part of the disconnect between how people behave in the walls of the church and how they behave on the pages of Facebook is because we see ministry or our commission as separated from our daily lives.

However, the great commission is not just about vocational ministry or about ministry done in the church. It is for every believer. Our primary calling is to make disciples, to be image bearers no matter where we go. We are to

---

1   Leslie Newbigin. *The Open Secret*. 54.
2   Ibid., 110, 139.

make disciples in our going; whether this is going to work, to the store, to a restaurant, to the gas station, to the DMV, no matter where we go we are to make disciples, to be God's image bearers in the world.

I remember when this really hit me for the first time. I had just returned from 15 years on the mission field to marry my husband. I was reading through the New Testament and came to Matthew 28:18-20. I thought to myself, "Been there, done that! No longer applies!" And in that moment, the Lord spoke, "What has changed?" I realized I had read this as a call to full time vocational ministry rather than the primary call on my life, to make disciples. My vocation may change, but no matter where I am, my primary calling was to make disciples.

Shortly after this God decided to give me an object lesson. I had a job cleaning rooms at the inn where missionaries were in transit on their way home from the field. As I was cleaning a toilet one day I remember asking God, "OK, Lord when are you going use me again?" And the answer was, "I am using you, and if this is the ministry that I intend for you for the rest of your life, are you willing to be content in this calling?" It changed my perspective to see cleaning rooms as my ministry versus my job. From then on, as I cleaned the room I prayed for the family, their safe travel, for their comfort as they stayed the night. I looked for ways to make the room feel special and for the guests to feel loved. So many times students are anxious to get through school or a job so they can get into 'real ministry' rather than seeing ministry is where God has them for now. We need to reimagine our jobs as where God has sent us to be image bearers. Can you imagine if everyone in our churches understood this? What would happen if we gathered the people in our churches and asked about the ministries outside the church that they were involved in? Or in September we called up teachers and commissioned them for their ministry? Or office workers? Or medical personnel? You get the picture. Not only would it require a radical change in how most people in the church view their vocation, but also how those in vocational ministry view their role.

This same principle also applies to our interaction on the internet, especially social media. Far too often people can divorce themselves from the pictures, opinions, or articles that they post on social media. However, just as in physical spaces, we are to be image bearers in cyberspace. We need to be intentional about how we use social media to be image bearers. For example, I belong to a large Facebook social media group Women for Tri, which encourages women in triathlon events. People post triumphs, questions, training successes, and race results. Last year I reentered the world of triathlons after a five year hiatus. I have discovered it has taken me a lot longer to get back into triathlon shape at my current age than when I was younger. For the first time in my life I DNF'd (Did Not Finish) at two longer races. I was extremely disappointed. I remember thinking I didn't want to really post my failure to finish my races. But after reflection, I realized that far too often we tend to project the image we want people to see on social image rather than vulnerability. I realized that there were a lot of younger athletes on the page that could be helped by my reflections and how I handled disappointment. I chose to be an image bearer to the group as I reflected on what I learned about myself and attitudes that God had graciously given me. Just as in physical space, we are image bearers on cyberspace. We can choose to use this space to divide people by our rhetoric or to build relationships by our postings. Rhetoric or relationships.

The third aspect of being the image of God is that this is the good news of the gospel. We, all of us, are created in God's image. The person who may think differently about a particular subject is not an issue, but an image bearer. John Wesley understood this and thought of people not as "lost" but as people whom God has created in His image. As Snyder notes, "This means that the first word in evangelism is not bad news but good news-not, 'You are a sinner,' but 'You bear God's image.'[3] The first thought in our interaction with others should not be to a category of people or an issue, but as someone who is created in the image of God.

If we say that we love God, we must also love the one who is created in his image (1 John 4:19-21). Period! It doesn't mean we have to accept what people have done, or what they believe, but we need to remember that every human is a unique reflection of the image of God. But we tend to objectify people in our debates. I have felt this often in the debate about women in the church. Many times when people are talking about 'the women issue' I have wanted to raise my hand and say, "I am not an issue, I am Sue, a real person." When we reduce people to liberal, conservative, left, right, gay, straight, feminist, racists, we have put people into a category and we have dehumanized them. We now respond with rhetoric rather than relationship. When Jesus says to love our neighbors as ourselves he is requiring us to treat others as people we know. We need to ask, would I want someone to treat my husband, wife, brother, sister, friend, like this? Would I say this to one of them? Until we personalize our responses we have dehumanized a person created in God's image.

Wesley and Radical Hospitality

The second theological foundation for civility is hospitality. I think right now the church is facing very difficult issues with people on both sides of those issues. It is very easy in our words and actions to divide rather than unite. It is easy to create a caricature of people and then label them as the 'repugnant

---

3   Snyder, Howard in *World Mission in Wesleyan Spirit*. 63.

other' and exclude them from our group. Note the contrast to this harshness and exclusion that is promoted by some on social media to the welcome that Christine Pohl so eloquently states about Wesley's view of hospitality:

> *"Many of John Wesley's most profound words of invitation and welcome occur when he is communicating God's love and welcome to sinners in need of grace. The tenderness and warmth by which he invited others into new life in Christ runs through his sermons and letters. He was passionate and compelling in his efforts to portray a God who genuinely welcomes all who would come to Jesus. He invited those who were strangers to God to find a divine friend. In powerful contrast to the spiritual apathy of so much of his society, and in response to the distance of persons from God, Wesley invited people into vibrant relationship with a loving and living God*[4]

This message of love and welcome to all contrasts starkly with the rhetoric of hate and exclusion found in so much of the media today. How can people hear about a God who welcomes them and loves them when they are rejected by those who claim to be God's people. George Hunter is his book on evangelism notes, "People have to belong before they can believe."[5] In today's ever increasing post-Christian environment, the way many people will come to Christ is as they are welcomed by those who love Him. The very foundation for welcoming others is based on the fact that God created us in His own image (Gen. 1:26).

None is to be excluded from this welcome. When Jesus told the story of the Good Samaritan, one of the things that is often overlooked is that Jesus never identified the man who was robbed, he was just a 'certain man'. We know nothing about his background, his ethnicity, his nationality, his hometown, his parents, his family, his wealth, his religion... all we know is that he was someone in need. I think this was very deliberate on Jesus' part, any kind of status markers would have allowed some in the audience to exclude him from their help because he didn't belong to their group. But all we know is that he was someone in need. When we think of hospitality, I think this is what Wesley meant. We weren't just to offer hospitality to people we know or can gain from, or who can repay us; we are to offer hospitality to those who are in need, to those who have different worldviews, those whom God brings along our paths, to our Facebook feed, to our twitter feeds, and Instagram accounts

This radical hospitality often requires deliberate choices to provide opportunities to welcome people. When I was hired at Asbury, my husband and I began to pray about where we should live. While at Biola we had my classes over each semester, hosted student meetings, and hosted department

---

4   Christine Pohl.
5   George Hunter.

parties. We estimate that we hosted approximately 4000-5000 students in our home while we were at Biola. When my husband and I were looking for a house in Wilmore we had two criteria; it had to be within walking distance of the campus and it had to have a large room where we could host groups of students. In a way that it was evident that God was leading us, we found the house that we eventually bought. As we renovated this house several people have implied that we were foolish to buy the house as a financial investment, since we will never get a return on our investment. But the Lord did not lead us to invest financially in a house but to invest into the lives of students to create a place of welcome; not only for students, but for our neighbors in Wilmore as well. Hospitality doesn't always make economic sense.

We need to learn ways to show hospitality no matter where we are interacting. Whether it is in our churches, in our homes, or in social media. The question we need to ask is how can we show hospitality in this situation, to these people, in this conversation. The following are a few principles from cross-cultural training that can be used in teaching students to engage their cultural 'other'.

Practical Application

Don't stereotype, humanize

The first principle is to humanize. We learn about stereotypes and ethnocentrism when we talk about cross-cultural missions. However, this same principle needs to applied in our conversations about groups in our own culture. Far too often it is easy to vilify people or a position when they belong to a category, a class of people. They are gay, or liberal, or feminist or _____ fill in your own category. We can also do this when we speak of the 'unsaved' or even the poor. By placing people in categories we problematize them or their opinions as problems that we need to fix or address. We need to talk about people. People who do not have homes. People who have immigrated to the United States. People who think that gay marriage should be legalized, or who have married a same sex partner. We need to give names to people, neighbors who are married, divorced, or who have recently immigrated.

The second step to humanizing is to build a relationship. This means getting involved with groups of people who are different than ourselves. I belong to a home group in Kentucky in which I listen to people who were raised in a different part of the country. I get to know my neighbors, hire people or get involved in the local groups of similar interests, in my case triathlon clubs. If our networks are only people who are like ourselves, we will never humanize people who have different opinions and values. I live in an area where we often take our dogs to a public beach. While our dogs play together, these have been some of the best times to listen to people who are different than myself.

When I teach this to my class, we talk about what it must have been like for John and Peter to hear that the Samaritans had received the gospel. Or how the church must have felt when they heard Peter had eaten with Gentiles. These were the 'repugnant other' for Jewish people and they could not imagine 'those people' being included as part of God's people. I ask them to think of who they think of as their 'repugnant other', their 'Samaritans.' I also ask them to think of people for whom they had stereotypes. Then in a living out of the gospel assignment, I ask them to start a conversation with someone they would not normally hang out with. Someone that they look at as the 'other.' On a small evangelical campus it is sometimes the athletes who are chosen, sometimes the popular kids, sometimes it is just someone from another dorm. They then are to write about the misconceptions they had about the person and what happened when they listened to their 'other.' Most found that they had misconceptions about this group and found them more like themselves than they imagined.

Listen and Learn

The second principle is to listen and learn from people different than ourselves. We often teach in missions that we need to spend time learning the language and learning the culture. But we don't apply that same principle when we are in our own cultural arena. We need to be able to understand issues from different perspectives and find our common humanity. Many times what we hear as rhetoric is really based in fear. For instance, I sat with a neighbor on the beach when I started my Sabbatical to catch up. He and his partner had been married for several years. He shared that many in his community were living in fear and he personally was in fear that he and his partner may lose their marriage license. My neighbor knows where I stand in my own beliefs, but I can share in the fear and hurt that he is experiencing. We all know fear, loss, and pain, and we need to listen to these fears. What was often expressed in anger on both sides of an issue is really fear and we need to be able to listen to people's fear. We need to listen to people who fear losing health care, fear violence, fear losing family. These are real fears and we need to listen to understand.

Let me give a cross-cultural example. The community I worked with in S.E. Asia, constantly feared harm from spirits. Their question was who was going to protect me from the spirits. This was not a question I understood or could relate to. However, my brothers and sisters in the church knew how to answer that question and were effective in their ministry because they understood those fears.

Far too often the church is addressing the wrong question. Abortion? The issue for many women on the prochoice side is not about whether killing a child is right or wrong, but rather why should men control my body? Or how can I afford to raise a child? When 60% of children raised in single women households live below the poverty line, perhaps the church is asking the wrong question. Or at least not all of the questions. But if we only vilify people who have a different view on an issue, rather than listening, we may not address other questions that need to be answered. The same could be said of the people who self-identify as homosexual, people who are in our country illegally, etc. It is only by listening to people who hold views different than our own that we can really understand the issues and the fears.

Listening to another's story is to provide opportunities for people different than ourselves to tell their stories, their experiences. For instance, students at Asbury organized a series of fireside chats in which minority students were given an opportunity to tell the stories of their experiences at Asbury. I was impressed by the number of students who came to listen to their stories. None of us likes to hear how our words and actions might have hurt another, but we need to be willing to listen to how we might have unintentionally hurt others. We have to be willing to accept that another person's experience is different than ours, particularly when we are the majority. Most of us are ignorant of people's experience. I don't know what it is like to be a single mother, or what it is like to struggle to put food on my table, or have to choose when I take my children to the doctor because I can't afford it. I need to listen to those who have felt left behind, who can no longer find good jobs, who find their beliefs are no longer widely held by others.

Be Honest, be vulnerable

One of the hardest things to teach to Western missionaries is to be vulnerable and honest. It is hard for many of us to be dependent, but at the same time we cannot have true partnership unless we also receive. In our own cultural context, we need to be honest with ourselves and ask what we are afraid of if a certain policy passes or changes. We need to look beyond our anger and look at our fear. True friendship is never one way. Just as we listen to another person's concerns we can also express ours, not as right or wrong, but as our fears. After I had listened to my neighbor about his concerns for his own marriage, I expressed mine about how some of the new laws would undermine the advances that Title IX had made for women in sports and education. As a woman athlete, I was concerned that now I would be competing against physiologically developed men who identified as women. I was concerned if gay men were a protected class, I would once again be competing against a privileged class of people. Because I listened to his fears he also listened to mine and I was able to bring viewpoints that he hadn't heard in his own circle of friends.

Find Common Ground

Finally, in building relationships we can find common ground. We might not agree on specific issues, but there is a middle ground in most issues. We might not agree on abortion, but we can agree that children should not be raised in poverty and talk about ways the church could address this. We might not agree on immigration, but we can talk about ways in which the church can help people who have come to our country find the resources they need. We may not agree on health care, but we can agree that the sick and the infirm need to be taken care of and discuss how the church can help with this. We may not agree about how welfare is handled, but we can agree that we need to help the poor even if we disagree on the means to do this. We might not agree on the death penalty, but we can agree that prisoners are created in the image of God. When we polarize issues, rather than see people in need, we may miss the vast middle ground in which we can build bridges. If we only stay on our one side of an issue, people may never be able to see and relate to an image bearer of God. We need to ask, what is more important, being on the right side of an issue or bringing someone onto the right side of a relationship with God? Sometimes we may win a debate, but lose the relationship.

Conclusion

The gospel of Jesus Christ does not say that we are to be on the right side of political issues, it says that we are to be on the right side of relationships with God and people. There are no boundaries in the Kingdom of God. When Jesus said to "love our enemies" he included everyone, even those who disagree with us. No one is to be excluded from our love. When we chose to love our enemies, to treat them with kindness, to listen and learn from them to find middle ground, we might just discover that they have become our friend. When this happens, the world takes notice. This is exactly what happened in the unlikely friendship that formed between Barry Corey, president of Biola University and Evan Low of the California Assembly, chair of the LGBT caucus as reported in the Washington Post. The relationship started in the assembly with a legislative debate that pitted a conservative college's religious freedom against LGBT student protections. Both sides feared what the passing or failure of the law would mean. It was a win-lose situation. However, Evan and Corey, in the process of listening, became friends. Listen as they reflect on how their friendship formed:

> What happened? Two leaders on opposite sides of a divisive ideological issue decided to talk to each other. We listened to each other's perspectives. We listened while wanting to learn rather than listening while waiting to respond. Generous listening helped deconstruct some of the wrong impressions we had about the communities we represented. Breaking bread sometimes breaks barriers.
>
> We both had notions that informed our initially defensive stances toward the other. It's amazing how quickly biases can be overcome when relationships are prioritized, when you realize the person you once thought an adversary is in many ways like you, with a story and passions and ears, and a hope that we can make the world a better place.
>
> Do we agree on everything? No. Do our ideas of how to make a world a better place align? Not on every issue. That's okay. But what we have discovered, in getting to know one another, is that two people do not need to see eye-to-eye in order to work shoulder-to-shoulder.....Few problems are best addressed by homogenous groups, closed off to the voices of alternate views.[6]

The article concludes, "Relationships like this, whether on university campuses or in the halls of government, are crucial in a democracy that thrives insofar as its citizens know how to disagree without demonizing and work together for the common good without diminishing differences."[7] Civility can only be achieved when we prioritize relationships over issues. It can be achieved only when we as image bearers reflect the generosity and hospitality of God to others who were created in God's image.

---

6   Evan Low and Barry H. Corey. "We first battled over LGBT and religious rights. Here's how we became unlikely friends." *Washington Post.* March 3, 2017.
7   Ibid.

"Teaching the Uniqueness of Christ in an Increasingly Polarized World"

Luisa J. Gallagher and Robert L. Gallagher

Introduction

In the last few decades there has been a Western cultural shift concerning the uniqueness of Christ. Teaching at Wheaton College Graduate School (Wheaton, IL) for the past 20 years, I (Robert, a baby boomer) have witnessed a sea change in the attitudes of the first-year students coming to campus who are predominately from evangelical families, churches, and schools. When I started teaching at the College in 1998, the incoming student questionnaire showed a majority of students believing that Jesus was the only way to obtain salvation from the one, true, and living God. Now the bulk of arriving millennials see the Lord Jesus as only one way to God; and that God should be "fair" in treating all people with justice and compassion; and that he would never send anyone to eternal damnation simply because they had never heard of his Son. In addition, I (Luisa, a millennial) have taught and worked with millennials for over fourteen years at George Fox University (Newberg, OR), Gonzaga University (Spokane, WA), Whitworth University (Spokane, WA), Westmont College (Santa Barbara, CA), and Wheaton College (Wheaton, IL), and have experienced an intensifying of the same trend that my father Robert has mentioned.

How do you present the belief that Jesus is the only way of salvation to your millennial ministry class? By using narrative reflection and focus group conversation, this essay will explore how to facilitate discussion and critical thinking among millennials in our global tertiary context regarding the uniqueness of the Lord Jesus. In this process, we (Luisa and Robert) will use andragogic methods that allow students to embrace a positive and trusting learning environment. Meanwhile, we will present an orthodox biblical apologetic that will give space to the Holy Spirit to guide students towards the Son of God who came to take away the sin of our world; a ransom for all languages and cultures. In broader terms, the procedure will assist tertiary instructors in what the teaching of mission and ministry should look like in an increasingly complex public arena; and how they can negotiate contemporary global landscapes with faithful Christian witness in their teaching, including models of dialogue and engagement.

After presenting the purpose of the study together with the guiding question, definitions of key terms, and the teaching challenge, the essay summarizes the three common approaches and four evangelical views of the problem of teaching the uniqueness of Christ. The chapter then deals with an analysis of the written reflections and focus group treatment of the participants, observing and interpreting the findings, and applying the results towards teaching implications. The study is of vital importance. If we are training future Christian leaders who do not have a clear understanding of the centrality of

Christ, then what will be the gospel motivation, method, and message that they are taking to their field of ministry? Moreover, what are the future prospects of the Christian church and its global missionary endeavors?

Purpose of the Study

The purpose of the investigation is to understand the interplay between the universality of God's love and the particularity of salvation via the narratives of peer graduate students, and how to communicate that relationship to Christian millennials in their spiritual journey. This enquiry is crucial to the Church since one of the most disputed questions facing our contemporary world is the query of whether Jesus is the only way for salvation. Amongst millennials there is a growing trend of interpreting Scripture through a post-modern lens of religious pluralism and universality, rather than through an orthodox lens that values the doctrines of the Christian church that have been embraced for over two thousand years, such as the preeminence of Christ.

Considering the desire for tolerance in our society, how do we teach mission and ministry in our Christian colleges and seminaries in a manner that is faithful to the biblical worldview, and at the same time remain culturally pertinent and respectful of all backgrounds? To facilitate the purpose of the study, we presented a guiding question to a graduate cohort: as a Christian millennial, how would you lead a discussion with your evangelical peers regarding the perspective of the uniqueness of Christ? We then collected the narrative data from twelve graduate students during a one-week period using the question to obtain individual written reflections before conducting a focus group dialogue on the subject. Before deliberating and evaluating the findings, it is important to consider the definition of the key research terms, evangelical and millennial, as well as the teaching challenge before us.

Definition of Evangelical

Who are evangelicals? The British church historian, David W. Bebbington, gives four characteristics of evangelicals. First, conversion: the belief that lives need to be changed; second, activism: the expression of the gospel in effort, especially evangelism and missionary work; third, biblicism: giving special importance to the Bible; and lastly, cruicentrism: Christ's atoning sacrifice on the cross is central.[1] Furthermore, John R.W. Stott identifies three theological constraints of evangelicals: the Gospel comes from God and not human ingenuity; the Gospel is Christological, biblical, historical, theological,

---

1   David W. Bebbington, *Evangelicalism in Modern Britain: A History from the 1730s to the 1980s* (London: Unwin Hyman, 1989), 2-17. Bebbington argues in his quadrilateral that evangelicalism began because of the Enlightenment.

apostolic, and personal; and the Gospel is effective because God himself revealed it.[2] Together these criteria offer guidelines for determining practices that we can identify as evangelical.

Definition of Millennial

First coining the term in their book *Generations*, historians Neil Howe and William Strauss described the generation born between 1980 and the early 2000s as millennials.[3] Making up over a quarter of the population in the United States, the 2015 U.S. Census Report noted that the millennial generation, with 83.1 million people, now outnumber their parent's boomer generation (born between 1946 to 1964) of 75.4 million. Millennials are more diverse than any U.S. generation prior, with 44.2 percent identifying as part of a racial minority group, or ethnicity. They are the most educated generation, with 63 percent having attended or planning to attend college.[4] In the workplace and in society, millennials are collaborative, accepting the rules and authority laid before them, while also choosing professions that bring a sense of meaning and purpose. A key distinguisher of the millennial generation is the emergence and use of technology. The impact of technology on this generation is already visible in its effect on popular culture, education, the workplace, and even mundane human interactions from dating to texting, Instagram, or gaming culture.

In the United States, millennials, ranging in age from seventeen to thirty-six, are a highly optimistic generation. More liberal than previous generations, millennials in the U.S. align more with the democratic party and socialist ideals than other generations, maintaining a strong concern for issues of justice and social responsibility. Much research remains to be conducted on the demographics of millennials globally, therefore, for the purposes of this study, we will use the above definition and generalized characteristics to describe millennials. Throughout the remainder of the chapter, we will employ these definitions of the expressions, evangelical and millennial.

---

2   John R.W. Stott, *Evangelical Truth: A Personal Plea to Unity, Integrity, and Faithfulness* (Carlisle, UK: Langham Global Library, 2013), 1-18.

3   Neil Howe and William Strauss, *Generations: The History of America's Future, 1584 to 2069* (New York: William Morrow, 1991). The authors explore the millennial generation in greater detail in their later book, Neil Howe and William Strauss, *Millennials Rising: The Next Great Generation* (New York: Vintage, Random House, 2000).

4   "Millennials Outnumber Baby Boomers and Are Far More Diverse, Census Bureau Reports," *United States Census Bureau,* 2015, Retrieved January 6, 2018 from: https://www.census.gov/newsroom/press-releases/2015/cb15-113.html

The Teaching Challenge

Similar to the challenge of defining terms, there is a parallel complexity regarding how we approach teaching the unique role of Christ to millennials. We will demonstrate this by quoting several millennial student responses from a book review assignment that involved this topic. Although not connected to the study participants directly, we believe this data will help explain the shift in thinking regarding the centrality of Christ in the salvation story. The following remarks are from a "Perspectives in Global Outreach" mission course I (Robert) taught at Wheaton College over the last ten years. These millennial students in this course have had no association with the research cohort.

In a book review of Bruce Olson's *For this Cross I will Kill You*,[5] an undergraduate comments, "One of the chapters deals with the exclusive nature of Christianity. We (Christians), are right and going to heaven, and they (everyone else) are wrong and going to hell. I have a hard time rationalizing God condemning the billions of faithful followers of other religions around the world simply because they do not know that Christ died for their sins. This is a seemingly absurd act of God." Another student supports these comments by continuing, "Devout people of other religions do not need to know Christ to be saved because that thought is not something they can discern from their position. I think that it is possible that not all practicing members of other religions will go to hell."

The quotation from the next evangelical millennial draws on the character of Emeth in C.S. Lewis' *The Last Battle* to whom Aslan (Lord Jesus) says, "You have been worshipping me all along; you just never knew it was me." The undergraduate concludes from the lips of Aslan, "Pagans too can gain salvation. There is only one God: meaning that Muslims, American Indians, and African tribes all worship God. I think if God sees that they have followed the truth as much as they could know (such as Aslan saw in Emeth), then God may extend his grace to them even if they have not seen the saving works of Christ."

Our last student summarizes the view of the majority of millennials in this review exercise regarding the saving work of Jesus. She contends,

> The fairness of God would require that they ['devoted non-Christians'], deep down, have some inkling of truth. How could they be judged for what they had no way of knowing? At death, would it be fair for them to immediately be judged for not having believed in Jesus Christ as their personal Lord and Savior? I don't think so! I believe that God is fair, and so,

---

5   Bruce Olson, *For This Cross I Will Kill You* (Carol Stream, IL: Creation House, 1973). Charisma House changed the title of the book to *Bruchko* in 1978.

> I feel that whatever happens must somehow make it possible for people to simply make a choice between God's will and their own.

Over the past twenty years, the stalwart beliefs of millennial evangelical students at Wheaton College has dramatically shifted. I (Robert) believe that there are a number of internal causes that add to the external influencers of culture and post-modern worldview. Besides being immersed in a culture of tolerance posturing towards religious pluralism, there is also an internal Christian movement away from biblical inerrancy. This internal Christian movement is one of the major contributors towards millennials' theological change of belief.

Biblical literacy has plummeted among Christian millennials in the last twenty years.[6] Bible professors at Wheaton College openly declare that incoming first year students have an appreciation of a few isolated scriptures in the New Testament, yet have little understanding as to how they are connected; and little to no awareness of any of the stories of the Old Testament. One of the prime reasons for this burgeoning dilemma is the practice of the Christian church to separate the Scriptures into ethical, moral, and theological bits and pieces; and then extract them from their original contexts to feed personal or cultural biases. This situation is so pervasive in Christianity that most readers of the Bible have little chance of grasping the overarching grand story.

This trend has escalated since the Reformation when the 1560 Geneva Bible divided the Protestant bible into chapters, verses, and study notes. With the history of a segmented biblical tradition, it is unsurprising that Christian young adults struggle with scriptural knowledge. Lacking a clear understanding of the bible, or life and ministry experience, young adults may easily default to society's metanarrative instead. Consequently, emerging adult Christians, who are in their late teens through to the early thirties, often have a small view of God, whose character mimics the fairness of our culture's tolerant-inspired message, rather than a Spirit-inspired illumination of God's person and attributes revealed in Scripture. In the following section, we will briefly examine three common approaches and four evangelical views of the argument, prior to analyzing the composition of the group and revealing the class' insights.

---

6   Glenn R. Paauw, *Saving the Bible From Ourselves: Learning to Read & Live the Bible Well* (Downers Grove, IL: IVP Books, 2016), 12-17.

Three Common Approaches and Four Evangelical Views

What is the destiny of the unevangelized? The answer to this question creates a tension between two truths: the universality of God's love (John 3:16; 1 Timothy 2:4), and the particularity of salvation (John 3:18; Acts 4:12). From this tension, there arise two problem questions: what is the relationship of the two truths, and what happens to those who never hear about Jesus? The three common approaches to this set of questions are: exclusivism, where a person knows Jesus, and they know they know him; inclusivism, whereby an individual may know Jesus, yet not know that they know him; and pluralism, where a person does not know Jesus, and does not know that they do not know him.

In addition to the perception of these three common approaches, evangelical Christians can hold one of four views regarding the destiny of the unevangelized: restrictivists believe that there is no other name; universal opportunists claim that God does all he can do; postmortem evangelists argue that there is hope beyond the grave; and inclusivists contend that God is not without a witness.[7]

One week before starting the research, the class read and commented on two essays related to the subject: Lesslie Newbigin's "The Gospel and the Religions" and Charles E. Van Engen's "The Uniqueness of Christ in Mission Theology," both found in *Landmark Essays in Mission and World Christianity*.[8] A student commented on Newbigin's article, "This chapter was very theological and interesting to read and digest. As someone who tends to fall on the inclusivism side of salvation, I appreciated how the author thoughtfully considered other ways of looking at interpreting Scripture and evangelism." Continuing, she contends with Van Engen's treatment, yet states, "The author does confirm one thing that we should all agree on—Christ is Lord, and there is only one God." Finally, a North American woman ponders, "I find it very odd that Newbigin is arguing against the exclusivist view that all who do not accept Christ are lost. I think the Bible is pretty clear about the fact that Jesus is the only way to God; the only way to eternal life." Thus, before the research began, the group had familiarity with some of the approaches and evangelical views concerning the question of the destiny of the unevangelized.

Composition of the Group

The students had enrolled in the course "Biblical Theology of Mission" in the M.A. (Intercultural Studies) program at Wheaton College Graduate

---

7   Gregory A. Boyd and Paul R. Eddy, *Across the Spectrum: Understanding Issues in Evangelical Theology* (Grand Rapids, MI: Baker Academic, 2009), 197-213.

8   Robert L. Gallagher and Paul Hertig, eds., *Landmark Essays in Mission and World Christianity* (Maryknoll, NY: Orbis Books, 2009).

School in Chicagoland, and were composed of nine women and three men from seven nations (China [2 students], Indonesia [1], Japan [1], Philippines [1], South Korea [1], Taiwan [1], and the United States [5]). All the graduate students were millennial evangelicals with cross-cultural experience. Eight of the twelve members of the class had worked in China. At times, there was more Mandarin spoken during class breaks than English, not only from the two Chinese men, but also from several Caucasians who were fluent in the language.

The ministry among Chinese-speaking people varied from children's ministry in underground churches to leading Bible studies and youth camps, and teaching English as a second language. Other countries of missionary activity and the respective tasks conducted as mission were medical-dental assistance in Honduras; conducting business ventures and English classes in Indonesia; facilitating worship in churches from 50 to 4,000 people in Los Angeles; teaching Chinese and English in Myanmar; children and youth ministry and instructing English to refugees in South Korea; working as a radio broadcaster and caring for hearing-impaired children in Taiwan; and teaching at a girls' junior high and high school in Tokyo.

The class's future ministry desires ranged from three students planning to teach English in China and/or Taiwan; working in a Chinese family church; starting a children's ministry, and medical outreach in the western region of China; ministering with the Chinese diaspora in the United States; teaching English in a restricted-access country; conducting ESL classes in Chicago's Chinatown; running an intensive English program in Texas; founding a house-of-prayer ministry in the Los Angeles suburbs; working with university students and starting business enterprises in Indonesia; and teaching at a girls' junior high and high school in Japan.

The group's ministry call is exemplified in the following prayerful desires to: "practice biblical theology on the mission field and in the market place;" "be bold and open enough to commit myself to the Lord Christ;" "use the Bible to teach about God's love for different cultures;" "appreciate the privilege of being in God's service;" "serve God, and put him first above all things;" "know our God deeper and through a broader horizon;" "learn theological principles, and how to apply them in real life;" "be wise in what I have learned in my own life, being open to new ideas and perspectives, and in discernment regarding where God is leading me;" and "grow in Christ, and find effective ways of doing mission that I can bring to my ministry context."

In this study, the research group was composed of millennials sharing the values and attitude of their peers, as well as themselves. We (Luisa and Robert) embedded the distinctiveness of the essay's exploration and included elements that considered the barriers of presenting Christ, together with the methods and approaches of discussing Christ with other millennials. As an Indonesian teacher contended in the focus discussion, "I need to present Jesus in a way that makes sense to this generation."

We have based our research on the limited insights of a representative sample of evangelical millennial graduate students to gain initial perceptions of how to communicate Christ to millennials. The participants in this study were graduate students who chose the field of cross-cultural mission and ministry careers. Therefore, their motivation to participate in ministry may be led by a stronger understanding than an average evangelical millennial student of the preeminence of Christ and an evangelical theology that takes Christ's exhortation to make disciples of all nations (Matthew 28:19-20) to heart. A comparative may be drawn between this graduate group and the undergraduate responses from the students in the "Perspectives in Global Outreach" mission course over the past ten years. The graduate students participating in this study are not necessarily typical students at Wheaton, as many already have ministry experience abroad, and have committed to a life of ministry on behalf of Christ and his kingdom.

An additional limitation of this study is the international composition of the participants involved. Since this study includes seven students from East Asia and five from the United States, we are faced with the dilemma of how to interpret and generalize the findings. The theological, religious and philosophical worldview of the global participant group has the potential to be diverse. Yet, the international makeup of the group did not hinder this study, as many students were in alignment despite cultural backgrounds. In an increasingly global education context, the international makeup of this graduate class is more of a norm than an anomaly. Although showing signs of flattening, in the 2016-17 school year, the U.S. hosted over a million students, with an increase of three percent from the prior year.[9] A benefit of the international makeup of the participants may make this study valuable not only for a North American higher education context which often includes international students, but also for a global teaching context.

The short essay responses of the twelve graduate student participants allowed us to view a broad cross-section of experiences from diverse ministry and educational backgrounds with a more limited representation provided by the focus group. We recognize that the analysis of the research will perhaps

---

9   "IIE Releases Open Doors 2017," *IIE, The Power of International Education*, Retrieved data Jan. 12, 2018: https://www.iie.org/Why-IIE/Announcements/2017-11-13-Open-Doors-Data

have limited relevance beyond Wheaton College. Yet, we believe that the findings may provide principles of teaching on the topic of the uniqueness of Christ that could be helpful to the global Christian community.

Insights of the Group

The findings of the international group described in the previous segment, both in written essay and open sharing, revealed three supplementary insights: the values of millennials, perceptions of millennials, and barriers of presenting Christ. We will now share these results before elaborating on the methodology of teaching about Christ, and ways of enabling discussion of the Savior such as philosophical, comparative, and theological approaches.

Values of Millennials

The values of millennials that the group identified as important were: building trust through vulnerability, being authentic or true to oneself, sharing authentic struggles, serving locally and thus being effective globally, justice and compassion questions, care for everyone, and the view that relationships matter. Accordingly, as one of the Asian women explained in her consideration, the values of millennials should influence how people present Christ to them. She states,

> This is Jesus, who loves everybody; who works in his community, yet brings a global effect; who fights for justice; who is for the marginalized as he comes to the world of sinners; he is also the One who wants to connect with this generation to help them with their struggles and sin. Bringing these topics and presenting related questions will be useful for teaching.

A male Caucasian provides further understanding of the values of millennials.

> Having the ability to reach and teach a millennial is something that is very hard to do. One thing that I find millennials hold to high value is trust. Trust involves vulnerability and authenticity. What I mean by that is you must be vulnerable with them about yourself. If we are constantly preaching to them about sin and forgiveness, then as a teacher, you must have a testimony to show that in your life. With vulnerability comes discussion and openness. You will find that more and more millennials will feel more comfortable and safe sharing when you set a precedent. Secondly, authenticity involves being true to yourself. There is nothing more off-putting to a millennial than trying to be someone you are not. Millennials value uniqueness, and they want to see truth through you. If

they sense you are trying to be someone you are not, then they will lose that trust. Trust is the foundation of connecting with a millennial.

Perceptions of Millennials

The graduate class not only assessed the values of millennials, but also reviewed the millennials' perception towards presenting Christ as the only path of salvation. The group believed that millennials would skeptically consider such an attempt as arrogant and narrow-minded since, as many post-moderns, they do not consider truth to be absolute, and would even challenge the term "millennial" as being legitimate. One of the Chinese students brought together philosophical and theological considerations in observing his contemporaries. He notes,

> One of my major mission fields is young adults in China. I think the millennials in China are quite critical, and in the meantime, they work very hard. They want to live a good life. So, I think one of the things that I can ask the class to do is to ask them to think about what is a good life. I am sure they have many good ideas. The next thing I would do is to see if they have any preconceptions about religions. I am sure many of them do. Because as far as I am concerned, some of them would look at religions when they have difficulties. Then I would like to ask them to talk about their perspective on religions to me, and try to connect these to the mighty power of Christ.

Barriers of Presenting Christ

In considering the barriers of presenting the uniqueness of Christ, the twelve students listed the following as negative millennial reactions that would serve as obstacles: reaction to conservatism, inclusivity leaning towards moral relativism, rules of religious legalism, and church hypocrisy that leads to an inauthentic lifestyle. The class observed that they had grown up with an increasing exposure to globalism, and various cultural and religious influences, and thus had to "wrestle with the uniqueness of Christ." Relativism had made it difficult to accept anything as uniquely true for fear of limiting alternate expressions of truth through the religions and cultural practices of others.

In the focus sharing, a student instructor explains her understanding of possible hindrances to teaching about Christ.

The format of the class should be approachable. When I teach, it is important to let them [millennials] know that I deal with real struggles too; being authentic when presenting myself helps my audience to know that I'm approachable. My personal journey of deciding that I need Christ for my salvation, accepting him as my Savior, and walking with him in ups and downs through the journey of my faith, are all important aspects to be open about.

Methodology of Teaching

Within the student focus group discussion concerning teaching methodology about Christ, seven women (Indonesia, Japan, Korea, Taiwan, and the United States) and four men (China and the United States) spoke of different means such as class discussions (open class [8 students] and small groups [4]), case studies (3), testimonies (2), individual reflection (2), readings (2), lecture (2), role-plays (1), simulations (1), videos (1), visual aids (1), and technology such as blog, live streaming, online forum, and Instagram (1). Students in the study primarily focused on relational teaching methodology, highlighting the millennial value on relationships.

Hence, conversations, both in open or group sessions, far outweighed any other teaching technique. Along these lines, a Chinese man in the focus dialogue suggested to connect personal experience with the message of the class by beginning with the teacher "telling their story about how they came to Christ. And then let the students discuss with a partner their experiences of knowing God and becoming a Christian." Supporting this teaching method, an Indonesian woman shared in the group, "With open discussions about Jesus, answer them based on the Bible, showing that Jesus connects to all humankind, showing [that] the need for salvation is real, [and] they [millennials] have a bigger purpose to impact the world. [These] are all themes I would like to have in my class."

Then followed in frequency, case studies ("from real everyday life of the young generation seeking the hope of salvation in Jesus") and testimonials ("bringing in millennials to ask him or her to share with the class"), which similarly provide occasions for sharing real struggles, talking about justice and compassion themes, and caring for everyone in the group. Relationships matter. A student suggested that in a more relational setting, "questions will arise to lead people to Jesus as the only way of salvation: Who is Jesus? What is his view of justice? What kind of love does he offer? What impact does he bring to humanity? Why does humankind need salvation? Why do I need salvation? How does Jesus help me through my individual struggles?"

Surprisingly, for a media astute age-bracket, technology played a lesser role as the vehicle of instruction, even though one student commented, "The millennial generation uses online and social media as a parameter to decide if something matters." Videos, visual aids, blogs, Facebook, live streaming, online forums, Instagram, and Twitter were low or non-existent on the list, as were interactive prospects such as role-plays, simulations, and projects to share online. Of note, the format of communicating truth that teachers use in the majority of classrooms was equally low on the list: the lecture. This is an interesting point. Certain mediums of teaching, such as a lecture, do not necessarily provide openings for personal conversation that promote deeper relationships, or inspire trust through vulnerability and authenticity. According to the students in this study, the participatory modes are of greater value in teaching than less personal and interactive activities.

Approaches of Discussion

In the previous section, the twelve millennial participants in the study brought valuable exposure to the methodology of teaching. Moreover, they also shared multiple styles to approach the discussion of Christ as the only way to salvation. In the next part of the chapter, we will unfold the musings and conversation of the philosophical, comparative, and theological tactics of the group.

Philosophical Approach

Three female students (Japan, Taiwan, and the United States) and one male student (the United States) highlighted the need for a philosophical understanding of the teaching challenge. The male student reflected,

> This discussion needs a prior discussion on truth and epistemology. Is there truth, and is it possible to know it? This would look different for Christians and non-Christians. I would take Christians to Jesus' well-known statements that he is the truth, which those who do what he says build on a solid foundation, that to know him is eternal life. With non-Christians, I would start with the discussion of truth and ask the question: If what Jesus says is true, then what does that mean for us? In both cases, I would ask the Holy Spirit to give me the words to say, and the ears to listen (to him and them).

The Taiwanese woman struggled with the question of the final state of the non-Christian after death asking, "What happens to the non-Christian after death? I want to ask God so many questions such as what happened to the Gentiles after their death who were killed by Joshua. They didn't even have a chance to listen to the gospel, and they were killed by the people of God."

The Japanese student pondered the same question. "We are bound to become judges of that which God only knows. Many Christians like to argue. We like to prove our justice. Thus, we are often tempted to ask, 'What happens to the non-Christian after death?' However, only God has the answer. We have to draw a line between us and God." These colleagues confessed that they often found themselves looking at people and their actions, and thinking whether they will make it to heaven. They concluded that as Christians they needed not to judge others, whether or not God had saved them, but instead they needed to view everyone as equal in God's eyes.

The final student drew upon her apologetic training by maintaining, "I would use C.S. Lewis' famous 'liar, lunatic, Lord' argument—Jesus himself claimed to be God (which is backed by Scripture). If he is not who he said he was, then he is either a liar (and therefore not God, or someone whom we should follow), or a crazy person (again, therefore he wouldn't be God). Based on Scripture, the most reasonable explanation we have is that Jesus is God."

Comparative Approach

Five women and two men within the class (China [2 male students], Indonesia [1], Japan [1], South Korea [1], and the United States [2]) responded with a comparative-religion approach to the question prompt. The typical attitude towards this approach of the focus group is illustrated in a statement by a student from the United States.

> I would compare Jesus to other religions to see how unique Christianity is compared to other religions. Jesus and world religions: cover the main religions, and how one finds salvation. Compare the teachings of Jesus versus the main leaders of the other religions. Reiterate that there is no other way to salvation than Jesus.

Continuing this line of argument, the Filipino female student declared within the focus group,

> All humans, both Christians and non-Christians, are sinners. Only God's grace can forgive sins. Every person's faith, regardless of religion, reflects God's grace. As Christians, we should welcome all the signs of the grace of God at work in the lives of those who don't acknowledge Jesus as Lord. Christians should open a dialogue, and share stories about Jesus with other faiths, and cooperate with them in all projects that are in-line with a Christian's understanding of God's purposes.

Lastly, within the focus group, there was a repetition of the importance of cooperating with people of all faiths and ideologies, especially in projects, which are consistent with the purposes of God. Instead of focusing on the doctrinal differences, Christians could agree with people of other religions concerning the struggles for justice and freedom, even though the Christian's ultimate goal is different in many issues.

Theological Approach

By far the greater number of students used the theological approach: seven women (Japan, South Korea, Taiwan, and the United States) and two men (China and the United States). They cited several scriptures to inform millennials of Jesus in both the Old and New Testament: Deuteronomy 6:4; Mark 12:29; Luke 6-9; John 2:23-3:21; 14:6 (2 students); 17:2-3; Acts 4:12; and Romans 10:9; as well as general references to the prediction of Jesus in the First Testament compared to the promised fulfillment in the Second Testament (3); the Gospels (3); Romans (2); and the Book of Acts (1). The student who encouraged the reading of John 2:23-3:21 followed with eight discussion questions. For example, how does Jesus respond to Nicodemus (3:3)? What does it mean to be born again? And, according to this passage, is Jesus the only way to God, or are there other ways?

The focus group reiterated the importance of the biblical truths about Christ, relationship with God, and an understanding that culture should influence the way Christians present the Gospel for the unreached millennial to understand. This view combats the ethnocentricity of Western Christianity since it demands that we learn from every culture. In particular, one student noted that Acts and Romans "addresses the meeting of the Gospel with culture by showing the distinction between the two." In this light, the Japanese woman comments on her cultural context,

> I understand why many Japanese people think that Christianity is not their religion. For them, a religion is a trademark of who they are. I think that for many Japanese people, what they most fear are their ancestors. They want to be faithful to their ancestors. In this society, we often say, 'Don't make your ancestors upset.' I believe [that] the truth, Christ's love, and eternal hope can reach out to the Japanese people's heart. However, at the same time, we need to understand the cultural context, and have the wisdom to share this good news.

She concludes that telling the truth—the story of the Bible—is the most powerful and ultimate message Christians can share with every one of every nation. Nothing can separate us from Christ's love. Moreover, it is only this love that is authentic to every people group.

A North American woman expanded her theological views in her written answer by supposing that if she were to teach on the uniqueness of Christ she would begin by explaining about the Lord Jesus in the First Testament using verses that prelude to Christ's coming; and in so doing, emphasize the need of a Savior, and that God planned Jesus' coming to this world. Next, the masters' student would refer to Christ in the Second Testament by declaring the seven "I am" statements of Jesus in the Gospel of John, the death and resurrection of the Lord from the synoptic Gospels, and Paul's Gospel message in Romans.

Generally, the focus group said yes to God's grace and activity in the lives of non-Christians, agreeing that God plants "Easter eggs" (his witness) in different cultures that can be redeemed to reveal more of him. Separating salvation, however, from an explicit confession of Jesus as Lord was a genuine concern among many of the students. They appreciated the warning against trying to judge on earth who will go to heaven, and would not presume to give final pronouncement of anyone's eternal destiny. Yet, they believed that Christians should hold to the standard given in Scripture that if a person openly declares that Jesus is Lord and believes in their heart that God raised him from the dead, then God will save them.

Teaching Implications

We accomplished our research aim to understand and communicate the centrality and love of Christ to millennials by conducting a study, consisting of a focus group with twelve graduate male and female students, and an analysis of participants' written narratives. In the prior sections, we discussed the values and perceptions of millennials and possible barriers of presenting Christ. We also shared how participants would approach teaching about Christ, and the ways of enabling discussion about Christ such as philosophical, comparative, and theological approaches.

The main findings of this study reveal that in teaching millennials, the approach of faculty should be highly relational. Faculty, students, and those ministering with millennials should take an authentic and vulnerable approach, sharing personally, including, as a student instructor noted, the "ups and downs [of] the journey of [your] faith." In a culture that is saturated with inauthentic Facebook feeds, and image-conscious celebrities famous for being famous, there is real power in being vulnerable with each other. By highlighting spiritual struggles, and a need for Christ, faculty should approach the conversation humbly, and with an attitude that comes alongside the student. Once relationships have been built and trust has been established in a classroom setting, teachers may approach a discussion about Jesus as the only way of salvation through various means. Individual discussions with students about the centrality of Christ should be led through building relationships, asking questions, and sharing of personal encounters with Christ.

In teaching pedagogy, there has been much discussion about creating safe and effective spaces for students in the classroom. Marcia Baxter Magdola lists four categories that promote inclusive classrooms: viewing students as capable participants with valuable experiences, providing students with reflective and analytical experiences leading to critical thinking, creating a community-learning atmosphere that inspires open dialogue, and encouraging students towards deeper levels of thinking.[10] In the desire to create safe spaces in the classroom, we also need to challenge students to have difficult conversations, and encourage them to grow. Assignments should enhance complex thinking skills, addressing multiple perspectives and empathetic abilities.[11]

In the classroom setting, three discussion approaches were highlighted: philosophical, comparative, and theological. The philosophical approach was not noted for being overwhelmingly convincing to millennials, while the comparative approach was deemed more helpful. Considering the intercultural makeup of the participant group, a comparative approach may be helpful in cross-cultural settings, or with student populations that are more diverse. Overwhelmingly, participants highlighted the inspiration of the theological approach. Considering that millennials often enter college as biblically illiterate, the affirmation of the theological approach by the student participants was a surprise. Through the reading and exploration of Scripture, however, Christ is readily revealed as the only way to salvation. The role of the Holy Spirit also serves as a teacher and guide in this learning process. Training students to think critically about how to engage in Scripture and how to dialogue with people of different beliefs is vital to the health of the church.

As our society and church is increasingly at odds with itself and the world, we need to train our students in how to approach relationships with convicted civility.[12] This view is not promoting relativism, yet holds the tension of having

10 Marcia B. Baxter Magolda "Teaching to promote holistic learning and development." In Marcia B. Baxter Magolda (Ed). "Linking student development, learning, and teaching," *New Directions for Teaching and Learning, 82* (San Francisco: Jossey Bass, 2000), 88-98.

11 David Schoem, Sylvia Hurtado, Todd Sevig, Mark Chesler, & Stephen H. Sumida, "Intergroup dialogue: Democracy at work in theory and practice." In David Schoem and Sylvia Hurtado (Eds.), *Intergroup dialogue: Deliberative democracy in school, college, community, and workplace* (Ann Arbor: The University of Michigan Press, 2001), 1-21.

12 For further information regarding convicted civility, read: Richard Mouw, *Uncommon Decency: Christian Civility in an Uncivil World* (Downers Grove, IL: InterVarsity Press, 2010).

real convictions, such as the exclusivity of salvation through Christ alone, with the respect offered towards other religions, beliefs, and ideas. In the classroom, teachers might also employ a dialogic approach. True dialogue provides room for open conversations, and allows for something new to be created. It is not an approach that tells people what to think, but instead teaches individuals how to explore and think critically, using theology, scripture, and logic. In this increasingly complex public arena, teachers might also direct students to look at the values that motivate them to do ministry and mission work. Millennial values of justice, compassion, and care for all, might be explored in alignment with Scripture, and God's own compassion and love of the poor and marginalized.

Conclusion

At Wheaton College, along with many evangelical liberal-arts campuses, we are faced with the task of teaching a population of students where many individuals are no longer convinced of the inerrancy of Scripture, or the central figure of Christ as the only means of salvation and eternal life. Our post-modern culture of tolerance and relativism has certainly influenced the church, and how many approach the topic of the exclusivity of Christ. Through relationship building, however, creating safe spaces in the classroom, and approaching difficult conversations with convicted civility, faculty can set the stage for open theological conversations about the role of Christ in Scripture.

In our churches and in places of learning, we must continue to engage students in the word of God, raising questions, and building students who are critical thinkers, able to adapt and teach others about the centrality of Christ. This question will continue to be of vital importance to the church, as the generation immediately following millennials, generation Z, or igen, will bring unique perspectives to the classroom, and the students we are now training will teach this new generation. It is our hope and our belief that with thoughtful dialogue and biblical exploration, students will continue to acknowledge and know Christ as Savior and Lord, to the glory of God the Father, God the Son, and God the Holy Spirit.

The Impact of Globalized Immigration on Mission and Missiology

CHRISTIAN DUMITRESCU, PhD, AIIAS

Abstract: The globalization process created a set of new challenges for mission and missiological thinking and teaching. Eastern and Western cultures influence each other. Immigration moves people from one side of the world to the other. Too often immigrants were taken advantage of for missionary purposes in their openness created by the transition to a new environment. Too often the Bible is offered to them in Western terms and logic, and mission is taught with Western philosophy and strategies. This paper will look at the challenges and opportunities created by immigration in both directions and look at how the process of contextualization needs to be adjusted to people who experience both rejection and gradual acceptance of new cultural values. What strategies may be both faithful to Scripture and to the culture and worldview of the guests in our culture? The paper will also assess the missiologists' current awareness of the new developments in immigration patterns and their responses.

Introduction

Globalization is defined today as "interconnectedness" (Tiplady 2003:2), as "complex connectivity" (Tomlinson 1999:2), or as an "intensification of worldwide social relations" (Giddens 1990:64). Tiplady describes globalization as a process in which "events and developments in one part of the world are affected by, have to take account of, and also influence, in turn, other parts of the world." He also notes that globalization creates "an increasing sense of a single global whole" (Tiplady 2003:2). It goes beyond internationalization where communication mechanisms enhance cooperation between different entities. Globalization implies that all nations, institutions, networks, and individual players become one. As Tiplady concludes, "Globalisation is about global interconnectedness, not global Americanness" (or Westernisation) (Tiplady 2003:4)

However, globalization is not unidirectional, it runs many ways: both from the West to the Rest and from the Rest to the West, as well as from the North to South and return. Tiplady cautions that "ideas and products . . . when they get to their new destination, are not imbibed wholesale. They are adapted to fit the local situation" (Tiplady 2003:4). This adaptation changes globalization into "glocalization," with its religious counter partner being the glocal church. Describing the glocal church, Dyrness and Garcia-Johnson portray it as "a sociocultural space that is diasporic, polyphonic, and polyvalent at its core" (Dyrness and Garcia-Johnson 2015:123).

Globalization and Christianity

Christianity was supposed to be global from its beginnings. When Jesus prayed for his disciples to be one, he wanted them to be part of the world. Obedience to the same Christ makes Christianity global. He often emphasized the importance of obedience to the Father for the sake of unity. When commissioning his disciples for mission, Jesus re-emphasized the global nature of the incipient movement in the light of the Adamic, Noahic, and Abrahamic blessing. Because of Israel's reluctance to go to the nations, people had to come to Israel in order to hear the good news of salvation, and too often they had to become Jews or proselytes to have access to the temple and sacrifices. Jesus restored the global nature of his people in light of his presentation of the divine beings as one. History shows that globalization happened cyclically, but today, as Shenk notes, "a new stage in this process toward an integrated world system has been reached. We have no choice but to recast knowledge and relationships in light of the processes of modern globalization" (Shenk 2006:9).

Today, no nation can survive isolated. But our sense of interdependence needs to evolve "into a compelling sense of solidarity across national boundaries. We have become interdependent with one another at the global level in all the important areas of life, in economics, politics, and culture, and the challenge is how to develop a sense of universal humanity in a way that does not either suppress legitimate differences or reify and absolutize such differences but sublates them into a recognition of common humanity" (Min 2008:189).

Mission cannot escape the "two-way street" context. From the beginning, Christians under persecution moved to other countries and cultures, and mission was done by im/migration. Today, refugees are forced to find shelter in Christian nations where locals may witness to them. In Scott Sunquist's words, "persecution is one of many causes of movements of people. From the beginning of time humans have been on the move, carrying their possessions as well as ideas and religious beliefs with them." In many parts of Africa, "migration, not intentional missionary activity, mostly explains this spread of Christianity" (Sunquist 2015:136). The current process of globalization brings back missional challenges and opportunities from past centuries at a larger scale. If history recorded most of these movements in the Western cultures, it does not mean they did not happen in other parts of the world, such as Asia or Africa. They were simply not so well documented or recorded.

Walls also observes that "Global Christianity is not a product of the twentieth century. . . . It is easily forgotten that the emperor of China was studying the Christian Scriptures at almost exactly the time that the king of Northumbria in Northern England was placing the adoption of the Christian way before his council, and that by the seventh century gospel preaching had spread across the whole Eurasian land mass from the Atlantic almost to the Pacific. Much of Asia had a millennium and a half of Christian history before the first Western missionaries reached there, and some parts of Africa have a continuous Christian history far longer than Scotland's. In those early centuries the gospel interacted with cultures other than the Greek and Roman, and theological developments took place in other cultures than these" (Walls 2012:28).

Comparing Christianity of the first centuries with Christianity today, Walls finds powerful globalization parallels. He notes that the church through the centuries "lived amidst religious plurality, where Christians had to interact with those of other faiths. Its theology faced issues arising from Chinese, Indian, and Buddhist language, culture, and religion, and it had to reckon with Islam, not as a rival but as a ruler" (Walls 2012:29).

The post-World War II migration to Europe, after the demise of Western empires and colonialism, is linked by Sunquist to the concept of "reverse mission." "Migrating largely from Hindu and Muslim cultures, they were coming to live in the shadow of cathedrals and monasteries. . . . Nearly 20 million Muslims from North Africa, Iraq, Turkey, and the Balkans as well as from West Africa have settled in Western Europe, so that in France about 10 percent of the population is now Muslim and in Britain about 4.4 percent" (Sunquist 2015:138). Sunquist notes fairly accurately that "In the past, the flow of people and missionaries was from the West to the South and the East. The present missionary movement does not follow the mass movements going mostly to the West, but most of the African, Latin American, Pacific Island, and Asian missionaries are working within their regions. . . . These are the major new twists of migrations and missions at the beginning of the twenty-first century. The result is a much more culturally diverse Christianity and a much broader missionary engagement with cultures and societies than the world has ever known" (Sunquist 2015:138).

Globalization changed the economic status of many non-Western countries, for better or for worse. The newly created imbalance impacted the worldview of people, especially in terms of education, church life and organization, and mission. Consumerism and secularism are piggybacking on globalization and producing what Valerio calls global mobility. She lists two sides of global mobility: "Firstly, there is the mobility of the wealthy: those who can travel to the UK (for example) to study and just visit. Secondly, there is the mobility brought by displaced peoples: economic refugees and asylum seekers. This mobility brought by economic globalization, whether positive or negative, allows for many opportunities, and mission agencies are well placed to help local churches, through their knowledge of people's homelands" (Valerio 2003:20).

Payne sees the hand of God behind global mobility, stating that "The Lord of the harvest has been moving some of the world's unreached and least reached peoples to countries where governmental opposition will not interfere with missionary labors and where obtaining a visa and the costs of travel are not issues. The church in the West must remember her missional nature and function intentionally, strategically, and apostolically" (Payne 2012:33).

According to Patrick Johnstone's demographic study (2011), migration is the second major global challenge. He challenges churches not only to be aware of the trend, but also "prepare for this inevitable, unstoppable reality" (Johnstone 2011:4). He warns that an aging Western society, due to falling birth rates, especially in Europe, "will have created a population deficit, which will be made up, legally or illegally, from the poorer parts of the world until the global population begins to stabilize" (2011:4). With a prophetic voice, Johnstone states that his predictions and charts may remain true if migration patterns are not upset by demographic catastrophes, "most of which would affect Muslim-majority regions . . . greatly increase that number and add to the large and growing Muslim communities that are least willing to assimilate into their host countries and cultures" (2011:4). Looking at possible migration patterns, he identifies Northern and sub-Saharan Africa and the Middle East as refugee reservoirs from those politically, economically, and demographically volatile areas. Notably, he predicts that "the global Muslim population is likely to grow as fast as the Caucasian population shrinks" until 2050 (2011:5). These demographic changes already happen today at an accelerated rate, due to conflicts and natural disasters, and missionaries and missiologists need to respond to the new realities and predictions.

For the past few years, as a result of war and conflict in the Middle East and Northern Africa, Europe witnessed an increased influx of immigrants from these areas. European governments and citizens reacted differently. While Germany and Austria encouraged immigrants to get to their countries, Hungary or Slovenia closed their borders. Although, generally, population in every country stepped in to help, immigrants seemed to reject the resources offered. Many Westerners became upset when media showed immigrants angrily throwing on railroad tracks the water bottles received as a gift. Quite a number of Middle Easterners, educated people, obviously felt humiliated to be treated as refugees. They demanded free transit, caring less about visa requirements or border control issues.

Not long after immigrants settled in Western European cities, European citizens discovered and watched in horror how media presented incredible scenes of sexual harassment in public square, and even rape, while police forces pretended not to see or be overwhelmed. In fact, reports filed by police officers were hidden while major media news channels refused to include such events in their news casts. Europeans started to have chills asking themselves how could immigrants be so ungrateful and respond with such barbarity to the warm welcoming in the very countries that offered them not only shelter but food and help for integration in the new society.

Something was obviously wrong, and many blamed the immigrants' lack of education, morals, or ethical principles. They were often portrayed as animals, and nationalistic political parties seized the moment to ask that the immigrants be sent back home. However, only a few faint voices talked about cultural differences, and even fewer had the courage to ask for an evaluation of the differences between the values of the newcomers and those of the local population.

Even before the recent wave of immigrants from the Middle East and Northern Africa, Europe discovered that the loudly trumpeted policy of multiculturalism was not producing the expected cultural or ethnical heterogeneity. Nationalistic feelings were more and more displayed, especially in countries with a history of ethnic cleansing. The melting pot was also a fiasco, because the individual entities did not merge together. Everybody started to ask the question, Why? Politicians claimed that legislation was the problem. Sociologists blamed the differences in cultures, traditions, and practices. However, the problem seems to be much deeper, and this paper would try to look at the differences in values and assumptions, and assess the level where the conflict really takes place. Unfortunately, very few people take the time to listen and understand how immigrants feel, think, and see the world around them. The cultural values and worldviews of these two worlds are different and only by understanding them a solution to the crisis may be found. How are Western nations responding to immigration woes? And how are missiologists and missionaries responding to the immigration crisis in the context of globalization?

Different worlds

Europe boasted the creation of a space without borders. But under the pressure of the new wave of immigrants it closed its outer and intra borders again. In every European country nationalism is on the rise. The question is How it affects mission? How are churches going to respond? And what about our theology of mission and our strategies? Do we use the historical windows of opportunity? We seem to be debating if a C5 insider movement approach is justifiable or not, while borders are closed and windows of opportunity lost. Are we prepared, pro-active, so when an opportunity arrives we already have trained people and contextualized approaches ready?

The cultural dimension of globalization is creating abysmal tensions. Since culture is so pervasive, the conflict between different cultural values challenges missiologists and missionaries. In Hanciles' words, "No aspect of the debate is more problematic then the now commonplace assertion that globalization is a homogenizing force ushering in a single global culture or universal civilization" (Hanciles 2008:48)

People from different cultural backgrounds do not live in the same world. Their worldviews are different, and they practically live in different worlds. If, for Westerners, rules and laws have as source of authority the judicial system and a constitution, "In traditional cultures, people validate actions and practices by appealing to tradition" (Shenk 2006:9). There should be no surprise that, for immigrants, rules are there to be bent or broken if personal face or the honor of the group needs to be defended.

Most immigrants feel depressed and lonely, in spite of groups or individuals that visit them. They clearly miss the community and lack their (extended) family that usually provides support. Due to the strong individualistic values, the society in the West assumes that immigrants feel content having a shelter and decent living conditions. Loneliness is widespread among newcomers regardless if one is an immigrant or a migrant (student, temporary worker, etc.). Individualistic societies keep individuals busy so they cannot even associate with their peers. From a mentality of survival, they find themselves having to compete for status and achievements. For many immigrants the language barrier adds to the isolation.

Most immigrants often seem claustrophobic because of the cramped apartments where they have to live or the cubicles in which they have to work. Space in the West has different meanings than back at home. There is no sacred space, and Westerners keep scrubbing every corner as if leprosy is endemic in their houses or countries. There are lots of private properties, and in general the idea of privacy is completely different.

Time is perceived differently by the two categories: for Westerners time is money, and it seems they never have time to talk, to enjoy life, or to meditate. An immigrant wants to communicate, to share his or her stories, but their hosts barely have time to exchange the mundane information of the day under the pressure of impossible schedules. A Westerner finds validation in the accomplishments of the future while immigrants are validated by their connections with their past.

For immigrants, shame is to be avoided at any cost and honor guarded fiercely and increased as much as possible. No effort is spared to avoid shame, even if one has to lie straight to someone's face. Such an approach is not accepted by Westerners who believe truth is the capital value and justice is the highest ideal. But what, is the immigrant asking, if you are right while all your friends are abandoning you and you are left isolated and alone? Relationships are more palpable and alive than abstract ideas of truth or righteousness. Conflict is in the air.

Equality is another important value for Westerners, but not in the non-Western world. Your family provides you with a quota of honor and status that you will have to maintain and increase. One will always be striving for a higher status. As a karmic believer, your concern is to insure your birth into a superior status. Even within the Indian society's caste system, one doesn't pretend or claim equality with Brahmins, but stays within the agreed social and cultural boundaries.

Equality between genders is a utopia in most of the world. Each immigrant arriving in the West has roles assigned depending on their gender. Even within the same gender, the place in the order of birth makes a huge difference. In polygamous families each wife has certain given duties made clear at the time of marriage or even implied by the ranking position. The first wife will always be the one in charge of the house, directing the other wives in their chores. It is the husband's duty to provide for living, women are not expected to look for a job. If a wife looks for a job, the husband feels ashamed and humiliated because the assumption is that he cannot provide.

Every female has to be attached to a male in order to have status in society, and wives should have children, especially sons. Wives without sons are often abandoned by their husbands, and widows without children are repudiated by the extended family and have a hard time surviving. Most of the times, especially when still young, these widows are seen as a potential temptation for other women's husbands, so the community expels them.

It is only "normal" and assumed for a Middle Easterner male, who recently arrived in the West, to sexually harass a lone woman on the street because to him such a woman is available or is a prostitute. No honorable woman, in his eyes, would walk alone in the public square without a male companion, or without dressing according to the honor and modesty code they were used to. Websites report daily violence against women or entire communities at the hands of immigrants in West European countries. There is a rise of hatred or demands that immigrants behave according to the ethical and societal agreed norms of the West. However, immigrants' worldviews and values do not change overnight, or even at all.

Face is the most important value in the majority world. Traditional cultures apparently embraced globalization, but in reality it was a polite way to receive the uninvited guest and save the face of both, at the same time fighting strongly to maintain identity and values intact. Often, Christianity has been accepted, but old traditions and beliefs continued more or less visible. Strong syncretistic cultures exist in many parts of the world that were Christianized during the past few centuries. Spirits became saints, incantations became hymns, sacrifices became offerings, while rituals have often been baptized. The Western emphasis on truth, understood as universal, clashed with the locals' understanding of face. Truth was to be avoided if face or honor needed to be saved.

The other side of truth is that it was never intended to be defined as a set of abstract principles or dogmas. Truth was always incarnated. Jesus described himself as the truth, at a time when the Pharisees and the scribes were debating principles of orthodoxy. Jesus never divorced orthodoxy from orthopraxy. As James stated in his letter, it is futile to prove the right faith without the right action. But Jesus always invited people to live by the right action in order to be consistent with their faith. He showed them how to save face and be truthful at the same time. Jesus himself denied he was going to be present at the Passover celebration in Jerusalem, only to show up there during the ceremonies. No one accused him of being a liar, everyone understood he needed to save his face and his ministry. For immigrants today, truth is incarnated in life, it is part of daily being and doing. Truth is not an attribute of religion; it is life itself. Truth is real.

It is not uncommon to see new Christian converts accepting the new religion but having problems living it. Ministers and missionaries are only too happy to baptize immigrants who accepted Jesus out of respect for their hosts and with the desire not to lose face. In the race for numbers, very few missionaries and evangelists ask questions to determine the real *metanoia* in the life of the new converts. In other words, Westerners take advantage of the values and assumptions of immigrants for their own very pragmatic purposes. Real discipleship takes time, and time is not to be wasted in the West. How many times did we hear horror stories about young converts from among immigrants who acted based on their unchanged assumptions and values? People for whom polygamy was normal, lying was necessary, and violence and bloodshed was required in order to wash away shame, showed up at our door and we assumed they shared our values and worldview.

The major current challenge I witness in the globalized village is a powerless Christianity. Other major world religions, especially outside of the Western world, are ways of life, not simply a doctrine or an intellectual assent. Too often Christianity is presented as a cover to other aspects of life. It is like a coat put on or taken off depending on the need. A Christian worldview is frequently described in biblical terms, but in reality those are systematic doctrines defined and interpreted over the centuries in the West. Most Christian principles are devoid of cultural context. Dichotomy and the separation of life into isolated compartments contributed to the dualistic identity of Christianity. Terry LeBlanc writes that "Dualism is comfortably embedded in the foundations of Western Christian theology. As a consequence, it has become increasingly difficult for Western Christians to make sense of what we are discovering, by means of contemporary science, to be a far more interrelated cosmos than we had ever imagined" (LeBlanc 2012:175).

Many times, new converts have been taught to read the Scripture with Western eyes, without realizing that two major worldviews clashed and different values had to be accommodated. Some assumptions and values went undercover, but did not disappear. When crisis hit, the old worldview was there and surfaced by default.

Missiology in the Global Context

Theology and missiology were historically defined by the West, according to the Greek philosophical understanding. Even the process of contextualization is a Western creation, due to centuries of lack of theological flexibility. The recent focus on humans, as a counterbalance to theology as the study of God, reveals the innate ability of human nature to adapt to newly discovered realities. Missiology itself went through an arduous process of transformation from understanding mission as belonging to the church to *missio Dei*. From mission to overseas territories to mission in the back yard. From unreached countries to unreached people groups. From pure exegetical theology to enlisting the support of anthropology and other social sciences. Missiology stands today as a multidisciplinary activity that intends to exegete both the Word of God and the World of humans.

The Enlightenment's project to provide universal principles and values evidently failed. Modernity's push for globalization managed to create superficial universals, but underneath the visible, the vast realm of differences and division remained alive more than ever. Modernity tried to offer universals removed from the cultural context, but cross-cultural encounters proved the limits and illusory nature of modernity's claims.

With the arrival of the internet and email communication, Westerners shared—or even imposed—their theologies, religious views, opinions, and hermeneutical approaches. Academic courses, literature, seminars, webinars flood today the internet "often at the expense of people from other countries developing their own material that would reflect their individual cultures more adequately" (Valerio 2003:19). Rich Christians from the West inevitably impose their agenda and views to the rest of the world. Valerio notes that "this domination inevitably affects mission thinking and practice." She proposes "'reverse missions,' whereby Christians from poorer countries live and teach in the wealthier nations. It is imperative that those from poorer countries be heard and that those from more wealthy churches/mission agencies find the humility to sit at the feet of these others and let themselves be taught by them. This would enable us to discover the positive side of globalization" (Valerio 2003:19).

My observation is that the Majority World Christians come to the West and teach the very conservative and fundamentalist theology and practice Western missionaries brought to the rest of the world decades or centuries ago. Reverse missions is not automatically the best solution, unless the same process of contextualization and understanding of Western values and worldview is taken into consideration by the Majority World missionaries. Unfortunately, immigrants and refugees tend to create their own ethnic churches and mostly stay separated from the host country Christians.

Frequently, Christian books dealing with immigrants advise discipleship. However, extremely few authors consider the different cultural backgrounds of the immigrants or how their value system conflicts with the Western discipleship and ethical expectations. As J. D. Payne explained, "Whether the new believers are literate or not, they need to know how to understand and apply the Scriptures, fast and pray, share their faith, and deal with spiritual warfare. They need to understand what it means to be a part of a local church, even if that local church is initially made up of just few other new believers" (Payne 2012:142). However, Majority World Christians may not worship like us, and may not read the Scripture with the same hermeneutical view. As Payne noted, we are in danger of teaching them our own Western preferences. "We end up teaching new believers an unbiblical—maybe even a syncretistic—understanding of the local church. In addition to providing poor biblical teaching, we also provide complicated structures and organizations that are difficult for new believers to reproduce among their people across the world" (Payne 2012:143). Although there may be nothing wrong with our understanding of the Bible or the way we do church, "we need to instruct others that our culturally preferred ways are not the only ways and simultaneously help those we are teaching to think through how they will apply biblical church-planting principles to their own contexts" (Payne 2012:144).

Theology in the Global Context

Globalization, inevitably, impacts theology. Andrew Walls (2012) rightly remarked that even "the theological agenda is ... culturally conditioned ... Each time the gospel crosses a cultural frontier, new issues will arise, first of the

"What should I do?" and then of the "How should I think?" category, many never faced by Christians before. Each time the gospel crosses a cultural frontier, a fresh set of intellectual materials is available for the task" (Walls 2012:26). Predictably, Walls notices that "the twenty-first century will face new theological issues that have little to do with Greek or Latin, and still less to do with the later developments of European and American thought. The issues will arise from the Christian interaction with the cultures and realities of life in Africa and Asia and Latin America" (Walls 2012:27). And these African, Asian, and Latin American realities are brought by immigrants to the Western world.

Walls counsels that "one of the best ways of preparing for the new age of global theology may be to develop the study of the history and literature of the former age of global Christianity. It is the joint inheritance of Western, African, and Asian Christians alike" (Walls 2012:29-30). He concludes on a positive note, looking at the opportunity globalization brings to the theological development. "The biblical and Christian interaction with the cultures of Africa and Asia has begun to open a whole range of new theological issues and the possibility of fuller and clearer thought on some old ones. . . . Much of Christian humanity lives in a larger, more populated universe than the Enlightenment one. As a result, Christians face countless situations to which Western theology has no answer. . . . The theological workshop is likely to be busier than ever before, its workers more varied in language, culture, and outlook" (Walls 2012:33).

Analyzing the early church's contact with the Gentiles, Lamin Sanneh (2012) noted that "uniformity of belief and culture was not what the Gentile breakthrough was all about. . . . In its most creative phases, Christianity has been an intercultural reality, and its doctrinal system remained plausible at all because of the rich variety of cultures upon which the church drew" (Sanneh 2012:41). He remarks, on the other hand, that "Christianity translated naturally into the terms of all cultures." What Sanneh points to is the fact that being translatable to different cultures, "Christianity was a stimulus on the vernacular. . . . Christian vitality tapped into vernacular springs. . . . Religion can bring about change by the influence it exerts rather than only by the instruments it controls" (Sanneh 2012:42-43). In the global context, theology needs to find its flexibility and relevance.

Hermeneutics in the Global Context

For Westerners, interpretation takes place naturally in the forensic context of their cultures. Laws, natural and scientific laws, are guiding theological inquiry. But the rest of the world looks at the same reality and the same revelation asking different questions. As Gene L. Green noted, "Asian Christians ask questions about the faith in a pluralist culture, African theologians grapple with the relationship between Christianity and African traditional religions, and Palestinians and Native North American theologians have deep concerns about land. Reading from their place involves asking questions that find little or no expression in the received texts from the West" (Green 2012:50-51). As a result, the global hermeneutic employed by immigrants is informed by the particular social and cultural context of the reader.

Due to the inclusive nature of reality, Majority World theologians "long for an *engaged* faith, but not a faith devoid of substance beyond the issue of the moment. . . . While upholding the normative role of Scripture, Majority World interpreters hear its prophetic voice speaking into their world" (Green 2012:53). They find inappropriate the cultural detachment of the Western hermeneutic. For them, "The biblical understanding of Jesus as Mediator, as in Hebrews, resonates with African views on mediation and the place of ancestors as mediators. Jesus then becomes the Ancestor. This inculturation hermeneutic has found wide acceptance, so that in India, Jesus may be viewed as a Dalit, and in First Nations theology, God is primarily known as Creator, resonating with the traditional indigenous concept of God" (Green 2012:57-58). Green concludes that "Meaning is only known and is only useful if it has efficacy for one's community and our world" (Green 2012:59).

Immigrants will find in Scripture plenty of support for their communal cultural values because the context of the biblical writers was similar. However, for people who treat laws as not so important as for Westerners there is hope: the gospel can be found through an honor and shame reading. Sin is not primarily breaking the law, but disobeying and dishonoring our heavenly father. The Majority World Christians understand much better why God required so much blood as a solution for sin, because they understand that the shame of sin can be washed away only with blood. The Rest of the World Christians understand what grace is, not so much intellectually, but in a practical way. They understand why Jesus is described as a mediator, since conflicts in their cultures are often solved with the help of third parties. Although different, non-Western hermeneutical approaches are as valid and legitimate as the Western one. In fact, they may have a better grasp of biblical concepts and principles because their cultural values come closer to the ones shared by the biblical writers.

Conclusions

Mission in the new globalization era needs to adapt to the cultural context. Relevance has to become the guiding principle. Missiology, as a multidisciplinary field, should balance the tendency of Western theologians to focus mainly on God by bringing the exegesis of people to the table. In the face of globalization, contextualization should be guided by a thorough understanding of how the Bible describes the incarnated Christ. Church growth and discipleship should pay attention to people's worldviews, building up the set of values they bring to the table. Theology can no longer be informed strictly by Western assumptions and categorization systems, but will have to answer multicultural questions that may open up new perspectives that were obscured because of lost cultural values. Theological unity will be achieved not through a unique statement of beliefs, but through a lively dialogue where there is room for a diversity of views supported by the Scripture. Hermeneutical approaches will support different emphases and values depending on the context where they are used.

Using Mark Labberton's suggestion, our primary attitude should be humility when it comes to doing mission and theology in the global context. "The diversity, range, and subtlety of contexts, history, issues, and challenges is breathtaking. Global theology demands particularity. And that particularity is itself 'global,' not least given the wonder and mystery of human beings who bear the *imago Dei*" (Labberton 2012:225). Reflecting on Psalm 8, he concludes that "Human existence, including global theology, involves acts of paying attention to God and paying attention to the world in God's name. . . . Ministry beckons God's people to pay attention to the particular world of people, relationships, culture, economics, religion, sociology, power, art, land, and more. . . . Paying attention is a continuous, communal act that is meant to be part of how our diversity of gifts enable the body of Christ to attend to God and the world more faithfully" (Labberton 2012:228-229). Immigration is the continuous result of globalization. Let's pay attention to it.

Works Cited

Dyrness, William A., and Oscar Garcia-Johnson.
　　2015. *Theology Without Borders: An Introduction to Global Conversations*. Grand Rapids, MI: Baker.

Green, Gene L.
　　2012. "The Challenge of Global Hermeneutics." In *Global Theology in Evangelical Perspective: Exploring the Contextual Nature of Theology and Mission*. 50-64. Edited by Jeffrey P. Greenman and Gene L. Green. Downers Grove, IL: IVP.

Hanciles, Jehu J.
　　2008. *Beyond Christendom: Globalization, African Migration, and the Transformation of the West*. Maryknoll, NY: Orbis.

Johnstone, Patrick.
　　2011. *The Future of the Global Church: History, Trends, and Possibilities*. Downers Grove, IL: IVP.

Labberton, Mark.
　　2012. "Some Implications of Global Theology for Church, Ministry, and Mission." In *Global Theology in Evangelical Perspective: Exploring the Contextual Nature of Theology and Mission*. 225-236. Edited by Jeffrey P. Greenman and Gene L. Green. Downers Grove, IL: IVP.

LeBlanc, Terry.
　　2012. "New Old Perspectives: Theological Observations Reflecting Indigenous Worldviews." In *Global Theology in Evangelical Perspective: Exploring the Contextual Nature of Theology and Mission*. 165-178. Edited by Jeffrey P. Greenman and Gene L. Green. Downers Grove, IL: IVP.

Min, Anselm Kyongsuk.
　　2008. "Migration and Christian Hope: Historical and Eschatological Reflections on Migration." In *Faith on the Move: Toward a Theology of Migration in Asia*. 177-202. Edited by Fabio Baggio and Agnes M. Brazal. Manila, Philippines: Ateneo de Manila University Press.

Payne, Jervis David.
    2012.   *Strangers Next Door: Immigration, Migration, and Mission.* Downers Grove, IL: IVP.

Sanneh, Lamin.
    2012.   "The Significance of the Translation Principle." In *Global Theology in Evangelical Perspective: Exploring the Contextual Nature of Theology and Mission.* 35-49. Edited by Jeffrey P. Greenman and Gene L. Green. Downers Grove, IL: IVP.

Shenk, Wilbert R.
    2006.   "Foreword." In Ott, Craig, and Harold A. Netland, eds. *Globalizing Theology: Belief and Practice in an Era of World Christianity.* Grand Rapids, MI: Baker.

Sunquist, Scott W.
    2015.   *The Unexpected Christian Century: The Reversal and Transformation of Global Christianity, 1900-2000.* Grand Rapids, MI: Baker.

Tiplady, Richard, ed.
    2003.   *One World or Many? The Impact of Globalization on Mission.* Pasadena, CA: William Carey Library.

Tomlinson, John.
    1999.   *Globalization and Culture.* Chicago, IL: University of Chicago Press.

Valerio, Ruth.
    2003.   "Globalisation and Economics: A World Gone Bananas." In Tiplady, Richard, ed. 2003. *One World or Many? The Impact of Globalization on Mission.* Pasadena, CA: William Carey Library.

Walls, Andrew.
    2012.   "The Rise of Global Theologies." In *Global Theology in Evangelical Perspective: Exploring the Contextual Nature of Theology and Mission.* 19-34. Edited by Jeffrey P. Greenman and Gene L. Green. Downers Grove, IL: IVP.

Persecuted Churches in the Public Square: Power Encounters in Context

PAUL HERTIG

Abstract: In teaching the Bible to persecuted church leaders in Ho Chi Minh City, Vietnam and Malacca, Malaysia during the past few years, I have discovered that the Southeast Asian Christian practice parallels that of the Acts of the Apostles. The faith of the community is laden with miracles, supernatural experiences, and the spread of the gospel in a context of ever-evolving complexity in their public arenas--governments that are suspicious or oppressive and religious pluralism that clashes at the level of power. I will interpret Paul's power encounter with Elymas (Acts 13:6-12), and incorporate parallel and powerful stories of faith from Southeast Asian contexts. I will also interpret Paul's effort to contextualize at Lystra, when Paul and Barnabas are misunderstood as Zeus and Hermes in the public square, after which Paul is stoned by a crowd of Gentiles and Jews (14:8-20). I will provide recommendations for teaching missions in North American contexts that consider how practitioners in non-Western contexts might encounter issues of power that include magic, shamanism, fortunetelling, and persecution.

Introduction: Upon retirement, a Chinese financial accountant at a Taoist temple in Malaysia immediately began suffering attacks from demons, getting only two hours of sleep, repercussions for no longer serving in the temple. Christians from the local church learned that he was not feeling well and visited. They prayed for him and shared the gospel, but the demon interrupted. As they shared the gospel, the man pointed to his ears, stating, "The devil is talking to me." The Christians were surprised by the simultaneous intrusion from the devil while they shared the gospel. Even more surprising, the demon also in some telepathic way, warned the son, the medium at the Temple. The son then rushed back home on his motorcycle to prevent Christians from sharing the gospel with his father. The son went into the kitchen, grabbed a knife and threatened the Christians, backed them into a corner, and they fled from the house.

When the first hand account of this story was told among my theology students in Malaysia, quite a lively debate ensued, even laughter at times, because one of the students, reprimanded those who had fled to have have stood firm, without fear, because Jesus is more powerful. This particular Christian, Barnabas, and his father had once been active in Taoist religion and at that time found that even a wielded knife was powerless before them. A thief once broke into their home and knifed his father, yet the blade could not penetrate. Barnabas' logic was that Jesus is more powerful than any force in the Taoist religion, and therefore, one should not back down during a power encounter, but instead let God exhibit the superior power. While the students who had fled did not agree with, or have the same faith of, Barnabas, the story illustrates the commonly experienced power encounter in persecuted church settings in Southeast Asia, rooted in the experiences of the earliest church.

Acts 13: Power Encounter at Paphos

On their first mission, Paul and Barnabas enter the city of Paphos and are confronted by a Jewish sorcerer and false prophet, the attendant of proconsul, Sergius Paulus. The sorcerer interferes the moment Paul and Barnabas begin sharing the gospel with a high official. It becomes clear that if the gospel will reach the widespread populous in the cities, power encounters will occur with those in leadership when existing structures, utilized as tools for evil, are threatened. God leads these new missionaries to people of high standing so that they might impact the core leadership. Paul and Barnabas are sent into the eye of the storm.

Sergius Paulus, the proconsul, served as a Roman administrator of a senatorial district. He wants to hear the word of God. Elymas attempts to disrupt the faith decision of Sergius. Notice, Paul charges Elymas with deceit and trickery, "making crooked the straight ways of the Lord" (13:10, *literal Greek*). This is a direct reference to Isaiah 40:3: "make straight in the desert a highway for our God." Three references to "the crooked" are found in Luke: John the Baptist, who preaches repentance and baptism, illustrates repentance this way: "The crooked roads shall become straight, the rough ways smooth" (Luke 3:5). Peter echoes John at Pentecost urging people to repent, be baptized, and save themselves "from this crooked [*skolias*] generation" (2:40). And now, Paul accuses Elymas, the magician, of making crooked the straight ways of the Lord (13:10). A contrast is made between the crooked people of evil intent and the people of the Way. The entire passage is rooted in Isaiah 40:3: "In the wilderness prepare *the way* for the LORD; *make straight* in the desert a highway for our God." Those who oppose Christians i.e. the Way, make crooked the straight Way of the Lord. This describes the battleground between good and evil, i.e., the power encounter.

Elymas, "Son of the devil," seeks to turn the proconsul from the true God to a false deity, to Elymas himself (13:8), paralleling Simon, another magician, called "the Great Power of God" (8:10). Light contrasts mist and darkness that hovers over Elymas. When Paul later testifies to his God-given mission, he incorporates these same contrasts: "to open their eyes and turn them from darkness to light, and from the power of Satan to God, so that they may receive forgiveness of sins and a place among those who are sanctified by faith in me" (26:18).

This definitive moment in Acts introduces the heart of Paul's mission that overcomes the power of evil and confronts false declarations of deity. In settings that are resistant to the Gospel, one often encounters strongholds of evil in high concentrations (cf. 14:1-2). In defeating the intentions of false prophets and magicians, the Way continues to proclaim Jesus who has power over all forms of evil. This legitimizes the disciples, who represent the Way, the true channel of divine power through the Holy Spirit.

We now explore comparisons and contrasts of Paul and Elymas. Both blinded, they had to be led by the hand. Both once served as instruments of the devil. Elymas made "straight paths crooked;" Paul was led to a street called "straight" (9:11). Paul's blindness led to radical transformation; the Elymas account leaves him lost in blindness. "The two paths diverge in directions as different as night and day" (Parsons 2008:190). Why does this story not end but leaves Elymas groping in blindness? Resembling the case of Simon the magician, the fate of the individual as tool of Satan is not Luke's focus; Luke emphasizes the warning (13:11; cf. 8:24) and that authority over evil proves God's servant as worthy of mission, leading to salvation: "When the proconsul saw what had happened, he believed, for he was amazed at the teaching about the Lord" (13:12). Note that in this case the sign (evil defeated) led to belief: he "saw what had happened" and "believed" because there was "teaching" that explained the sign (Elymas groping in blindness). Deed and word go together. Also interesting, when it comes to the encounter of evil and magic, we have a black-and-white world, good and evil, without gray areas. When it comes to culture (which contains both good and evil), however, Paul utilizes those gray areas to communicate the gospel, which is seen in the next passage at Lystra.

Summary Pattern of the Power Encounter (Acts 13:6-12)

1. The Gospel goes to new territory (Paul and Barnabas travel to Paphos).

2. Immediately, evil presents itself (a sorcerer/false prophet) to block the progress of the Gospel; Elymas interrupts the proconsul who desires to hear the word of God (the power encounter is *not* initiated by Paul).

3. Paul, filled with the Holy Spirit, declares that Elymas is a child of the devil, and that he will go blind "for a time" as Paul did on the road to Damascus: "'You are going to be blind for a time, not even able to see the light of the sun.' Immediately mist and darkness came over him, and he groped about, seeking someone to lead him by the hand" (13:11).

4. Evil is defeated and salvation unconstrained; the proconsul believes. In a summary statement after this and other forces of evil are overcome, the pattern continues, and, Luke states, "The word of the Lord spread through the whole region" (13:49).

Southeast Asia Power Encounters

Many of the power encounter descriptions I researched from Christians in Southeast Asia emerge from the backdrop of war. A Korean pastor and missionary to Cambodia, grew up with nightmares of North Korean communist soldiers harassing him. He lived in a region that was a battlefield where many people had died. His bad dreams always included images of menacing soldiers. He thus grew up with a disposition to the spiritual world and became a missionary in Cambodia. He set up the mission facilities in Phnom Penh for those orphaned in the aftermath of the killing fields, and the church walls were adjacent to the living quarters of a national champion boxer. One day, while they were worshiping, the wife of the missionary was returning from an errand, and several boxers emerged and beat her up before she entered the missionary church, and she nearly died. "Normally when we pray there is not such a backlash; but when we sang praise songs about the blood of Jesus they went crazy and beat her up," said the pastor. The pastor reported the incident to the police; the boxers bribed the police immediately and there was no further violence. The pastor asked for an apology, but the boxers ignored him and began harassing the orphans instead. Having no fear of the boxers, the Pastor told the coach how shameful it was to demean weak people, and "the thugs disappeared one by one," he said.

As in this contemporary story in Cambodia, the following story from the book of Acts illustrates that when a mission of healing is set up in new territory, violence can ensue as a backlash from strongholds of evil.

Paul and Barnabas: Worshipped and Stoned in Lystra

At Lystra, Paul heals a man crippled from birth. When the man jumps up and begins to walk, before Paul could say, as when Peter and John healed a cripple, ... "not by our own power ..." the crowd shouts that "the gods have come down to us in human form!" (14:11). They determine from their own religious framework that Barnabas is Zeus, and Paul, Hermes. Then the priest of Zeus prepares sacrifices to make to Paul and Barnabas (14:8-13). In cross-cultural mission contexts, best to expect the unexpected, predict the unpredictable. All chaos breaks loose:

> Paul and Barnabas tore their clothes and rushed into the crowd, shouting: "Friends, why are you doing this? We too are only human, like you. We are bringing you good news, telling you to turn from these worthless things to the living God, who made the heavens and the earth and the sea and everything in them. In the past, he let all nations go their own way. Yet he has not left himself without testimony: He has shown kindness by giving you rain from heaven and crops in

> their seasons; he provides you with plenty of food and fills your
> hearts with joy." Even with these words, they had difficulty
> keeping the crowd from sacrificing to them. (14:14-17)

Paul and Barnabas stress that they are only human beings, urging them to turn away from "these worthless things," a reference to idols, and onto the true God. But then the sudden shift, due to a Gentile audience, a strategic adjustment: "Yet he has not left himself without testimony: He has shown kindness by giving you rain from heaven and crops in their seasons; he provides you with plenty of food and fills your hearts with joy" (14:17). Stunningly, in the middle of this crisis moment when Paul and Barnabas are being worshiped as gods, Paul begins to speak about nature--including rain, crops, and food. Something this unusual indicates its importance. Desperately and deliberately, Paul, in a crisis moment seeks to connect with a culture that believes in a world filled with various gods. Paul makes reference to natural revelation and speaks directly to the Gentiles' belief that the earth teems with representations of God. Paul affirms that God's kindness and glory has manifested in creation and provides plenty, everything needed, filling their heart with gladness. Knowing that fertility gods of weather and vegetation were worshiped in local temples of Zeus in Asia Minor (Parsons 2008:201), Paul provides an alternative perspective.

Nature, and its plenty can be appreciated as signs and gifts from God, "who made the heavens and the earth and the sea and everything in them" (14:15c). Paul urges a shift from nature and the divine as one, to a supreme God active in and above nature. This shift is understandable for Paul and his rural audience, but difficult for a contemporary audience to understand for these reasons:

> References to nature in the New Testament, especially
> the Gospels, have been persistently understood from the
> perspective of modern urban people, themselves wholly
> alienated from nature, for whom literary references to nature
> can only be symbols or picturesque illustrations of a human
> world unrelated to nature. (Richard Bauckham 2012:111)

Paul shifts the mindset to nature as a *sign* of God, providing blessings flowing from God.

The crowds respond according to their own cultural assumptions. As in other texts (10:25, 28:6), God's servants become mistaken for deities. "Greeks portrayed their deities as coming in disguises" (Craig S. Keener vol. 2 2013:2142-3). A relevant myth: Zeus and Hermes came to Phrygia, north of Lystra and Iconium, testing hospitality. To those who did not respond with hospitality, the gods destroyed them in a flood (Ovid 43 B.C.E.-17 C.D.). People from the region of Phrygia and nearby regions of Asia minor had strict moral codes, and confession records portray suffering as divine punishment, and due to fear of divine vengeance, they chose to show respect to these gods who had come in human form (Keener 2 2013:2146-7). Jews believed in a similar concept of entertaining angels unaware (Gen 18:2-16 and Heb 13:2).

The apostles, already chased out of town by fellow Jews in Acts 14:2, are acclaimed as gods in this subsequent town: "they preach monotheism to idolaters, then are further assaulted by monotheistic (Jewish) enemies who join forces with the idolaters to attack them" (14:5; Dunn 1996:189). The deliberate irony portrays blind resistance to the Messiah (Keener vol. 2 2013:219). People see but do not see; they hear but do not hear! Truth and reality have no significance. To the reader the whole episode seems humorous, but Barnabas and Paul recognize this as "blasphemy" exhibited when they tore their clothes, appropriate to a mourning context.

Paul's natural theology, further developed in Romans, demonstrates that the revelation of nature gives humans moral responsibility for their behavior (Rom 1:19-25) and lays the groundwork for the gospel of salvation (Rom 3:22-24). Paul shares common ground with the listeners regarding nature and agriculture. Polytheism, more popular than monotheism, even among intellectuals, represented the entrenched beliefs of dominant culture. Icons that represented spiritual intermediaries, common in public places and at entrances to homes, were associated with nature and agricultural fertility.

> Intellectuals could normally distinguish between a deity and its statue; such images were simply symbols of, or pointers to, a deeper reality. The statue should seek to accurately portray the deity's attributes, but statues cannot adequately portray deity, and when in human form, they simply offer humanity's best illustration. Nevertheless, even intellectuals who offered such distinctions might insist that such humanly made images were useful for allowing mortals concrete ways to honor their deities. (Keener 2 2013:2163)

Thus to surrender polytheism was to concede an entire way of life, relinquishing puzzle pieces to a coherent worldview that provided tangible explanations and meaning in daily life. Jews and Christians challenged these deities and myths, believing that nature gave witness to God's character and glory (14:17).

Paul understood that the creator of heaven, earth, and sea (14:15) spoke directly to Greek myths about Zeus that divvied up the reign of heaven, earth, and sea to Zeus (heaven), Hades (underworld), and Poseidon (sea); none of these three were distinctly sovereign, though Zeus was "increasingly viewed as an all-powerful supreme deity" (Keener vol. 2 2013:2167). Therefore, the time and context were ripe for the Gospel. Not addressing the issue of idols would completely disconnect Christians from the public arena, leaving them discredited and without influence in a polytheistic society. Furthermore, Paul and Barnabas understood that God allowed past generations and nations to follow their own lifestyles, "let all nations go their own way" and "overlooked such ignorance" (14:16; 17:30). There's a certain "kindness" and patience toward nature religions and fertility rituals because what they honored in nature was God's very own testimony and provision of "rain from heaven and crops in their seasons" (14:17) since God intended to one day usher in a new era of salvation in Christ (cf. 17:30). They worshipped the very elements granted as testimony to God's love, kindness, and provision. Now they needed to see these as signs of God and not gods themselves. In this power encounter, Paul tactfully and contextually laid the groundwork for this shift, a change of allegiance from worshipping the wonders of nature to worshipping the maker of all wonders of the earth. Gifts from heaven should turn the heads of curious creatures to the source of those gifts, since blessings from God indicate traces of deity.

Phrygia was fertile and replete with rural farmlands. Greeks invoked Demeter prior to sowing crops. Thus, an urban address from Paul would have disconnected him from his audience. Instead, Paul built bridges to this agricultural community by talking about nature and crops, spiritually connecting with their world.

In this narrative, the testimony of God came through immediate and miraculous signs and wonders (14:3), but also through Paul's proclamation of creation and God's indiscriminate gifts to all. This general revelation provides humans a glimpse of God's existence and kindness, which should lead to a responsibility to serve God with reverence and repentance (Romans 1:20, 2:4). Philosophers laid this foundation: "Stoics believed that the universe's order and signs of benevolence indicate the divine mind that established and sustains it." (Keener 2 2013:2169-2170). Paul utilized this philosophical connection to the universe to bring about a reversal in which people no longer took care of God, but God took care for them.

That "he provides you with plenty of food and fills your hearts with joy" expresses the joy that God shares with humanity in providing the rain, vegetation, fruit and food (14:17). It conveys God's kindness to those who do not even acknowledge or appreciate God. "Filled with gladness" also implies being filled with the joy that comes from living according to God's purposes (13:52). Paul's words are "strikingly relevant in their local setting" since "Phrygian and Pisidian inscriptions praise Zeus Kalakagathios, a deity of good things and fruitfulness" (Keener vol. 2 2013:2172). Paul utilizes local religious thought to connect spiritually. The missionary does not just say what's wrong, but also what's right.

Urban Madness (14:19-20)

The crowd, barely restrained from worshipping Paul and Barnabas, respond to the apostles' signs more than their words. A sudden turn of events occurs when the crowds who respond with worship, turn to stoning. It reveals the unpredictability of the masses in a context of power and healing. The unmistakable irony at Lystra: local Jews gang up with Gentile worshipers of idols in opposition of a monotheistic missionary. In other words, enemies unite as friends when they have a common enemy, setting up a power encounter. Paul consistently proclaims that he preaches a message of true Judaism, but these leaders who represent Judaism subvert it, even banding up with 'idolaters.' Also tragically ironic, stoning is typically the sentence for blasphemy (Lev. 24:16), yet Paul and Barnabas tore their clothes as an appropriate response *against* blasphemy (Acts 14:14). Possibly the Jews convinced the crowd that Paul rejected their local gods as well as the Jewish God. (Keener vol. 2 2013:2175-6)

A final irony: Paul, after stoned to the point of death "got up" and went back to the city, paralleling the lame man who "jumped up" (14:10). Whether Paul was healed from death or delivered from near death, the story begins and ends with images of the resurrection power of Christ. Then Paul and Barnabas return to the city, fearlessly, as the missionary to Cambodia responded after boxers beat up his wife—knowing God's protection. Paul and Barnabas leave town the next day, onto their next adventure in mission.

God's Glory in Nature: Vietnam

A contemporary story of God at work in nature occurred recently in Vietnam during the construction of a house of prayer in an undeveloped plot of land surrounded by a farming community. A young Vietnamese Christian leader, John, who lives by faith, obtained a piece of land and organized his youth group to begin construction of a prayer chapel, though he had no experience in architecture or construction. Once the building project was underway, it began raining. The land was soft, and not suitable for building and he realized that the cement foundation could be washed away in the rain. John hurried to the construction site and asked all the church youth to participate in overnight prayer. One youth had worked in construction and was available to help and knew how to prepare the cement. A Christian neighbor also helped. But the rain put the construction project in jeopardy, so John prayed for the rain to stop.

"God showed me a vision of Moses raising his hands," said John. "Early in the morning, I raised two hands and prayed that the rain would stop. Only at our location it did not rain, but it rained heavily all around us. For two weeks every day this continued, and the sun shined only on us. I departed to my home in Ho Chi Minh City but it rained again, so the workers pleaded for me to came back. I returned and fasted and prayed and raised my hands, and we were able to complete the project successfully."

I asked John, "What about farmers who needed rain? Is it fair for you to ask God to stop the rain?" His answer: "The rain only stopped at the prayer center; I saw it raining on the surrounding farm lands." Along with the struggle to build the prayer center in the rain, another challenge is the backdrop of war. While preparing the land for construction an unexploded U.S. bomb from the war was uncovered and safely removed. Furthermore, while engaged in prayer in the new prayer chapel, there was once a knock on the door and soldiers with guns appeared, apparently as an apparition, indicating that the trauma of war still left its mark, in this case the lingering images of those engaged in the combat of war remained, long after the war. The healing of war-torn nations does not happen overnight, but it influences the spiritual battle of contemporary Christian practice in Southeast Asia.

The Power of Contextualization in Acts and in Vietnam

The account of Paul and Barnabas in Lystra indicate the importance of contextualizing in mission. Paul speaks in a way that his Gentile audience can understand God in their context, particularly, God in nature and above nature.

In a remarkable development, a former drug addict initiated a ministry for drug addicts in communist prisons in Hanoi. This Christian leader has access to do ministry in communist prisons due to his success in reforming drug addicts like never before, in the context of ineffective government rehabilitation programs. He goes into drug rehabilitation prisons and conducts worship services, baptisms, and rehabilitation, bringing Bibles with him. All of this is unlawful, but the government officials permit these exceptions because of the phenomenal results not only in the prisons, but also in some of their own offspring. Ministry must walk the fine line of not only gaining access but also maintaining access. Thus, the leader of the ministry recently spoke to a large gathering of government officials and brought 100 former drug addicts to the front of the room and made this statement: "These men and women were once your enemies, destructive to society and now they are good people and have a positive influence on society." He effectively defended his ministry through contextualizing his appeal to the government, showing that his ministry produces good, and not harm, for society. He utilized the civic argument, as the early apostles did in Acts. Peter defended his healing ministry to the civic leaders, when "filled with the Holy Spirit" and said to them, "Rulers and elders of the people . . . we are being called to account today for an act of kindness" (4:8-9). Tabitha "was always occupied with works of kindness and charity." (Acts 9:36). Thus, an important way to overcome power encounters, or even bypass them, is through demonstrating that the values and ideals of civic life are being upheld and propelled by the ministry of the church, which meets the needs of society. "The gospel in prison is already a live witness to many government leaders," says the prison rehabilitation ministry leader. "We received many calls from officers, even in high positions, saying, 'Please come and help our children,' and they send their children to the Christian rehabilitation center."

Power Encounters and the Western Classroom Context

The accounts above, in Acts and in Southeast Asia, are often seen as outside the paradigm of Western contexts. Yet, as a Global Studies professor at Azusa Pacific University, I feel obliged to prepare Global Studies students for intercultural encounters in various contexts around the world, and thus include teachings on signs, wonders, and power encounters that are prevalent in Southeast Asian contexts, and in the Bible itself. After assigning my students to read Paul Hiebert's essay, "The Flaw of the Excluded Middle," we then discuss their discomfort with the realm of the supernatural as well as any experiences. Surprisingly, there are always many students who, from a Western point of view, have had explainable experiences. We then discuss these experiences that often have been compartmentalized into the realm of the unexplainable; we do this to prepare them to engage in global and biblical contexts that do have explanations for these experiences.

For instance, just one month ago, when discussing the "excluded middle zone" in the class, Global Engagement in the 21st Century, one student said that when she was a young child, her neighbor was throwing out some beautiful pillows and she retrieved them and slept on them. But that very night, she saw a face in her fan, and her fan was talking to her. The parents talked to neighbors and found out that the neighbor who threw out the pillows had engaged in some form of practice of 'voodoo' with those pillows. As this story was being recounted, one of the students said, "this is getting creepy" and started walking toward the door. I told her to feel free to get some fresh air. But she decided to return to her seat and began talking and laughing about her cat who had died, but for one month after its death, would show up running across the floor at night, even though the windows and doors were closed. As she was laughing about this, I asked, "why were you 'creeped out' by the story about the pillows, but you are laughing about the story of your dead cat running around in your house." She said, "Well, that's different; my cat was cute." This led to an important discussion about how we compartmentalize experiences of the supernatural as unexplainable and do not really process them or take them seriously. Maybe the reason why signs, wonders, and power encounters seem so rare in the West is not because they don't exist here, but because we do not pay attention to them or take them seriously.

References Cited

Bauckham, Richard
    2012. *Living with Other Creatures: Green Exegesis and Theology*. UK: Paternoster.

Dunn, James D. G.
    1996. *The Acts of the Apostles*. Valley Forge, PA: Trinity Press International.

Keener, Craig S.
    2013. *Acts: An Exegetical Commentary, Volume 2: 3:1-14:28*. Grand Rapids, MI: Baker Academic.

Parsons, Mikeal C.
    2008. *Acts (Paideia: Commentaries on the New Testament)*. Grand Rapids, MI: Baker Academic.

Historical Models of Engagement to Teach Mission in the Complex Public Arena

DR. SANTHA K. JETTY, PH. D

Designing contemporary Missiological studies and curriculum became a crucial aspect for the continuity of missions' work worldwide. As a Christian missionary historian, I have examined the historical models of missionary engagement by the 19th and early20[th] century missionaries in the Asian context particularly in India. My Ph. D thesis on *"Christian Missionaries and the Birth of New Social Consciousness among the Depressed Castes: A Case of the Malas and Madigas in Colonial Coastal Andhra, India 1850-1950"* was submitted to a public research university where an effort has been made to make the study of Christian Missions an academic field of study and created a space in the Social Sciences' research field in contemporary India. Simultaneously, there has been an increasing amount of scholarship and research interest into World Christianity themes in recent times. Missions and Missionary work are prominently taking place in the complex public arena where public engagement models are needed. The question is what should the teaching of mission look like in our increasingly complex public arena? An attempt has been made to reinvent a few historical models of engagement to teach mission in the complex public arena, especially in educational institutions by combining both social and missional aspects. The paper exemplifies models which the late 19th and early 20th century Protestant Christian missionaries used in public ministry and some of these models could be used to teach future mission personnel.

The nineteenth century was a great century for Protestant missionary work and Christian missionaries acted as *'agents of change'*, through their evangelistic and philanthropic activities towards the growth of education and economic mobilization. Christianity as a 'social religion' created institutions for the betterment of society. The reasons behind winning the trust of future converts by the Christian missionaries was their understanding of the former's social problems and the fulfilment of some social obligations that came with an opportunity. They found no excuse to serve humanity where it was dutiful to feed the hungry, give drink to the thirsty, visit the sick and so on (Taylor 1913:88). Christian missionaries in India conducted their ministry activities as evangelistic missionaries, educational missionaries, medical missionaries, and itinerant missionaries with a primary aim of Gospel acceptance by the people. The aim and method of Christian mission is always evangelism or evangelization (Horner 1968: 122). For God and God's Mission (Frances Adeney), the development of a theoretical framework for teaching Mission involves a multi-modeled approach in the Divinity Schools, Schools of Religion, Theological Seminaries and Theological Schools of Colleges and Universities and such a model comprises a combination of multiple approaches that could be found in the history of missions. We confess in the Triune God: Father, Son, and Holy Spirit and believe in the Gospel as the power of God for the salvation of human kind. In preparing members for mission in the teaching of Missiology, we foster unity and public engagement by ecumenical and interreligious dialogue. The following models are suggested and adopted from my thesis with sources and citations.

Ecumenical Teaching Model:

This type of methodology for missionary teaching will bring out any conflicting differences among denominations and foster unity in teaching practices. Adopting to the grassroots ecumenical missional practices followed by pioneering missionaries is a way to ecumenical rapprochement. Good faith, a zeal of the missionary spirit, a desire for fruitful work, mutual accord, ability to see the opposition in a fuller light and respecting 'otherness' would promote a continual growth of ecumenical spirit and learning (Ratzinger:1987).

As a precursor to the World Missionary Conference in Edinburgh in 1910, the foundational activities of the Christian Missionaries in India serve as a classic example of the early ecumenical spirit among the missionaries. Anthony Norris Groves indirectly accomplished the establishment of the American Lutheran Mission near Guntur and Rajahmundry. He wrote a letter in 1834 to the Synod of the American Lutheran Churches seeking support for German CMS missionary Rev. C.T.E. Rhenius of Tinnevelly. The Church Missionary Society at Madras had advised the collector of Guntur, Mr. Henry Stokes, to persuade Rev. Heyer of the General Council of the Pennsylvania Ministerium to be stationed at Guntur. This initiative may be termed as one of the first examples of perfect ecumenism in the Mission history of India. Rev. Heyer was a pioneer missionary who can be considered the founder of the Guntur Mission of the American Evangelical Lutheran Missionary Society in 1842 where for over a year after his arrival, he conducted worship services for the English officials and European residents of the East India Company. A geographical arrangement of mission engagement was done in good faith with friendly understanding and cooperation. The World Missionary Conference in Edinburgh (1910) launched an ecumenical movement that attempted to coordinate the institutionalized revival evangelistic movements such as that of the Student Volunteer Movement for Foreign Missions (Stanley: 2009). In seminaries and in academic institutions, ecumenical cooperation and coordination in the training of teachers and scholars on ecumenical Christian doctrine promotes the betterment of one another's observations and mutual appreciation. Going beyond one's denominational learning levels in areas of missional education, social action, and theological dialogue fosters interdependence and a multi-dimensional perspective among the participants.

Apostolic Teaching Model:

"The missionary is a necessary person, involved in essential functions in the life of the church, because it is through him the church fulfills its obligation to reach out in the mission" (Horner 1968:122). Among the manifold motives that drove the Christian missionaries for far off countries was their passion for the spread of Christianity through "apostolic fathering." They found no excuse to serve humanity where it was dutiful to feed the hungry, give drink to the thirsty, visit the sick and so on.(Taylor 1913: 88). The missionaries used the evangelistic practices of conversionism and activism while discharging their evangelistic services. The late 19th and early 20th century Christian missionaries conducted their ministry activities as evangelistic missionaries, educational missionaries, medical missionaries, itinerant missionaries, and as industrial missionaries with a primary aim of Gospel acceptance by the people. With remarkable qualities as those of self-denial and selfless devotion, the missionaries discharged their daily duties with unquestioning fidelity for the establishment of the missions in the world missions arena. The modest and unwearied attitude of the missionary (often accompanied by his amiable wife) together proved themselves to be the right people for the missionary calling. During natural calamities like famines and diseases, the charitable conduct of the missionaries was appreciated by not only the depressed castes but by the higher caste people as well. While touring the villages, the missionaries lived in tents which were pitched just outside the village, or in the open field, or under tree shades.

As teachers of the gospel and to prepare student-missionaries to undertake the comprehensive objective of evangelizing the nations, training on the apostolic calling in matters of educational ministry, medical ministry, agricultural and industrial ministries is to be taken to a new level with practical and apprentice training. This contribution alone is more than the agenda of direct evangelism. Also in the 'Apostolic Tradition' of life-transforming catechism instruction model, the Bible is given a prominent place followed by gospel hearing, baptism preparation, admission of baptism and become mature disciples in Christ. Through a 'lived experience' the preachers proclaim, 'love one another,' 'encourage one another,' 'greet one another,' 'forgive one another,' and 'bear one another's burdens' (Kreider 2014: 259).

Language Acquisition Teaching Model:

At the beginning stages of missionary work, teaching of Gospel was much hindered due to language barriers where the missionaries needed to learn the local languages. In 1840, Rev. Samuel. S. Day (American Baptist Telugu Mission in Nellore) had acquired proficiency in the Telugu language in order to increase his interaction with the local people. (Orchard and McLaurin

1925:128). Likewise, other missionaries gave their utmost attention to the study of local languages and met constantly with the natives to achieve progress in the spoken language. When they were able to speak fluently, they started visiting the surrounding villages and preached the Gospel. Some missionary societies decided on a two-year language examination comprised of the study of native languages and native religions.

Students of mission are increasingly paying attention to learn at least one new language for future mission positions. With the help of newly emerging audio-visual technologies and instruction by native language teachers, a positive impact on quick language learning can be achieved. Language missionary activity can be divided into two areas: the Translation Model (William Carey's Model) and the Functional Proficiency Model (Samuel S. Day's Model). As the majority of Bible translation has already been completed in major world languages since the beginning of the 19th century, we tend to pay more attention to the Functional Proficiency model. Foreign language instruction begins with the learner's interest levels and choosing a language that is relevant to their proposed missionary undertaking. All through the five stages of language acquisition (Pre-production, early production, beginning fluency, intermediate fluency, and advanced fluency), a dynamic process of comprehensive teaching can be done by native speaking teachers. A reexamination of the methods and outcomes of new language learning is critical and an important part of the linguistic model. In an applied linguistics model, the understanding of the language structure, epistemological rules, articulation and similar procedural criteria define the general character of the right language acquisition skills by mission personnel. While in foreign lands, preaching in local languages is preferred as incorporating the use of indigenous tongues into the worship services makes the target audience feel "I have maintained my language, I still maintain my culture today, and I'm proud of the fact that I have."

Indigenous-Driven Teaching Model or Non-Ethnocentric Teaching Model:

During the early part of the 20th century, World Christianity quickly moved from a "missionary-driven" model to an "indigenous-driven" model. Increasingly indigenous people are more and more connected to their past with pride, despite accepting the gospel teachings and becoming followers of Christ. This is due to a drive towards primordial and culture-preserving techniques (including worship styles) and a heightened awareness within native and tribal communities. In the light of emerging nationalisms, the politically deconstructed identity-based native Church represents the actual indigenous model. Instead of teaching along the line of forcing change on indigenous Christian communities (as with the traditional ethnocentric models), mission practitioners allow local cultures to flourish simultaneously with bringing people to accept Christ as their personal savior. Any attempt of manipulation and exploitation of the native cultures and attempts to show 'otherness' as "inferior to that of the dominant society" are not recommended and to be discouraged. Students of Mission may understand ethnography as a study of the principal characteristics of the social and cultural life, and an examination of the human agencies that shed light on the relationship between social life and social structures. They study ethnography to explore the scope and dimension of an explicitly ontological status of distinct social groups. The students will know the anthropological assumptions of the nature of the society within the spheres of the social, religious, material, and cultural life of the indigenous peoples.

Missionaries in foreign lands have an important role in preparing their communities for an eventual transfer to the indigenous model by providing in-depth training to native leadership and helping make internalized development a priority among indigenous converts. The aim is to evangelize and still leave native cultures intact. However, any practices that are incompatible with the teachings of Christianity, for example the practice of idolatry and image worship, are advised to be discarded. Keeping in view the quickly changing self-governing patterns among the indigenous peoples, mutual respect is to be fostered between missionaries, cultural groups, missional anthropologists, and lay leadership.

Self-Offering Teaching Model:

In the utmost imitation of Jesus Christ who made the ultimate gift to mankind, the purpose of the missionaries is to offer themselves in a self-giving model and are meant to love, accept, embrace, receive and welcome "others." The late 19th and early 20th century missionaries showed "pietism" and offered their "whole person" to missionary undertakings. Mission students are to be taught along the lines of self-giving, self-denying, and self-disciplined ideals to live to the level and work among the people. The spirit of love, penitence, and prayerfulness are to be taught for spiritual awakening and renewal.

"Social Change Agent" Teaching Model:

Christianity as a "social religion" and Christian missionaries as "social reformers" created institutions for the betterment of converts and aspirant converts in the second half of the 19th and early 20th centuries. The philanthropic activities of the missionaries in areas such as education and economic development played a major role in the improvement of the material lives of the converts. The growth of social consciousness and an aspiration for social change among Christian converts was a byproduct of the Christian missionaries' evangelistic work. Social change is a process where an idea of social consciousness is a medium through which people consciously attempt to minimize their deprivation, to secure social justice, and to uphold themselves to a differentiated status. It is an organic solidarity that covers the consciousness of the individuals endowed with unity for possible inductive results. (Gehlke 1915:161). Students of mission are taught about understanding peoples' structural determinants, processes, and the directions for social change. To make mission practitioners into social change advocates, they are given training as educational missionaries, medical missionaries, industrial missionaries, and so on.

Inculturation Teaching Model:

For its long-term continuation on foreign soil, Christianity needs to be naturalized for its adoption, and students of mission are taught on similar grounds for "intercultural openness." Christianity in a contextual undertaking adopts and assimilates into the indigenous customs and cultural patterns of the people in question. Contextualization of Christianity calls for dynamic changes by incorporating the customs of the land to assist non-Christian relatives and their extended families to join the ranks of the Church. "Indigenization of Christianity" is a better way for converts to embed their faith in the indigenous and social order of their society. Elements of native traditions and ceremonies are retained in worship practices and social relations. Varied forms of social imagery are also retained such as music, architecture, attire, and other such practices (Woodburne1921:75). New approaches of contextualization and inculturation are invented while presenting the Gospel message to non-Christian cultures. The forms of native worship and meditative elements found in world cultures may be retained as a direct approach to God.

Ecological Mission Teaching Model:

In his work *The Eternal Now*, Paul Tillich affirms the biblical idea that human beings have dominion over all things-in the sense that humankind has the power to save or destroy all things (Tillich 1963: 55). As part of liberation theology, the Ecological Mission Teaching Model imbibes a balanced responsibility towards our creation. Denominationally adopted themes, such as caring for creation, vision, hope and justice, and the stewardship of creation, explains ecology as grounded in the biblical vision of God's intention for the balance and wellness of creation. This model provides us with a Christian understanding of the human role in creation and the ways we care for it for a sustainable future. The ELCA's *Caring for Creation* expresses a call to pursue justice for creation through active participation, solidarity, sufficiency, and sustainability, and states the commitments for pursuing wholeness for creation, which is expressed through individual and community action, worship, learning, moral deliberation, and advocacy (ELCA). Missional practitioners may understand the earth as a living system within which we humans live in a relationship of interdependence with other members of the earth's community. (Conradie 2006:70). Relationship between human-kind and nature are taken to the level of tree-planting projects, sustainable agricultural practices, and recycling materials, which are taught to the students. Awareness about ecological integrity models of social justice, non-violence, and caring for our creation addresses the issues facing the global ecological imbalances. Further, students will take part in ecumenical dialogues and inter-religious pacts with an ecological worldview and perspective. Missiology conferences should make a point to incorporate ecological themes and discussions into their agendas.

Conclusion:

The above-mentioned models are useful for Christian mission teaching in seminaries and theological departments that have ranged from social, cultural, and theological aspects to face the challenges in teaching Christian mission in the complex public arena. Theological instruction in our currently diversified society is to be carried out on functional lines by denominations beyond their own characteristic doctrines with a combination of knowledge and practical training.

References Cited

Bebbington David W.
    1989. *Evangelism in Modern Britain: A History from the 1730s to the 1980s*. London, England: Unwin Hyman Publishers.

Brewer John D.
    2000. *Ethnography*. Philadelphia, PA: The Open University Press.

Gehlke, Charles Elmer.
    1915. *Emile Durkheim's Contributions to Sociological Theory*. New York, NY: Columbia University.

Haferkamp, Hans and Neil J. Smelser (ed).
    1992. *Social Change and Modernity*, Berkeley, CA: University of California Press.

Harpster Julia M.
    1902. *Among the Telugoos: Illustrating Mission Work in India*. Philadelphia, PA: Lutheran Publication Society.

Horner, Norman A.
    1968. *Protestant Cross Currents in Mission: The Ecumenical-Conservative Encounter*. New York, NY: Abingdon Press.

Kreider, Alan.
    2014. "Ressourcement and Mission" In http://www.anglicantheologicalreview.org/static/pdf/articles/kreider.pdf

Mosse, David.
    1986. *Caste, Christianity and Hinduism: A Study of Social Organization and Religion in Rural Ramand*, Oxford, England: University of Oxford.

Taylor, Graham.
    1913. *Religion in Social Action.*, New York, NY: Mead and Co Publishers.

Tillich, Paul.
    1963. *The Eternal Now*. London, England: SCM.

Woodburne, Angus Stewart.
    1921. "The Indianization of Christianity" In *The Journal of Religion*, Vol.1, No 1, January. Accessed on 28 May 2013, 66 -75. http://www.jstor.org/stable/1195391.

Past is Prologue: Student Christian Movement Women Leaders, 1880-1920

DR. THOMAS A. RUSSELL

Abstract:

The focus of this presentation is to tell the previously untold story through narratives of three courageous women who served as leaders in the early international Student Christian Movement (SCM). Women served in the SCM's three major leadership capacities: committee member, secretary, and pioneer. Committees were the central governing bodies that directed local, national and international student groups. Secretaries were pastors to students and pioneers were developers of new ministries for the movement. I have selected three women, Winifred Mary Sedgwick, Grace Helena Saunders and Frances Cousins Gage, who I feel best shed light on how this generation of missionary women negotiated their "contemporary landscape." Drawing on historical records of the SCM, these stories establish the role of women in the organization from its inception, stressing not only the pressures and prejudices they faced but also the pioneering work and the valuable contributions they offered. To grasp exactly how these SCM women impact our thinking today, we will deal with how they handled cultural awareness, ecumenism and dangerous political contexts.

Introduction

If they could come back to life, women leaders of the late Victorian Era Student Christian Movement (SCM) would feel right at home with the themes of this conference. They would resonate with our fixation with how to navigate our "increasingly complex public arena," and how they could be missionally faithful and yet respectful of social differences. They might even be surprised that we in 2017 are still asking these questions. On the other hand, precisely because these questions have plagued each generation of missionaries and missiologists, they might not be surprised at all.

Because the SCM's women leaders faced these same questions, they provide historical models for how to deal with complex public life, missional faithfulness, and respect for social differences. They can help us prepare our students for faithful global mission work. For our purposes, like Shakespeare said, "What's Past is Prologue" (Shakespeare 1610-1611: Act 2, Scene 1).

Background

The movement that these women served was called the Student Christian Movement. The SCM began in earnest the late nineteenth century as a missionary movement to a fast-growing college and university community. In its heyday between 1880 and 1920, the SCM spread across the globe with its goal of reaching the student world for Christ and through students, triggering a transformation of the world. The SCM combined a rather dizzyingly array of local, regional, and national societies into one very large international student movement which both men and women could join and lead.

Groups falling under the SCM umbrella included the student departments of the Young Men's Christian Association (YMCA) and the Young Women's Christian Association (YWCA), the Student Volunteer Movement for Foreign Missions (SVMFM) and their non-North American counterparts, such as the Student Volunteer Missionary Union (SVMU), SCMs in different countries, and the global World Student Christian Federation (WSCF).[1]

Picking which stories to tell from over thirty-five women's biographies from my upcoming book, *Women Leaders in the Student Christian Movement, 1880-1920. American Society of Missiology Series (Maryknoll, NY: 2017)*, is a difficult task. Women served in the SCM's three major leadership capacities: committee member, secretary, and pioneer. Committees were the central governing bodies that directed local, national, and international student groups, secretaries were pastors to students and staff and pioneers were developers of new ministries for the movement.

I have selected the stories of Winifred Mary Sedgwick, Grace Helena Saunders and Frances Cousins Gage because I feel they best shed light on how their generation of missionary women negotiated their "contemporary landscape." Drawing on historical records of the SCM, these stories establish the role of women in the organization from its inception, stressing not only the pressures and prejudices they faced, but also the pioneering work and the valuable contributions they offered. To grasp exactly how these SCM women navigated their contemporary contexts, we will explore how they handled cultural awareness, ecumenism, and dangerous, life-threatening political contexts.

Developing Cultural Awareness

For our purpose, culture refers to those attitudes, feelings, values, and behavior that characterize and inform a particular social group and/or geographic location. SCM women leaders were forced to become acquainted with several cultures because of the internationalism of the SCM's membership and its locations for ministry. They had to understand the student world as a whole as well as the cultures from which students came from and in which students now lived. So, the SCM's women had to ask themselves, "How do I go about becoming culturally aware?"

Winifred Mary Sedgwick (1880-1922)

Although she never used the term cultural awareness, Winifred Mary Sedgwick had a definite strategy that would allow her to understand the attitudes, feelings, values, and behavior found in her SCM ministries in Geneva, Switzerland (1905-1906) and Moscow, Russia (1907-1909). Because of the rich sources available, particularly her official reports and letters, Sedgwick's efforts offer a substantive picture of a how a missionary can develop cultural awareness in a given location or with a given social group.

Of medium height, with slightly round-shoulders, an oval face, very large brown eyes, and golden brown hair, the humorous but always frail Sedgwick was born into a comfortable Birmingham, England family. Baptized into the Church of England in 1880, Sedgwick remained a devout member of this church throughout her short life. About her faith, she said, "To me it is huge comfort that God intends my perfection and does not adapt His standard to mine" (Tatlow 1933: 495). Sedgwick received her education at Somerville College, Oxford (1899-1903, BA, 1921 with Honors in Modern European History, Class II) and Dublin (BA, 1905). Inside SCM circles, Sedgwick played a variety of roles. At Somerville, Sedgwick was treasurer of the Christian Union (1901-02) and then with the British movement, co-secretary, traveling secretary, and evangelist for women students (1903-05 and 1909-14), and finally, with the WSCF, a pioneer (1905-09). After 1914, Sedgwick became warden of Duff House London, a YWCA training center, which offered training classes for YWCA leaders. She was honored by the British government with a British Military Medal for her service in Étaples, France from 1917-1918. Working as a YMCA canteen worker, Sedgwick furnished frontline soldiers with food, fellowship, classes and religious activities. Sedgwick contracted influenza and died in 1922 at the young age of forty-two. She left an estate worth £398,000 in 2016 pounds.

Because of her personality, Sedgwick had the skills necessary for a culturally-aware missionary. About her, Tissington Tatlow, the former general secretary of the British SCM, said:

> One's first impression of Winifred was likely to be that she was making a mental analysis of you. She had an incisive, analytical mind... She was immensely interested in people, watched them, considered their motives, and tried to find the principles, good or bad, on which they lived. Some found her critical mind a barrier, but her love of people was deep and true, she had a wealth of kindliness and sympathy, and students sought her help in large numbers... The friendship she gave to her friends was stimulating and bracing. She gave her friendship freely to both men and women... She had all

the qualities needed for friendship at its best—steadfastness, insight, candor, patience and tenderness. Perhaps her chief characteristic as a friend was to stimulate. 'I always feel as if I had had my head shampooed when I have seen Winifred Sedgwick... This gift never failed her, it was partly due to the quality of her mind, and partly due to her vivid interest in everything around her. (1933: 490-491, 494-495)

The first step Sedgwick took to become acquainted with her local contexts was to learn to speak a local language. This helped the missionary communicate and, more importantly, understand her environment, since words often convey the subtleties of a locality's culture. In her February 22-March 6, 1908 comments, Sedgwick was forthright about her struggles with Russian: "My Russian gets on slowly, and I feel I have to give much time to it. It is an awful language. I find I often understand the gist of conversation without knowing the actual words—so that I believe the girls here think I know far more then I say—and that I understand all their conversation. It is rather a joke!"

To fully appreciate the setting of their ministry, a missionary like Sedgwick had to be able to distinguish between local customs and their own. Sedgwick was shocked by some varying local customs. On November 26, 1905, she observed about a fellow resident at her lodging: "She is very dear, very attractive but my stars—talk of the sex question—she is the whole sex question in herself. There are two men in this pension, to whom she is very attractive— and I can't cry 'wolf' too often, but not too much 'a l'anglaise.' The continental ideas of propriety differ from ours! Then she is a little pagan."

Given that the SCM was a religious organization, it was imperative that one of their missionaries understood local religious beliefs and practices. In her February 22-March 6, 1908 comments, Sedgwick described a conversation she had with a man named Bulgakov, who came to her because he thought she was an expert on English religion.[2] The two discussed the influence of the Church of England on the WSCF, and he asked her what she felt about the value of church life. Bulgakov and Sedgwick also had a heated debate about whether the statement of faith of the St. Petersburg SCM was acceptable. He felt that "I have repented, I have given myself to him and believe that he has accepted me" was "unwarranted daring on our part and very alien to the Slav temperament." She, on the other hand, believed that this statement summarized what God expected Christians to believe. At the end, all Sedgwick could say was, "We discussed it for a long time, but I am afraid he did not understand."

In her March 25, 1908 letter to Rouse, Sedgwick gave her opinions about differences between Russian Orthodox and Protestant Christianity. She believed that Orthodoxy stressed modeling one's life after Christ and the saints, while Protestantism emphasized putting one's faith in Christ's redeeming work. To her, this meant that Orthodox Christians focused on changing outward behavior, Protestants on changing the inner spirit.

Making individual and group contacts was one of the most crucial tasks carried out when learning about a new culture. "Hanging out" with the locals provided all sorts of insights into local and group values and behavior. On the other hand, "hanging out" with only one's kind severely limited cultural awareness. Contact work required a certain personality type which combined friendliness and the "gift of gab" with a strong faith and courageous spirit that actively sought out new people despite the possibility of rejection.

Sedgwick worked hard to establish relationships with individual students in Geneva and Moscow. Her contacts began at her residence, where she spent most of her time. In a February 22-March 6, 1908 letter from Moscow, Sedgwick wrote about the struggles she was having developing relationships in her pension. She felt her only point of contact was through music. Often eating alone, she observed the women around her and noticed a difference between her and other residents: "I do not feel I am getting on very well yet. I think, it has a special atmosphere of its own and a rather frivolous one—chiefly balls, and theater and young men. I think getting to know them is a slow process." As a whole on March 25, 1908, Sedgwick noted that Russian women "generally post themselves as being utterly indifferent." Yet, she did have some success in a two-hour debate with a "weird specimen," who appeared to take the entire matter without any seriousness. Sedgwick wrote that the two reached an understanding, and then talked quite honestly, even though they got no farther.

Sedgwick's ministry with Russian men seems to have been more successful than her work with women. Writing to fellow SCM women leader Ruth Rouse, she observed, "Last night, the President of the Society which runs this 'intranat' came here and sent for me... He asked me various questions as to my reasons for coming here and I told him quite frankly... at the end of our interview, he gave me his card and asked me to call next Thursday."[3]

In order to more fully understand local life, Sedgwick also labored tirelessly to improve existing student groups and to develop new ones at the Universities of Geneva and Moscow. In group activities, she could learn about many different beliefs and practices found in her mission field.

Sedgwick contacted student groups outside her residence. Following John R. Mott's tactic, she sought out "strategic points" or places where students gathered that were especially advantageous for reaching them. In a November 26, 1905 note, Sedgwick reported that a family's monthly open house for students was such a location: "I rather fancy that to Mott this house is a strategic point." She joined student groups, like the Libertas (a temperance club), a study group, and attended lectures. Sedgwick joined a group of eight students and one professor, where she labeled herself the lone feminist.

Sedgwick's ministry at what was later called the Brasserie Meeting in Geneva, Switzerland was one of the most important examples of how she contacted groups of students. The gathering got its name because it was held at the Café Brasserie, a local pub well-known as a gathering place for socialist agitation.

The Brasserie Meeting was held on January 30, 1906 and was the result of the efforts by a small Christian group composed of Sedgwick and a group of men. Planners hoped the meeting would permit them to preach the Gospel or, at least, become acquainted with more students. Sedgwick and the men were shocked at the size of the crowd. From estimates, one-third of the university packed the café with an even mixture of foreign and Swiss students. The audience consisted of "long-haired men and short-haired women; faces stamped with sin, suspicion, hatred, sorrow and despair" (Rowland 1937: 211).

During the meeting, Sedgwick and three men each spoke for about ten minutes, giving a simple, direct account of what Jesus Christ meant to them. The audience greeted each speaker with rounds of applause, and mocking laughter. However, one older woman, "a well-known feminist," told the crowd that she was bothered by the tone of the audience. The Christians had spoken honestly and were quite fair and serious. Yet, the crowd had made violent, mostly unfair attacks and had derided the speakers. In the end, according to Rouse, the older woman made the audience listen politely (1937: 211).

The meeting triggered a variety of responses. Sedgwick observed that the general opinion of the university community was that the Christians had made fools of themselves. Her public stance also changed her relationships with other women. On February 13, 1906, she noted that some women viewed her now as an "object of curiosity, a little mild surprise." Some former acquaintances ceased to relate to her, while others became new friends.

Most important, contact work at the Brasserie Meeting paid off because it launched a series of meetings in which Sedgwick played an important role. She helped plan the first gathering that followed the Brasserie Meeting, but chose not to give a speech as she had at the earlier one. On February 13, 1906, she wrote, "The very thought of it makes me shiver (giving a speech)—one gets so sick of controversy! But it is obviously the right thing to do and if only as a result of it small groups may be formed for study, won't it be worthwhile." The meeting was attended by two hundred to three hundred students and afterwards most of the crowd remained to discuss future plans.

The group decided to hold regular meetings on announced topics directed by an oversight committee with representatives from the Christian and free-thought groups. When it was suggested that women be placed on this committee, Sedgwick was the logical person. Her enthusiasm was palatable in her February 28, 1906 note:

> The first committee is to meet tomorrow and I am to be there to represent feminine Christianity... Isn't it thrilling? Or isn't it simply splendid? I could dance a jig of joy—I don't believe you would find such a society anywhere else—and if only it works and if only we can keep up this "entente cordiale" and meet each other fairly regularly just think of the possibilities of it. The audience seemed to think it was quite a good idea. Of course, we can't say a bit how it will actually work, but as a net result of our experiment, it is simply astonishing. It has been worthwhile.

Sedgwick was a good example of a missionary who developed cultural awareness in her mission field. Examples of how she did this include her attempt to learn Russian, local customs, the differences between Eastern and Anglican Christianity, and her contact work with individuals and groups.

Forging Ecumenical Relationships

One of the SCM's founding principles was inter-denominationalism. Instead of having students from only one religious persuasion or making members ignore their denominational distinctives, the movement felt that students should bring the strengths of their denominations to the SCM. As the movement spread around the world, this Protestant movement encountered Eastern and Roman Christians. So, SCM women had to ask themselves, "How broadly constructed should the SCM be?" How can it minister to Eastern and Roman Christian students? What beliefs and practices from the East and Rome should be incorporated into this distinctly Protestant movement?

Grace Helena Saunders (1874-1970)

Grace Saunders had a very clear sense of how she should handle these ecumenical questions. Because of her official WSCF and YWCA reports and her own articles, she presents a clear picture of an SCM ecumenist.

Funded jointly by the WSCF and the World's YWCA, and armed with the SCM's widened ecumenical spirit, Grace Saunders served as a "kind of area-secretary" in Bulgaria from 1912-16 and again in 1919. She served in Serbia, Romania, and Hungary as well. Saunders had official funding, but there appeared to be a lack of clarity about her position. In periodicals, Saunders was the Organizing Secretary for the Women's Students' Christian Association or YWCA Women's Secretary at Sophia University, Sophia, Bulgaria or maybe both.

Tall, blond, very confidant, and artistically-inclined, Saunders was born into an extremely wealthy, large West End London family with royal blood. In 1874, she was baptized in the Church of England. One of her sisters, Una Mary Josephine Saunders, was also an SCM worker. Like her immediate neighbor, celebrated author Beatrice Potter, she was widely traveled. She took the famed Orient Express on her trips to and from the Balkans. She was a graduate of Kensington High School. Saunders never married and died at ninety-five years of age in Marylebone, London, not far from where she grew up next door to Potter.

To develop new ecumenical relationships, Saunders used a flexible, courageous leadership style. This was demonstrated by the following story:

> She has developed greatly in powers of leadership and in general adaptability... To give you an example of the kind of things she is up to now--She came home steerage from America, just by way of a social experiment and on board ship indulged in public controversy with an anarchist, who was attacking Christianity and amongst all things marriage, in his address on deck. Grace ascended the tub to answer him in public. Various lines of thought that have been brought into her life have prepared her curiously well, I think, for dealing with some of the moral questions which are bound to come up. (Rouse 1910: 2-3)

Also, Saunders recognized and appreciated the existence of the Christian world beyond Protestantism. In her June, 1919 WSCF report on her ministry in the Balkans, Grace Helena Saunders wrote, "It is important that the YMCA and YWCA leaders should keep clearly in mind that 'Christian' is not synonymous with Protestant" (Saunders 1919: 7).

Saunders made this case because she was a realist and recognized the failures of the missionary movement because it had not moved beyond Protestantism in her heavily Eastern Christian context:

> American and Congregational and Episcopal Methodist missions have been doing educational work in the country for fifty years, but the fact of their having formed Protestant communities, has been deeply resented by the nation as a whole. The Bulgarian YMCA (it is really a Young People's CA, as it includes girls) has grown up around these mission churches, and uses Protestant hymns and extemporary prayer,

which are regarded as foreign practices... It is owing to the Protestant associations of the name that is seems unlikely that the Bulgarian Student Association will be willing to affiliate, at least for a considerable time, to the YMCA or YWCA. (1919: 4)

To model her ecumenical spirit, Saunders developed her student ministry along distinctly Orthodox lines in terms of membership (i.e., more Orthodox than Protestant members), and atmosphere (i.e., she hung icons in the meeting rooms). She encouraged its members to participate in their local Orthodox church. Finally, Saunders advocated Orthodox Christians reach out to other Orthodox Christians.

Finally, Saunders fostered cordial relationships with Orthodox, Roman Catholic, and Protestant leaders. In 1919, she received the endorsement of Orthodox Bishop Miron Christea of Karansehes, Romania.[4] In a formal letter to other Orthodox bishops, he wrote that he was pleased with her explanation of the aims and methods of SCM work. He also officially welcomed other SCM workers and hoped that other bishops would also. During the same period, Saunders met with Sister Augustine, a well-known nun of the St. Vincent de Paul Convent, a man named Bates of the British YMCA, and a man labelled Mr. Masterson and a woman named Mrs. Williams of the American YMCA.

In sum, Saunders was a good example of how a missionary can forge ecumenical relations. Her understanding that Christianity was bigger than her own version, her recognition that the dominant version of Christianity in her mission field was different than her own, her modifications of her own practices to fit the practices of her area of ministry, and finally her fostering of cordial relationships with local Christians representing different branches of Christianity demonstrated this fact.

Confronting Dangerous and Life Threatening Situations

SCM women ministered in a world filled with menacing political situations. Examples include the Boer Wars, the Boxer Rebellion, the Balkan Crises, the Armenian Massacre, the oppressive climate of Tsarist Russia, the "scramble" for colonies, the arms race between Great Britain and Germany and World War I. They even faced oppressive local, petty dictators. So, SCM women had to ask themselves, "Should we send our missionaries to potentially life-threatening locations," and "How do I as a missionary remain faithful to my call and yet handle these?"

Frances Cousens Gage (1863-1917)

The story of Frances Cousens Gage was one of the most hair-raising tales in SCM history. Gage was a YWCA student traveling secretary in North America and Turkey. In SCM circles, the traveling secretary served as a pastor. While carrying out her ministry Gage found herself in the midst of the Marsovan Massacre and the Armenian Genocide. She became the first overseas American YWCA missionary to die while in service to the YWCA and the SCM. In all these, Gage navigated these treacherous events and yet maintained her committed Christian stance. Her life provides a lesson on how to do this.

At 5 ft. 6 in. in height with light hair and complexion, Gage was born into a middle class family in Quincy, Massachusetts and spent her life in Minnesota and Oregon. She attended Carlton College in Northfield, Minnesota. Gage graduated as Valedictorian with a BS (1890) and afterwards was elected to Phi Beta Kappa as an alumni member. After college, her career involved teaching high school in Minnesota (1890-1891) and at the Girl's school in Marsovan, Turkey (1893-1898 and 1913-1916), working with the YWCA Student Department in Washington, Oregon and Idaho (1898-1913) where she was a traveling secretary in Oregon for the YWCA Student Department and a member of the executive committees of the northwest field committee of the YWCA, and ministering as a traveling secretary for the Foreign Department of the YWCA (1913-1916), where she was also a member of the general committee for the Christian Associations of the Turkish Empire. Wherever her career took her "the outlook of her heart was toward Turkey" (Wilson 1918: 55).

In North America, Gage faced a potentially life-threatening situation while serving as the YWCA traveling secretary on the Pacific Coast sometime between 1898-1913. At this time, she displayed one of her most outstanding qualities, her ability to face a problem that needed solving and then fixing it. She did not "take things laying down." Gage found that girls under her care could not ride a particular steamboat because it was not safe. So, she went straight to the headquarters of the Steamboat Company and told the company's president directly, "Your boats aren't safe for my girls to ride on." When the president said he agreed and said "Tell them not to use them," she responded quickly, "You've got to make your boats safe for my girls." And the president dutifully did what she demanded (*The Woman Citizen*, 1918: 474).

Gage had a firm faith commitment. Despite being raised in a Christian home, Gage later claimed that she did not want to become nor did she become a Christian until college. The impact of this may be what a later report noted about Gage's college years. She was said to have "inspired interest in missions among the students, all of whom admired her fine intellectual abilities, her earnest spirit of consecration and her beautiful and attractive personality (*Mission Studies: Woman's Work in Foreign Lands* 1918: 27)."

In 1893, the Women's Board of Missions of the Interior (A Congregational missionary society) appointed Gage to teach at the Girl's School in Marsovan, Turkey.[5] Upon arriving in Turkey Gage was witness to what has become known as the Marsovan Massacre. That year, Ottoman troops took many Armenian students and faculty to jail and damaged some college buildings. This occurred because Armenian activists had displayed posters supporting Armenian rights. The Turks accused some of the school's Armenian students and faculty of colluding with the activists.

A *Los Angeles Herald* article in 1895 included a description of the massacre's events very close to the school from an unidentified person at the school (*Los Angeles Herald*, 1895: 2). This person might have been Gage herself, but since they are unidentified, no one will ever know. The article said, "A storm broke over Marsovan." The article's witness said that slaughter, shrieks, and yells could be heard close to the school. "Bullets came humming and struck the girl's school." The noise of soldiers banging on nearby doors could be made out also. The cries of a wounded woman could be heard just outside the school gates one entire day. About twenty-five soldiers guarded the institution and no one was permitted to attack the school nor harm the students or staff. Students and staff were huddled in a room. Several years later, because she was a woman of prayer, Gage would recall praying for protection in that room during the massacre.

Because she was a realistic person, in the fall of 1898, Gage came back to the United States and she was not sure she would ever return to Turkey. If she had lived one-hundred years later, she might be diagnosed as having Post-Traumatic Stress Disorder. The combination of her teaching load, the death of a close colleague, and the massacres had taken their toll.

Since the "outlook of her heart was toward Turkey," Gage was faithful to her call and returned there in 1913 or 1914 depending on which account one accepts. Gage's desire to return to Turkey, in particular Marsovan, was strengthened by her previous experience of living in Turkey and her knowledge of the Turkish language.

Travel was fraught with danger and it was difficult for missionaries, particularly women. Journeys inside Turkey and around the world included rough roads, exposure to all kinds of weather conditions and diseases with the absence of accessible health care, poor sanitation, and a lack of protection from robbers. During her first months in Turkey,

Gage spent eleven weeks traveling, checking out local associations and also examining the conditions of Turkish women. This trip included ten days of sea travel, twenty of wagon, two by horseback and twelve by rail. All-in-all she traveled over 2500 miles. She visited with a mix of Orthodox, Roman Catholic and Protestant believers as well as members of other religions. Gage had to be sensitive to the beliefs and practices of all these groups. During her travels, Gage generally spoke on "The Preciousness of Womanhood" to large audiences. In local associations, she gave evangelistic and inspirational speeches and she spoke in Armenian, Greek, Turkish, Islamic, Roman Catholic, and secular schools.

In 1915, Gage was caught up in what is known today as the Armenian Genocide (or the Armenian Holocaust, Armenian Massacres, or the Medz Yeghern, in Armenian, the "Great Crime").[6] Her part in the Armenian Genocide occurred in 1915 when the genocide came to Marsovan. With the assistance of fellow teacher Charlotte Willard, her actions were considered to be "one of the most thrilling stories of women's work during the war." To many, it made her and Willard real life heroes.

One day in the summer of 1915, a force of Turkish soldiers came into the school compound. Armenian men and boys had already been taken. This time they came for Armenian women and girls. Depending on which account is to be believed, sixty-two or sixty-three were taken in fourteen open carts. Gage herself went to the classroom mentioned in the 1895 account to pray. As a result, she reaffirmed her belief that she had to defend all girls, including the ones just kidnapped.

Gage and Willard devised a plan to get the kidnapped women and girls back. They had to wait around six days to get the travel permits they applied for. But once they received these, they were off on the approximately one-hundred and thirteen mile journey. Fearlessly, Gage and Willard passed large groups of refugees as soldiers let them pass. The roads were crowded, dusty, and dangerous. They telegraphed the Governor of Silvas, an upcoming town, and asked him to hold the kidnap victims there. About an hour after their arrival there, most of the women and girls appeared. Undeterred by the violent reputation of the Governor and his soldiers, she had a "momentous interview" with them (1918: 99-100).[7] In the end, she convinced the Governor to let forty-eight women and girls return with Gage and Willard to Marsovan.

Recalling how the men listened to her and Willard, Gage would later say. "You might say that the Boli courteously gave us back fifty girls." But to her intimate friends, she said, "The result was directly of God, nothing we could do was even slightly adequate, so many had tried and failed. This was just one of God's miracles" (Wilson 1918: 99-100). Typical for her, Gage gave God all the credit for the rescue.

Gage's reputation for all these things followed her when she died on July 15, 1917 in Marsovan at the age of fifty-one. Her funeral the next day had a crowd of over three-hundred men and women in a small local cemetery. In her honor, the Portland, Oregon YWCA started a Frances Cousins Gage Club and established the Frances Cousins Gage Memorial Fund. Soon after her death, *The Woman Citizen* observed:

> Among the women who deserve to be held in remembrance...
> is Frances C. Gage, who has laid down her life in Turkey
> since the war began. Miss Gage was a Y. W. C. A. worker in
> Marsovan... There are many incidents which show Miss Gage
> as a path breaker in the woman movement. A feminist? Yes,
> of the old-fashioned pioneer sort, like Frances Willard and
> Susan B. Anthony, women who pushed the world along until
> it has become almost safe for women. (1918: 474)

Gage was a bit more humble in assessing her own gifts, saying, "I am not very brave, but I realize that a missionary's life is by no means an easy one, and after looking at the matter in the face, I believe, God helping me, I can meet the emergencies He may send me (1918: 28)."

In conclusion, Gage's story is more than a heroic tale of daring deeds in the face of life threatening challenges. Her ministry shows the tools one humble woman missionary used to confront kidnappers, difficult and unsafe travel, human suffering, and evil while maintaining her faith commitments.

Final Thoughts

Recounting the lives and ministries of Winifred Sedgwick, Grace Helena Saunders, and Frances Cousins Gage, hopefully has shed some light on the themes raised by this conference, such as handling today's "increasingly complex public area," and "negotiating the contemporary landscape." Whether developing cultural awareness, forging ecumenical relationships, or traversing dangerous and life-threatening political terrain, these three women were able to respect differing beliefs and customs while at the same time, maintain their missional commitment. The successes and failures of their engagement provide a backdrop for facing contemporary versions of the same concerns for us and for our students. Many of their strategies are still relevant and of universal value, regardless of the era and particular cultural struggles. As William Shakespeare said, "What's Past is Prologue" (Shakespeare).

Endnotes

1   Or the World's Student Christian Federation.

2   Even though Sedgwick does not identify Bulgakov, one wonders if this man was Sergei Nikolaevich Bulgakov (1871-1944), a Russian Orthodox theologian, philosopher, and economist with ties to the SCM inside and outside Russia before and after the 1917 Russian Revolution. He was chair of Political Economy at Kiev Polytechnic Institute (1901-1906) and chair of Political Economy at the Institute of Commerce at Moscow University (1906-1911). This conversation appears to have occurred in Moscow when he would be in Moscow, but it is only speculation.

3   An internat was a student hostel, pension or small residential house with student bedrooms and a common dining hall.

4   Miron Christea (1868-1939), a bishop of Transylvania, became the Metropolitan-Primate of the Orthodox Church in Romania in 1919. In 1925, he was enthroned as its first Patriarch. In 1938, Cristea became the Prime Minister of Romania. His term was quite short because he died within a year.

5   In 1840, Bebek Seminary was established outside Constantinople by the American Board of Commissioners for Foreign Missions. In 1862, this school was transferred to Marsovan. In 1886, the Anatolia College was established there. Students were mainly Greek and Armenian. Most were boarding students because they came from outside Marsovan. Students quickly numbered one-hundred and fifteen and in 1893, a girl's school was founded.

6   This was the Ottoman government's systematic extermination of its Armenian population. Victims are estimated to number 800,000 to 1.5 million. April 24, 1915 is considered the first day of this genocide. On that day, the Turkish government rounded up, arrested, and deported between 235-270 Armenian intellectuals and community leaders. The majority of this group were later murdered. This extermination program was conducted during and after World War I. The first part involved the killing of able-bodied males through massacre or forced labor. Then women, children, the elderly, and infirm were sent on death marches to the Syrian desert. These individuals did not have food or water and were subject to robbery, rape, and massacre.

7   The man referred to as the "governor" or "vali" may have been Ahmed Muammer. He was the governor of the Vilayet of Sivas from 1913-1916. Muammer has been accused of complicity in the killing of the Armenians, which would make him particularly dangerous to Gage and Willard. Sivas was a town in north central Turkey located in the Sivas Vilayet, one of the six Armenian districts of the Ottoman Empire. It is located southeast of Marsovan. Gage's use of the term "boli" is unclear and why she used it may never be known. However, there are at least three possibilities for its use. Boli is the older name for the Bolu Province northwest of Marsovan, the term "boli" is slang for confirming a person agrees with something someone else is saying (i.e., someone being "dead right" or "on point") or the term is a misspelling of the word "vali" or governor.

References Cited

Anonymous.
n.d.   Archives of the WSCF, Record Group 46 (Box 167, Folder 1194; Box 100, Folders 816 and 819).

n.d.   "Massacre at Marsovan," *The Los Angeles Herald* 45:58. December 8, 1895: 2.

1918.   *Mission Studies: Woman's Work in Foreign Lands*: 27.

Rouse, Ruth.
1910.   "Ruth Rouse to Winifred Sedgwick":1-3. Archives of the WSCF, Record Group 46 (Box 210, Folder 1600).

Rowland, Wilmina M.
1937.   "The Contribution of Ruth Rouse to the World's Student Christian Federation." M.A. thesis, Yale University, New Haven CT.

Russell, Thomas A.
2017.   *Women Leaders in the Student Christian Movement, 1880-1920*. American Society of Missiology Series. Maryknoll, NY: 2017.

Saunders, Grace H.
1919   "Miss Saunders' Report on the Balkans" (March to June): 1-8. Archives of the WSCF, Record Group No. 46 (Box 284, Folder 2496) Special Collections, Yale Divinity School Library.

Shakespeare, William.
1610-1611   *The Tempest*. Act 2 Scene 1.

Tatlow, Tissington.
1933   *The Story of the Student Christian Movement of Great Britain and Ireland*. London, England: SCM Press.

Wilson, Elizabeth.
1918.   *The Road Ahead: Experiences in the Life of Frances C. Gage*. New York, NY: The Woman's Press, 1918.

1918   "Some Women." *The Woman Citizen: The Woman's* Journal: 474.

APM

Conference
Proceedings

First Fruits Report for the APM

ROBERT DANIELSON, *ADVISORY COMMITTEE MEMBER*

In 2013, First Fruits Press at Asbury Theological Seminary partnered with the APM to produce a digital and print version of the association's proceedings, with the digital version to be shared freely in open access and the print copies to be purchased through an on demand printer for the cost of paper and binding only. This project resulted in the publication of the book, *Social Engagement: The Challenge of the Social in Missiological Education* in October of 2013. The second proceedings called *Transforming Teaching for Mission: Educational Theory and Practice* published in 2014 were followed in 2015 by the third proceedings, which were published as *What's in a Name? Assessing Mission Studies Program Titles.* The 2016 proceedings will come out as *Teaching Christian Mission in an Age of Global Christianity,* which is about ready to be released. In each case, both the entire volume and the individual articles can be downloaded separately. The following chart shows the current status of downloads:

Year	Title	Volume Downloads	Article Downloads	Total Down-loads
2013	*Social Engagement: The Challenge of the Social in Missiological Education*	1,012 (In 52 countries)	2,015	3,027

2014	*Transforming Teaching for Mission: Educational Theory and Practice*	463 (In 61 countries)	2,889	3,352
2015	*What's in a Name? Assessing Mission Studies Program Titles*	36 (In 15 countries)	774	810
2016 Forth- coming	*Teaching Christianity in an Age of World Christianity*	0	0	0

For the past couple of years, we have been working on republishing of the Past Proceedings of the Association of Professors of Mission in two volumes (1956-1958 and 1962-1974). Using hard to find mimeographed copies of the originals in the library at Asbury Theological Seminary, we were able to reformat these proceedings and they have been through two rounds of editing already. We are waiting for the final edit and corrections, which has taken a bit longer then anticipated, but we expect these to be available by the fall of 2017.

I am continuing to seek for six more mission related books to complete my promise of making books available for the generous gift APM gave two years ago to Asbury Theological Seminary to be used for the work of First Fruits Press. In addition, I am continuing to look at the possibility of republishing Wilbur C. Harr's 1962 book, Frontiers of the Christian World Mission Since 1938: Essays in Honor of Kenneth Scott Latourette, which was the publication of the fifth proceedings of the APM from 1960. But there may be some copyright complications here.

This year has been a rather difficult year, both in terms of workload and personally with the unexpected loss of my mother-in-law in El Salvador. Due to a number of issues, I am unable to be with you in person this year, but I continue to feel that this work has been very successful and beneficial. I want to continue to seek ways of linking our material more effectively on the website, and I will continue to investigate that. Needless to say, I continue to look forward to working with APM this year to produce a fifth volume of the proceedings for the 2017 Conference in Wheaton.

Minutes of 2017 Meeting

1.   The APM meeting was held at Wheaton College, Wheaton, IL. The meeting was called to order by Larry Caldwell, APM President, 2:30pm, June 16, 2017.

2.   Minutes for the 2016 meeting were submitted by David Fenrick, Secretary-Treasurer. Motion to approve the minutes, seconded. Minutes were approved.

3.   The Secretary-Treasurer's financial report was submitted. Motion to approve report, seconded. Question about $25.00 Membership Dues. Will refer back to David Fenrick for explanation. Report approved.

4.   The next APM Annual meeting will be held, June 14-15, 2018, Saint Mary's College – University of Notre Dame, South Bend, Indiana.

5.   Executive Committee Report: Nothing to report, meeting went over the annual meeting program; no new business.

6.   Report from Robbie Danielson that the 2017 APM Annual Meeting papers will be published by Frist Fruits Press at Asbury Theological Seminary. Plenary sessions and parallel sessions will be published. Data on previous annual meeting papers: 2013 – 3000 downloads, 52 countries. 2014 – 3000 downloads, 61 countries. 2015 – 810 downloads, 15 countries. 2016 papers will be available soon.

7.   Other Business and Announcements:

    a.   Midwest Mission Studies Fellowship Meeting. Theme: Mission in the Age of Refugees and Immigrants. November 11, 2017, Andrews University, Berrien Springs, MI.

    b.   Eastern Fellowship of Professors of Mission meeting, October 27-28, 2017, at Maryknoll, NJ. Theme: Looking at the Past and Looking to Future - 100 year anniversary of Fellowship (oldest in US).

    c.   Question: Are we still holding to rotation in leadership? Answer: Yes.

    d.   Comment: It is Important for Executive Committee to meet in January. We are looking to fund mid-year meeting: $6000.00/year.

8.   The report of the Nominating Committee regarding the election of officers was submitted by Linda Whitmer.

    a.   Linda Whitmer, Johnson University President, was elected president

    b.   A. Sue Russell, Asbury Theological Seminary, was elected First Vice-President

    c.   Margaret Guider, Boston College, was elected Second Vice President

    d.   David Fenrick, University of Northwestern, was reelected Secretary-Treasurer.

    e.   New Members of the APM Advisory Board were introduced and approved:

        • Craig Hendricksen, Moody Bible Institute

        • Enoch Kim, Fuller Theological Seminary

Nominations closed, seconded. Slate of officers elected.

9.   Larry Caldwell thanked the Executive Committee and Advisory Board, as well as the presenters for their contribution to the annual meeting. He also introduced the new APM President, Linda Whitmer.

10.   Linda Whitmer thanked out-going President, Larry Cadwell. She presented the theme for the 2018 Annual Meeting: *Teaching Mission in a Technological World.*

11.   APM noted the death of the following colleagues this past year, and their unique and enduring contributions to the field of missiology and proclamation of the Gospel.

- Fred Morris, Manna Publications
- Alan Krieder, Anabaptist Mennonite Biblical Seminary
- Manny Ortiz, Westminster Theological Seminary, founder and senior pastor of Spirit and Truth Fellowship.
- Robert Linthicum, World Vision International and Partners in Urban Transformation

12.   Linda Whitmer closed the meeting with prayer.

Respectfully Submitted,

David E. Fenrick

Secretary-Treasurer

2017 APM Annual Meeting Minutes recorded by A. Sue Russell

Secretary-Treasurer's Report

	Credit	Debit	Balance
Opening Balance: June 17, 2017			3,817.39
Receipts			
Transfer from ASM	2,258.48		
Expenses			
APM 2016 Meeting Honorarium & Expenses		2,168.00	
Mission Studies Renewal		338.00	
Total	2,258.48	2,506.00	**3,569.87**

Balance at Wells Fargo Bank, Minneapolis, MN, as of June 16, 2017: **$3,569.87**

Respectfully Submitted,
David E. Fenrick
Secretary-Treasurer

Conference Schedule

APM Association of Professors of Mission

2017 Annual Meeting—Wheaton College

Wheaton, IL

"Developing Missiologically Informed Models of Engagement"

Thursday, June 15

2:00pm	Advisory Committee Meeting
2:00-3:00 4:00-5:00	Registration
5:00-6:00	Dinner
7:00-7:15	Welcome to the Conference
7:15-7:45	Worship

7:45–9:00	Plenary Address – D.A. Carson, *What We Should Look for in Those Who Teach Mission*
9:00	Announcements, APM Informal Gathering

Friday, June 17

7:15–8:00	Breakfast
8:00–8:30	Registration and check-in available
8:30–8:45	Worship
8:45–9:40	Plenary Address – Michal Meulenberg, *What Do You Mean by That? When Words Can Make the Difference between Violence and Peace*
9:40–9:55	Break
10:00–10:50	Parallel Paper Sessions

Pluralistic Landscape	*Identity and Otherness: Missiological Explorations of Engaging and Embracing the Other in a Pluralistic World.* David Moe, Asbury Theological Seminary	
Political Landscape	*Teaching Civility in an Age of Conflict.* A. Sue Russell, Asbury Theological Seminary	*Teaching the Uniqueness of Christ in a Politically Correct World.* Robert Gallagher, Wheaton College Graduate School
Cross-Cultural Landscape	*The Impact of Globalized Immigration to Mission and Missiology.* Christian Dumitrescu, Adventist International Institute of Advanced Studies	*Persecuted Churches in the Public Square: Power Encounters in Context.* Paul Hertig, Azusa Pacific University
Lessons From History	*Historical Models of Engagement to teach Mission in the Complex Public Arena.* Santha Jetty, World Christianity Researcher and Presenter, Atlanta, Georgia	*Past is Prologue:Victorian Women Leaders of the Global Student Christian Movement.* Tom Russell, TN eCampus and University College, the University of Memphis

11:05-12:00   Plenary Address – Daniel White Hodge, *"No Wild in the Church: Missiological Education in a Post-Civil Rights Era"*

12:00-1:00pm   Lunch

1:15-2:05   Panel Discussion: "The Intersection of Scholarship and Mission"
John Hubers – Northwestern College (Iowa)
Jim Rohrer – University of Nebraska (Kearney)
Respondent – Charles Van Engen, Fuller Theological Seminary

2:15-3:00   APM Business meeting and Conclusion

www.ingramcontent.com/pod-product-compliance
Lightning Source LLC
Chambersburg PA
CBHW071527040426
42452CB00008B/911